DISCARD

TASK FORCE
BLACK

Also by Mark Urban

SOVIET LAND POWER

WAR IN AFGHANISTAN

BIG BOYS' RULES: THE SAS AND THE SECRET
STRUGGLE AGAINST THE IRA

UK EYES ALPHA: INSIDE BRITISH INTELLIGENCE

THE MAN WHO BROKE NAPOLEON'S CODES:
THE STORY OF GEORGE SCOVELL

RIFLES: SIX YEARS WITH WELLINGTON'S
LEGENDARY SHARPSHOOTERS

GENERALS: TEN BRITISH COMMANDERS
WHO SHAPED THE WORLD

FUSILIERS: HOW THE BRITISH ARMY LOST
AMERICA BUT LEARNED TO FIGHT

TASK FORCE BLACK

THE EXPLOSIVE TRUE STORY OF THE SAS AND THE SECRET WAR IN IRAQ

Mark Urban

Little, Brown

LITTLE, BROWN

First published in Great Britain in 2010 by Little, Brown

A CIP catalogue record for this book
is available from the British Library.

ISBN 978-1-4087-0265-9

Typeset in Bembo by M Rules
Printed and bound in Australia by
Griffin Press

FSC
Mixed Sources
Product group from well-managed
forests and other controlled sources
Cert no. SGS-COC-005088
www.fsc.org
© 1996 Forest Stewardship Council

Little, Brown
An imprint of
Little, Brown Book Group
100 Victoria Embankment
London EC4Y 0DY

An Hachette UK Company
www.hachette.co.uk

www.littlebrown.co.uk

Contents

Baghdad

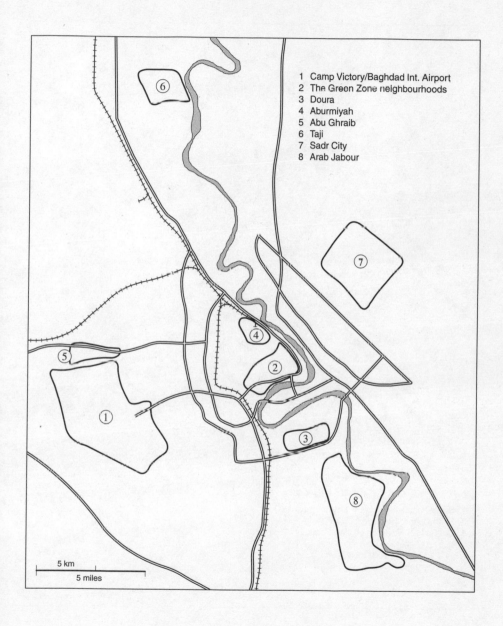

1 Camp Victory/Baghdad Int. Airport
2 The Green Zone neighbourhoods
3 Doura
4 Aburmiyah
5 Abu Ghraib
6 Taji
7 Sadr City
8 Arab Jabour

5 km

5 miles

Basra

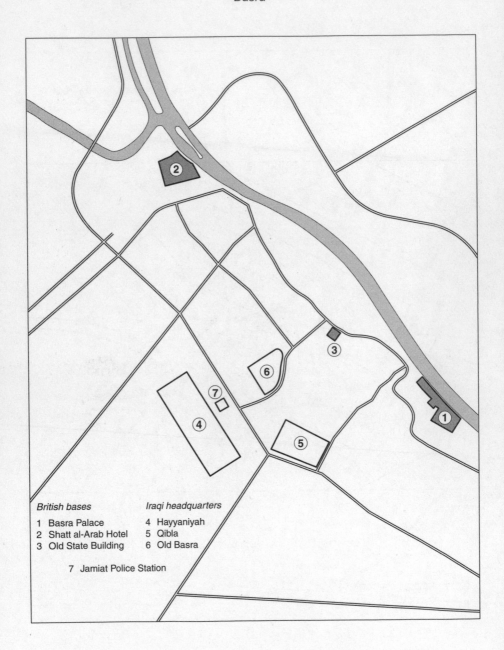

British bases

1 Basra Palace
2 Shatt al-Arab Hotel
3 Old State Building

Iraqi headquarters

4 Hayyaniyah
5 Qibla
6 Old Basra

7 Jamiat Police Station

Operation ABALONE, Ramadi, 31 October 2003

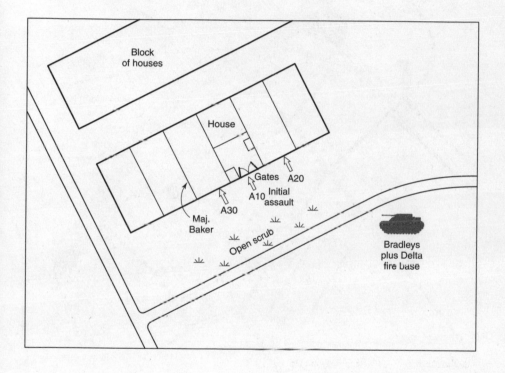

Operation LARCHWOOD 4, Yusufiyah, 16 April 2006

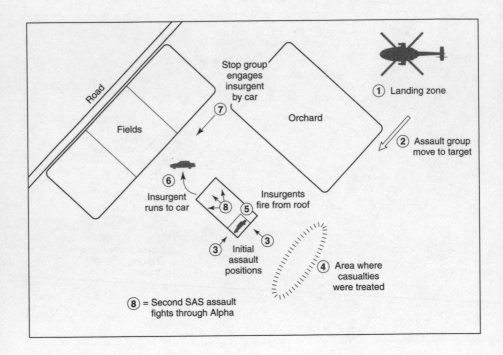

Arab Jabour Operation, 21 November 2007

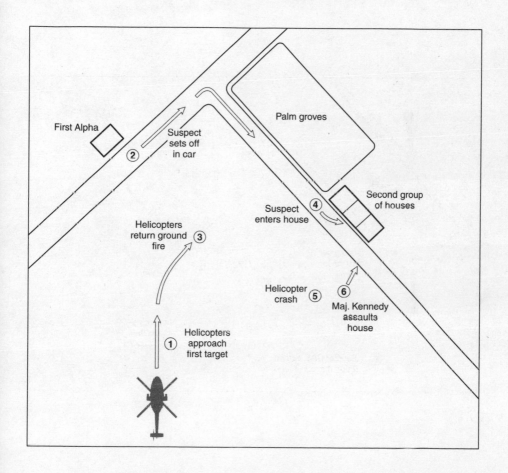

Preface

Late in 2005, I was waiting for an RAF plane home from Iraq when a large group of passengers arrived in the tent at Basra airport. There were about sixty men, divided evenly between an older heavier-set mob and younger, more sprightly-looking types. They were respectively members of the SAS and the Special Forces Support Group.

In their appearance these special forces seemed to be completely 'out and proud'. For one thing, they were all wearing civilian clothes, whereas all other passengers for the Tristar home were following the rules about uniform. For another, many had chunky labels on their daysacks with things like 'Jim, A Squadron, Hereford' written on them.

During our wait for the flight I was joined in the struggle to get hot water out of a faulty boiling vessel by one of the squadron members, who had a few weeks earlier been held prisoner in the Jamiat police station several miles away in the centre of Basra. I had seen his undisguised face on TV pictures as they were pulled down into the BBC, and we briefly shared our frustration at the brew famine.

Since my encounter with A Squadron, members of UK special forces have adopted a different camouflage pattern from the rest of the British Army – but the same as is often used by top-tier US special ops soldiers. In short, then, the SAS or SBS, by using these outfits or civilian clothes in certain military situations, for example in camp or when travelling on forces' flights, revel in their reputation as their country's military elite and, you might say, why shouldn't they?

The odd thing about this brazen attitude is that it sits uneasily with the culture of secrecy which many of those involved in the world of intelligence and special operations would like to impose. Members of Britain's special forces are expected to abide by a lifelong duty of confidentiality in much the same way as those who work for MI6 or GCHQ. But there are two obstacles to this being achieved: in the first place, many of those on the inside allow the ego that comes with their 'special' status or superb physical fitness to evolve into a desire for publicity. One only has to look at the many SAS books or newspaper articles relying on well placed leaks to see this.

A second reason for the high public profile of the SAS in particular is the lethality of their business. This is not a matter of discreet agent recruitment or coming up with a clever computer algorithm, as the intelligence professionals' world is. Special forces soldiering, particularly in the conflicts since the 9/11 attacks, is a high-intensity, deadly business involving face-to-face confrontation with some of the world's most ruthless terrorists. It is unsurprising, then, that the public interest in what these soldiers do is very high. Combine public interest with the desire of many in the military to talk, and you have fertile ground for a book like the one that follows.

My desire to write it came about on another Iraq trip – one

to Baghdad in September 2008. As coincidence had it, I ran into a succession of former intelligence and military types who had read *Big Boys' Rules*, my earlier book on covert operations in Northern Ireland, were keen to shake the author's hand and egged me on to write something similar about Iraq. Mark McCauley, the cameraman working with me on that trip (and during quite a few scrapes in Iraq and Afghanistan), added his weight to the argument, noting that my various trips to Iraq had given me the level of knowledge and access necessary to carry out such a sensitive project. So I began my own reconnaissance – to see whether it would be possible to write such a book.

It was clear to me that the scope for this would have to be far wider than just the SAS, as indeed my earlier work *Big Boys' Rules* had been. The special forces sometimes see themselves as the scalpel wielded by other hands, the senior commanders and intelligence types needed to gain the information vital for success. Indeed, without this direction 'the Regiment' can seem, as one Northern Ireland policeman once rudely put it, like 'plumbers who think they are brain surgeons'. As will become clear in this narrative, this was also true in Iraq, where the flow of accurate intelligence and evolution of a strategy to target certain elements of the insurgency were the essential preconditions for success. So while many may see this as an 'SAS book', I would argue it is something far wider and indeed more significant than that.

As I began my research, two things soon struck me. The first was that many people were willing to talk, in part because they believed great things had been achieved secretly by Britain around Baghdad. The second was that Britain's campaign in Iraq was already in its closing phase when my research was getting under way in earnest. This would allow certain final judgements to be reached and reduce the sensitivity of the contents to a level where many would be prepared to see it published, since continuing operations would not be endangered.

The story that emerged was a quite remarkable one of high risks and extreme violence. In this sense, Iraq presented a completely different arena from Northern Ireland where considerations such as the legality of the use of force ranked much higher. The truly disturbing (to those of a liberal mind, in any case) thing about the special operations campaign in Iraq is that it suggests a large terrorist organisation can be overwhelmed under certain circumstances by military force. The story of how far this was done is of course the main narrative of this book.

From the outset I decided to take certain steps to allow me to tell the story while protecting the lives of those – including insurgents as well as soldiers – who had been involved in these extraordinary events in Iraq. For those below a certain rank or status whose names had not come into the public domain, I would use pseudonyms denoted in the text by italics, such as Major *Smith*. I later added a few more senior officers who were still serving at the time of writing to this list, using pseudonyms in relation to the period of their special forces commands. Non-italicised names are of course real ones. I would also be very careful not to describe the limitations of intelligence or other capabilities used in this struggle, since many are still in use elsewhere.

When my research was already largely complete it became clear to me that there was also a body of opinion that was far less happy than those who had supported me in my work. In one sense this was a surprise, because I had come to assume that there was an official acceptance that it was not in the public interest to prevent my book's publication. Quite a few sources indeed told me that they had checked before speaking to me and had been given the go-ahead. However, it is always a mistake to assume that in matters of special forces and intelligence Britain practises joined-up government. As the tone of official letters became harsher it became clear that one hand did not know what the other had done. I could see that the kind of objections from officialdom that had accompanied my earlier books about Northern Ireland and on the intelligence services (*UK Eyes Alpha*) was likely to be repeated with *Task Force Black*.

I never had a problem with the idea of the Ministry of Defence reading my manuscript before publication because while I had been careful not to give away what I considered sensitive, I did not want to make inadvertent mistakes that might endanger lives. This indeed was why I agreed to make many changes, despite the fact that I considered many of those requested to be essentially pointless. However the reaction to my text in certain quarters – essentially of making demands for hundreds of changes, backed by the threat of legal action – did surprise me because it soon prejudiced the kind of reasonable discussion that I had hoped to enjoy. Horns were locked, lawyers engaged and the whole thing became an unpleasant confrontation.

Of course, I realise that many people will not only sympathise with Whitehall for trying to make changes to sections of the book, but will argue that it is the type of work that should never be written. I don't accept that, obviously. Whether the story of covert operations is essentially a critical or searching one, as my work about Northern Ireland was, or a somewhat more positive one, as this is, these histories must be told. They are about extraordinary deeds performed and lives taken or altered for ever by people who act in the country's name. The truth will out. It is simply a case of how soon, and how full a telling the narrative will receive. Many of those who cooperated with me were not only keen that these facts come to light but that I, as an unofficial person, should tell the tale.

In the end, it became possible to tell the story (for the most part) after a difficult and expensive (to the taxpayer) process. I would like to thank those who were essential to this process and of course the wider one of preparing this book: Ursula Mackenzie, Tim Whiting, Zoe Gullen and Siobhan Hughes at Little, Brown; David Hooper and his legal team at RPC; my ever-supportive agent Jonathan Lloyd; and of course my wife Hilary and my children for seeing me through once more. My *Newsnight* editor Peter Rippon was endlessly understanding in allowing me time off to write the book. Publishers, lawyers, family and indeed the BBC all gave me magnificent support. I suppose thanks are also due to the team on Operation ABER-RATE, whom I may have considered occasionally misguided but were motivated by honourable considerations.

Preamble: The Secret War

High over southern Baghdad an aerial dance was taking place. Flying at the top of the stack, a lumbering Hercules command aircraft banking in a figure-of-eight pattern was coordinating the planes with the assault force on the ground. Then, circling a couple of kilometres off to the west, was a group of Puma helicopters that had just dropped off the SAS and their supporting Paras. Closest to the ground, Lynxes were orbiting the target, each with a sniper peering out through an open side door.

If everything went to plan, their target would be picked off, cuffed and on his way to the interrogation facility within hours. If it turned into a drama, the air commander could call in anything from helicopters to F-16s. The outcome could vary from a swift night-time stroke that even the target's neighbours would be unaware of to the total obliteration of his farm.

The whole scene, at two o'clock on a summer's morning in 2007, was viewed through the green and black contrasts of night-vision goggles by pilots straining every sinew, scanning the

1

horizon of this unmanaged airspace, desperate to avoid a mid-air collision. Suddenly, a banking Lynx flashed in front but just below them, causing the pilots to tense momentarily. It was the ultimate flying challenge for these aviators, one of whom described it as 'a fucking awesome adrenaline frenzy – ten to fifteen air assets all stacked up on each other in the same air space, all doing a job. You would not believe the amount of time, energy and love that went into lifting one man.'

Down below, in the dusty farm compound that was his home on the edge of the Iraqi capital, that target was still unaware of what was about to happen. He was asleep, and so used to the sound of Coalition helicopters wheeling over the city by night that he did not stir. On the table next to his bed his mobile phone was still switched on. One of the brothers might call.

Across a plantation of date palms a few hundred yards from the farm, assault teams of British special forces soldiers stepped off their Pumas into the darkness. All of the men had state-of-the-art night-vision goggles and an assault rig carrying body armour, grenades and magazines, as well as plastic ties for their prisoner. Written on each man's forearm were the grid references of their target, as well as details of call-signs and timings.

Walking towards the objective was the Team Leader. He had been studying the target for weeks, learning who he was, where he operated and his place in the al-Qaeda setup. He had also gathered information on the community around the farm – if things went wrong, they did not want to get caught in a hornets' nest. 'You have to be driving ops with timely and accurate intelligence,' says one Team Leader. 'If it's flawed, people die on both sides.'

The target that night had been identified by intelligence as the administrator for a car-bombing cell. He put the vehicles, explosives and martyrs together to execute the attack. His people had already mounted several attacks on American troops and the market in the suburb of Doura a few miles to the north. Dozens of people had been blown apart in these bombings.

As the soldiers reached the farm they moved into position. The entry team had approached the chosen entrance. Up above the airborne commander was receiving reports from a surveillance aircraft. 'You are thinking about the individual you are after,' recalls the Team Leader. 'You are listening to the intelligence coming through from the aircraft above you. At a certain point you say "OK we're ready".' The door was blown and within seconds the SAS were in.

The mission that night was part of a secret war in which the SAS were effectively placed under the control of a classified American command working for General Stanley McChrystal. The gaunt American general would later emerge as a central figure in the Afghanistan conflict but at this time he was regarded with awe by a select band – the brotherhood of special operators he led in Iraq. McChrystal's people waged a campaign in which the old rules of counterterrorism were torn up and a devastating new style of operations emerged.

It was not easy for the British to adopt this new thinking. Many of them thought they knew better. But the sprawling suburbs of Baghdad or the alleyways of old Basra had little in common with Belfast or the Balkans, where the SAS had perfected its techniques. This was not a European battlefield, but something altogether more alien; a crazy jumble of baking heat, strange smells, and extreme violence. America's invasion of Iraq had drawn in thousands of jihadists, people who expressed their zeal for the cause in the willingness to cut off heads or drive cars full of explosives into crowded markets. Faced with a mounting disaster, the Americans were ready to kill these extremists by the thousand, harnessing all of their formidable technology and knowhow to the task. For the British, at times, the argument

3

between those who wanted to follow McChrystal's plan and those who opposed it threatened to tear the UK special forces community apart. In the end, the British task force found its way through the political minefield. Although it never numbered more than 150 people, it managed to play a key role in the battle for Baghdad and the suppression of al-Qaeda in Iraq. What follows is the story of how that happened.

1

MISSION PARADOXICAL

Early in April 2003 an RAF Chinook flew through the darkness towards Baghdad. It had set out from a remote airstrip in western Iraq and was heading for the city's airport. The pilots, highly trained special forces aircrew, scanned the land below through night-vision goggles, trying hard to keep low while racing over a desert so featureless that those who misjudged their height could easily fly into the ground.

BIAP (Baghdad International Airport) was the objective for one of the US armoured brigades that had sped up from Kuwait. But although the armour had reached it, the place was far from secure. Mortar rounds dropped in as the capital of Iraq tottered between decades of authoritarian rule and its uncertain future. The US 3rd Division's race to the capital had been part of the overt military campaign. It came up from the south,

5

accompanied by dozens of embedded reporters. The RAF Chinook, on the other hand, was arriving from a different point of the compass and had been part of an effort that was rarely talked about publicly.

A few minutes out from their destination, the passengers in the British helicopter started to glimpse the sprawl below. Tracer fire from heavy machine guns snaked into the sky, fires were visible across the city and the desert too. Disbanded Republican Guards, Fedayeen Ba'athist irregulars, and the criminals let flooding out of the jails were vying for the streets, turning the city into a cauldron of violence.

The Chinook came thumping over the apron, its twin rotors producing a huge cloud of dust as it came close to the ground. Taxiing to a halt, the passengers glimpsed more signs of America's eviction of Saddam Hussein. A couple of shot-up Iraqi Airways aircraft, one a Boeing 727 with its tail jutting awkwardly into the air could be seen in the darkness. As one of the early British arrivals recalls, 'The airport was a defensive perimeter under blackout conditions, with people in shellscrapes and Bradleys in defensive positions.'

The Americans were taking Baghdad. It wasn't a matter of marching straight in but a process of probing attacks. The airport had already served as the launching point for several thunder runs. These were strong armoured reconnaissance missions to test the mettle of those who had vowed to turn the city into a new Stalingrad. Although many Iraqis emerged to take pot shots at the passing tanks, the level of resistance was far less than the Americans, who had planned for 120 days of fighting, had feared. But as the Iraqi capacity for organised violence ebbed away, disorder was breaking out. Well-to-do businessmen were hauled from their cars and dispatched with a shot to the head by those who wanted their wheels. Looters carried off the contents of museums, Ba'ath party offices and even hospitals. The settling of scores was beginning too: between those who had been oppressed and the overlords who had trodden them down without mercy. The Sunni minority, and in particular members of Saddam's tribe, the Tikritis, braced themselves for payback from the Shia majority and the Kurds too. Too many had been tortured, bombed or killed for the thing to pass without bloodletting.

Out of the British Chinook stepped a group of officers with a handful of civilians and some well-armed SAS troops. One of the civilians on board, a young MI6 officer who had not been to war before, questioned whether the machine-gun fire they had seen had been evidence of celebrations. 'That's one celebration you don't want to be on the end of,' quipped a special forces veteran.

Among the party was Brigadier Graeme Lamb, Director of Special Forces (DSF). Lean and obsessively fit for a man of forty-nine, Lamb had started his military career in the Queen's Own Highlanders. The product of a Spartan Scottish boarding school, he had been reared to shun the rat race and crave adrenalin. He had commanded a squadron in the SAS and later, his regiment of Highlanders. Having experienced command at these levels, Lamb's ambition was almost spent. Friends say he never thought of himself as a general, and had assumed that he would leave the army as a colonel. But Lamb's superiors had other ideas. They had detected that, with his reputation for toughness, easy way with soldiers and special-forces mystique, he was a man whose services needed to be retained. He was one of the few people in the army with the self-confidence, as well as the respect of the old sweats of the SAS, to carry off the job of Director of Special Forces. The brigadier was given to blasphemous plain speaking, and his dismissal of overcomplicated ideas as 'bollocks' made some think of him as anti-intellectual. But as those who knew Lamb would attest, what he always sought was clarity, robustness and the avoidance of bullshit.

Not long after his appointment as DSF, the world had been shaken by al-Qaeda's attacks on New York and the Pentagon. Summoned to a weekend meeting to brief Tony Blair at Chequers, Lamb surprised the Prime Minister by turning up wearing Bart Simpson socks. As Blair listened, his eyes occasionally turned to the brigadier's ankles. Lamb laid out the ways in which the UK special forces might support the American effort in Afghanistan swiftly and effectively. The briefing carried the same message as his socks: 'no problemo'. He had made his mark with the Prime Minister, whose own world view had been altered dramatically by 9/11. Although the invasion of Iraq would involve much larger conventional forces than the toppling of the Taleban, that early meeting at Chequers had defined a relationship; Blair would take a personal interest in special forces throughout the Iraq campaign.

As DSF, Lamb had overall responsibility for the various regiments comprising Britain's military elite: the regular and two reserve regiments of Special Air Service; the Royal Marines Special Boat Service; a specialist surveillance unit; and the signallers who supported these forces on operations. The overthrow of Saddam had involved a big military operation of 'shock and awe' air strikes, divisions racing to Baghdad and the thunder runs that had sealed the city's fate. Britain's contribution, exceeding forty thousand servicemen and women, had taken southern Iraq, including the ancient port city of Basra. But Brigadier Lamb's role in this business was part of a different war – the mobilisation of hundreds of special forces troops for a secret campaign codenamed Operation ROW.

In essence Operation ROW was Britain's part of a larger Coalition effort designed to take large parts of the west and north of the country. This would pin down several Iraqi divisions, stopping Saddam either reinforcing his effort against the main invasion, from the south, or thickening Baghdad's defences.

The mission of the US, UK and Australian special operators moving in from the west and north was thus to take on entire Iraqi divisions by applying a level of force out of all proportion to their numbers, a task they took on with alacrity. The seizure of large tracts of Iraq – perhaps one third of the country – bordering Saudi Arabia, Jordan, Syria and Turkey by two special operations task forces totalling a couple of thousand men required them to advance with relentless aggression. With the offensive about to start, and a couple of weeks before his own arrival in Baghdad, Lamb had sent a final message to the UK special forces about to enter battle. Urging them forward, he signed off, 'Remember, the faint-hearted never fucked a pig!' This soldierly exhortation became something of a catchphrase among the special operators.

Milling about at Baghdad airport, the members of D Squadron of the SAS exchanged greetings with Lamb and the others who had come in on the Chinook. It was a chance to hear news of other elements of the covert offensive. The troopers who had flown in were just a few dozen who had set off from another Middle Eastern country on 19 March. A few of their D Squadron mates were down south as part of an SAS and intelligence team that had been detached to support the advance of the UK's 1st Armoured Division. This team infiltrated the city of Basra, where they brought in strikes against the local Ba'athist leadership. Apart from that small band, however, the majority of Britain's special forces had been part of joint Coalition special ops task forces that were supposed to take the place of divisions that would ideally have attacked from the north and west, but which political sensitivities had made impossible. While the rulers of certain countries did not want to risk the wrath of the Arab street by allowing overt movements of US troops through their ports towards Iraq, they had been prepared to accede to the launching of highly secret Coalition attacks from their territory. It was a typical double-dealing Middle Eastern approach, but the commanders of the UK and US special operations forces were used to that from years of operating in the region.

Most of the British – including B Squadron of the SAS – had come from the west. This force, including supporting aircraft, Royal Marines and RAF Regiment soldiers, had been limited because of regional nervousness about showing support for President Bush's war. B Squadron drove into the western Iraqi desert in its modified SAS Land Rovers festooned with weapons, looking for ballistic missile launchers along the way. They were still out in the desert when Lamb arrived in Baghdad. Meanwhile, most of D Squadron had been used as a heliborne force in a set-piece operation to seize a desert airfield before pushing on to the Iraqi capital.

Whereas the SAS had fought mainly in the west, the SBS had joined an American-led taskforce coming from the north. Because of the traditional rivalry between the special forces organisations, by the time the SAS reached the airport there was already much noisy comment about what had happened to the Marines. One of the SBS's sub-units, M Squadron, had staged through Cyprus, before insertion in northern Iraq, where it had come off badly in an unequal fight against a Republican Guard brigade. The commandos had extracted themselves rapidly without losing any people, but leaving behind most of their vehicles and much kit. In fact, Lamb's entire Op ROW force had not lost a single soldier in combat during the taking of Iraq (although two members of D Squadron had died in a training accident before the invasion).

Arriving in Baghdad, Lamb needed to do several things. He intended to support the Secret Intelligence Service (more usually known as MI6) in re-establishing a station. Nobody knew quite what the future held in Iraq, and that very uncertainty made the British intelligence operation all the more important. Given the possible dangers to the agent runners, they would need protection. The DSF also needed to link up swiftly with Lieutenant-Colonel *Charles Beaufort*, the Commanding Officer of 22 SAS and the key man on the ground, to canvass his views about what should come next. Lamb found *Beaufort* at the airport that night and one soldier recalls watching the two of them scaling the vantage point of the airport's control tower to scan the glow of Baghdad on the horizon. Just as the city they tried to make out in the darkness was entering a period of flux or uncertainty, so their own mission had gone beyond the original remit of Operation ROW, which was really no more than staging noisy diversions in the west and north of the country. Moving a couple of dozen troopers from D Squadron to Baghdad airport had been a flyer in the literal sense, but it typified the SAS spirit of wanting to get where the action was.

Both men knew they had no real mandate to operate in Baghdad, but both were convinced it was the right thing to do. As one who heard their expressions of determination to enter the Iraqi capital explains, 'Baghdad had the potential to be an intelligence Aladdin's cave of documents, evidence of WMD and evidence of Saddam's possible connections to the wider transnational terrorist campaign.' But *Beaufort* and his DSF knew that there were already plenty in London who were critical of Operation ROW because the campaign had been fought largely in the west and north, away from the main British advance. The argument that special operations tied down thousands of Iraqi troops who might otherwise have been sent south cut little ice with those who complained about Brigadier Lamb's troops 'screwing around on their own axis'. Lamb and *Beaufort* would have to couch their arguments for an ongoing Baghdad operation carefully, and Lamb would have to return to the UK to make the case in Whitehall, where many regarded the war as done and dusted.

Owing to the size of Operation ROW, *Beaufort* had deployed with the headquarters element referred to by British special forces types as TGHQ – Task Group Headquarters. This included the Commanding Officer, Regimental Sergeant-Major and Operations Officer of 22 SAS as well as several other key figures who usually resided back at the regiment's base in Herefordshire. Although the TGHQ could consist of as few as half a dozen people (though it was larger in this case), its use in any operation was always an important sign of scale and the UK's commitment, since most special forces operations tended to be run by the majors commanding special forces squadrons, which, depending on task, numbered a few dozen troops. The Americans had designated the SAS element in Iraq Task Force 14, and this name, often abbreviated to TF-14, came to be used by the SAS during its early months in Iraq.

Beaufort was a quite different figure from Lamb. Whereas Lamb's Scottish accent was slight, and sometimes lost in a relaxed drawl, *Beaufort* spoke with clipped precision. *Beaufort* embodied gen-erations of military service. Scion of an old West Country family, he was descended from a general who had once ruled Canada and an admiral of Nelson's era, and had progressed into the special forces via a top private school and the army's Household Division. One British general described him as 'a superb soldier, very urbane, very able, very clever, destined for the top'. Among the SAS commander's skills was a political instinct sharper than that of anyone else in the British special forces community. What Lamb and *Beaufort* had to do when they met in Baghdad was define more closely what the rationale for a continuing SAS role in the capital, away from the main British sphere of operations in Basra, should be.

One who watched them recalls, '[Lamb] did not want to end up supporting British forces in the south. He wanted to play the strategic game of supporting SIS in Baghdad'. In the short term, MI6 needed help to protect its people as they met with the agents that had supplied them with information prior to the fall of Saddam. Tony Blair's government had set such store in the argument that the Iraqi dictator needed to be toppled because he was continuing to develop Weapons of Mass Destruction that the imperative to find some actual proof of these claims was, to put it mildly, pressing. An SAS operator paraphrases the message from Brigadier Lamb in these early days: 'The strategic partnership with SIS is paramount and they're in the shit.' And even after the WMD issue had been dealt with, the spooks would need help.

TF-14 soon found themselves shifting from the mission of running around in heavily armed Land Rovers to the more subtle business of accompanying MI6 officers as they toured the city's better suburbs (and further afield) meeting their sources. This was a task often best conducted with a low profile. The decision was taken to start sending B and D Squadrons home. These two elements had spent months working up to the invasion with intensive training and were exhausted. By early May, a month after the SAS had arrived in Baghdad, G Squadron, which had impatiently sat out the invasion of Iraq as the regiment's counterterrorist stand-by force in the UK, started filtering in to take over as TF-14. In fact, it was not the whole squadron, for the system *Beaufort* had put in place as he took TGHQ and the others home was that a single squadron should be responsible for both of the regiment's main operational commitments, Iraq and Afghanistan. These SAS squadrons had an establishment, on paper at least, of around sixty men. With around a dozen men in

Afghanistan, this meant that the UK's special forces contingent in Iraq was soon down to twenty or thirty 'badged' – fully fledged – members of the regiment, with a few more from the supporting cast of signallers and medics. Of the four Sabre squadrons, G sometimes fancied itself as the most sophisticated in its approach. Certainly, the record of its squadron leaders succeeding to the overall command of 22 SAS was a good one. The 'G' commemorated the incorporation decades before into the regiment of the Guards Independent Parachute Company and there was a preference for having Guards officers in command of G Squadron.

Although *Charles Beaufort*, himself a graduate of G Squadron, would take a close interest in Iraqi developments, making frequent visits, it would be the squadron Officer Commanding who would become the ranking member of the SAS in-country.

Besides *Beaufort*, one other SAS officer of note was frequently in Baghdad during those early months. Major Richard Williams would become the third key player, with Lamb and *Beaufort*, shaping the SAS's operations in Iraq for years to come. The same general who extolled *Beaufort* above describes Williams as 'a superb field soldier. He wears his heart on his sleeve; he's very much an open book.' Tall, with dark tousled hair and blue eyes, the OC's demeanour was one of boyish enthusiasm. Williams had won the respect of his men the previous year, during an epic fire fight in southern Afghanistan. Tasked to assault a hill defended by dug-in Taleban but to do it without air support, Williams had led his soldiers up its slopes despite being hit by four bullets – none of which penetrated his equipment. He was awarded the Military Cross for his valour. Like many who serve with the regiment, Williams was driven. He told friends that the men who got through the arduous SAS selection process and prospered in the regiment were those who did not respect any limits: physical, psychological or of fear. 'Richard is a buccaneer, a pirate,' says a former colleague. 'He goes for the opportunities and the adrenalin every time.'

It did not take long for Williams to spot his, and the regiment's, opportunity in the growing chaos of Iraq's streets. The orgy of looting triggered by the collapse of Saddam's state had given way to all manner of violence. Williams wanted British operations to generate greater understanding of who was taking pot shots at Coalition troops, and why. It was equally apparent that the search for WMD, which was ostensibly their main task, was turning into an unproductive run-around. The debriefing of agents who had provided the British intelligence service with eye-catching lines in the government's Iraq dossier – such as the suggestion that WMD could be ready for launch in forty-five minutes, or that Saddam had resumed the production of chemical and biological weapons – was to produce some awkward scenes in Iraqi living rooms. As the sources of this dubious information drew from their cigarettes, shrugged their shoulders and confessed they had little idea where the stuff was, it became clearer just how deeply 'in the shit' MI6 were. The service eventually had to officially withdraw the intelligence of several of these key sources that had been used so publicly in the run-up to war.

The G Squadron Sergeant-Major, *Mike Page*, had to set his people up for business in a city in which Coalition combat units were laying claims to palaces and people were abandoning their luxury homes. There was no telling where the next day's mission might take them. Air mobility was critical so they would have to be ready to deploy from Baghdad airport at a moment's notice. On the other hand they did not wish to sit on the airport apron in the baking heat of an Iraqi summer, and the word from Delta (more properly 1st Special Forces Operational Detachment – Delta) was that they were finding quarters downtown.

Examining where Delta Force had lodged, *Page* discovered that a neighbouring villa was empty. He laid claim to it, arguing that the logistic and operational advantages of being next door to Delta would be considerable. Necessity had to be the mother of invention for *Page* and his men because once the war, or the Operation ROW deployment, was over, the SAS had no helicopters, or indeed armoured vehicles, of its own, just a handful of Land Rovers and SUVs. A further property was requisitioned by the Rangers – American special operators who support strikes by top-tier US troops – and the special operations village close to the centre of power began to take shape.

The SAS bashed a hole in the wall separating their property from Delta Force, and soon there was frequent two-way traffic between the neighbours. The British settled into the habit of Thursday night barbecues, raucous occasions that included beer, something forbidden to their Delta or Rangers neighbours. Each unit naturally equipped itself with an operations room, a gym and a television room. A landing pad big enough for several helicopters was laid out at the back of the row of houses. The whole complex was christened Mission Support Station (MSS) Fernandez, in memory of Master Sergeant George Fernandez, a Delta Force operator who had been killed in April fighting members of the jihadist group Ansar al-Islam in northern Iraq. The battle in which Fernandez died was a portent of the struggle that Task Force Green, as Delta was often called, and the rest of the special operations community in Iraq would face.

Having found a home at the MSS, G Squadron initially kept its HQ element and much of its gear at BIAP. Both the OC and the sergeant-major judged it better to keep their heavy stores in position there, ready for rapid deployment anywhere in the country. During the early months of the SAS operation in Baghdad, there was frequent shuttling between the airport and the MSS several miles to the east, in what soon came to be known as the Green Zone. The airport road would become one of the most dangerous stretches in Iraq, but as one SAS man said of those early months, 'I used to be able to drive on that road, on my own, at night'.

For G Squadron, the first significant operation of their tour came on 16 June. The US had issued its deck of cards of wanted Ba'athists and Lieutenant-General Abid Hamid Mahmud al-Tikriti, a key associate of Saddam Hussein, ranked as the fourth most important. He was indeed a High-Value Target, and British intelligence had picked up a trace of him. The takedown in Tikrit that night was a joint UK/US operation. A couple of dozen men from G Squadron sped north in their Land Rovers, meeting up at an airbase near the city with operators from B Squadron of Delta Force. They formulated an attack plan in which one group would be landed by helicopters while others assaulted on the ground. The place was taken without resistance and, after a brief comedy in which Tikriti had been identified wearing a bad wig, the Coalition operators had their man. Given that only Saddam and his two sons ranked higher in the HVT pecking order, it was considered a highly successful operation. The SAS had got started in the business many of them would call 'man hunting'.

Just over a week later, a disturbing event in the south drew in G Squadron and graphically demonstrated to British commanders the enormous potential for violence in Iraq. It happened in the town of Majar al-Kabir, in Maysan Province, one of those in the south that had been taken over by British forces. Arriving in Maysan, the British had soon become aware of its reputation for uncompromising lawlessness and banditry. The people there insisted they had liberated themselves from Saddam and did not want Coalition troops. British sweeps for guns, often using dogs – a tactic particularly inflammatory for Muslims – had caused local anger, and when six Royal Military Police soldiers had gone to a police station in Majar al-Kabir on 24 June a mob of several hundred attacked them.

What followed shocked the British army. Owing to poor coordination with the ground-holding unit (1st Battalion of the Parachute Regiment), nobody came to help the lightly armed RMPs, who took refuge in the police station. The crowd stormed the building and some of the Red Caps were shot, others beaten to death with fists and stones.

A couple of days after the incident, half a dozen members of the SAS descended on Majar al-Kabir. The Paras declined to support their sortie into the town. Pressing on without a Quick Reaction Force to come to their aid was hazardous, but the SAS men went on and, in their own style, made enquiries about who had been responsible for killing the British soldiers. It didn't take them long to get some answers, but gunmen were also appearing on the streets and it became apparent that they would have to shoot their way out.

The soldiers gathered their information, quitting the town under a hail of fire. But those running the British division in southern Iraq discouraged the SAS from going back in to arrest those responsible for the 24 June killings. The guidance to the special operators was just the same as it had been to 1 Para – stay out until the situation calms down.

In these few days in June 2003, the SAS team had seen the way things were going to play out. The future lay in Baghdad.

Those who ran UK special forces knew well enough that if they wanted to mount successful takedowns good, timely intelligence was critical to success. The more operations you wanted, the more intelligence you would need. As SIS started to set up shop, it was apparent that its variety of tasks, ranging from trying to find WMD to gathering political intelligence or predicting what might happen in the post-Saddam power vacuum, meant they could throw TF-14 the occasional bone but little more. And even if they did bring in a good tip, how would the SAS get there without its own helicopters, how would they fit in with the other troops operating there and who would back them up if things went wrong? These questions could be answered in part by sticking close to the Americans: if they were involved in every operation they could provide choppers and liaise with the local US ground-holding unit. But if the SAS worked like that they could show little independence and might be completely scuppered when operating in the British-held areas to the south. And if they could do so little on their own, what point was there in adding a few dozen British special operators to the huge killing machine already set in motion by the US?

To Williams, *Beaufort* and Lamb, the answers to these questions suggested that the SAS either develop its capabilities or give up the game. Since none of them were quitters by nature, they needed a stand-alone operation – or at least elements of one. The first step consisted of forming a special Iraqi unit as part of TF-14.

During the invasion of Iraq the British had assisted Scorpion Force, a special intelligence collection unit bankrolled by the CIA and manned largely by Iraqis. Much of the raw material for this outfit had come from the exiled Iraqi opposition – the mostly Shia and Kurd anti-Saddam parties on which the Pentagon set great store in those early days after the invasion. Scorpion Force was not considered a success for many reasons; many of its men disappeared soon after the invasion and others were considered to be political hacks rather than soldiers.

Starting afresh, the British set about assembling a different team of Iraqis. They found a dozen, so the unit was immediately christened The Apostles. The Apostles would emerge as the unsung heroes of what was to follow. They were used for everything from interpreting for SAS teams on the ground to more sensitive operations. Their singular advantage in all these missions was an ability to blend in on Iraqi streets in a way no foreigner could manage.

As the operation built up, the obvious question was, what was it for? The search for WMD soon became the kind of dispiriting exercise that many in the forces are used to but special operators, with their thirst for action or other tangible successes, carry out on sufferance. It was obvious with the killing already breaking out on Baghdad's streets that it had political undercurrents. What was going on? Coalition forces had already killed hundreds, perhaps thousands of irregulars, from the Fedayeen Saddam and other groups during the invasion. Were the people who the Pentagon high-ups liked to call 'Ba'athist dead-enders' going to rally resistance to the invaders? Or what about the jihadists, religious extremists like Ansar al-Islam, whom intelligence suggested were summoning mujahedeen from across the Middle East to do battle with Americans in Iraq?

The top brass back in the UK didn't seem to care about the answers to these questions. 'There was a sense of apathy in the UK about why any of this mattered,' recalls one special operator. 'We were going into soft hats.' The view of those watching the glue of Iraqi society dissolving on the streets of Baghdad was quite different from those back home, who just wanted to move on. With a bewildering array of possible enemies – from jihadists to demobbed officers or Sunni tribes – the SAS needed proper authority to shift from the war and WMD missions to something new. Major Williams took the initiative. In June 2003 he sent up a request for a new mission. It went through the command machinery back in the UK and was duly authorised under the codename Operation PARADOXICAL. Those who know about the contents of this secret order say it was very broadly drawn, allowing the SAS to target 'threats to the

Coalition' without defining exactly what they were. While others debated whether an insurgency had really broken out, Britain's special operators had already written their own marching orders.

2

INTO THE BLOOD

On 31 October 2003, Halloween, the SAS set out from the Big Brother House, as they had dubbed their modern-looking Baghdad mansion. They were riding in a handful of Land Rover WMIKs – Land Rovers mounted with heavy machine guns – and other Land Rovers. They nosed through the traffic in a city that was changing by the week.

The old government quarter on the west bank of the Tigris was already being sealed with concrete T-walls, concertina wire and roadblocks. At its centre was the Republican Palace with its giant sculptures of Saddam's head on each corner. The special ops complex that the SAS had left that day, MSS Fernandez, was also walled into the four square miles of the Green Zone.

As this part of the city centre was sealed off, traffic started slowing and choking because of all the detours. Outside the

Green Zone the oases of calm or pleasure that the city's five million inhabitants had enjoyed were being smothered. As one bomb followed another at the main entrance to this fortified area, the once-bustling shops on nearby Haifa Street became too dangerous for most. Across the river, on Abu Nawas Street, there were restaurants where wealthy Baghdadis sat drinking arak or beer and downing *masgouf*, a local carp dish. But Abu Nawas Street was close to the Sheraton and Palestine Hotels where many foreign visitors were, and foreigners had become targets. As the road was closed with barbed wire and concrete, one by one the restaurants shut up shop.

There had been pleasure in Saddam's Iraq as well as pain. But as the summer of 2003 wore on, all of the characteristics of life as it used to be – from fear of the secret policeman on the corner to the delights of washing down your *masgouf* with a bottle of beer – were disappearing. Through the carrots and sticks of Ba'athist Iraq, Baghdad had functioned as a multicultural metropolis, but with the arrival of the Americans this era was over. In this new world of uncertainty everybody seemed to be staking their claim with violence. In the east of Baghdad, in Sadr City – home to hundreds of thousands of Shia – gangs of looters had armed themselves with everything up to and including heavy machine guns and mortars. And while the Shia political parties had not yet turned on the Coalition, whom they thanked for toppling their oppressor, they were busy forming armed militia groups.

The western districts of Baghdad, through which the SAS column made its way, were predominantly Sunni. In these areas, attacks on passing Coalition forces had already started. The SAS was keeping itself busy responding to this emerging disorder, though as special forces they weren't specifically focused on this street-level aggro, but rather the underlying strategic connections, for example those emerging between jihadists in Iraq and men coming in from other countries. Their broadly drawn post-invasion mission, Operation PARADOXICAL, gave them great latitude to operate with US classified forces prosecuting the best available intelligence. That was just how the regiment liked to do business.

Britain's hand-picked troops headed west in their Land Rovers, under blue motorway signs that marked the way to Fallujah and Ramadi. The mission that night was to mount a raid on a compound near Ramadi. There were about two dozen 'blades' or fighting members of the regiment (the term coming from the designation as Sabre Squadrons of its four fighting sub-units A, B, D and G) in the convoy. G Squadron had left Iraq in August and it was the turn of A Squadron to go out looking for trouble. Being technically the senior of the regiment's four sub-units, A Squadron fancied itself as the best, but naturally every other squadron would have disputed it. There was a steady banter in the vehicles – humour was rarely in short supply on these ops and A Squadron could never have been accused of taking itself too seriously. Its badge, semi-officially at least, bears what looks like a red scorpion on a blue background but, legend has it, the creature is in fact a pubic louse removed decades before from the moustache of a squadron sergeant-major.

The road running west through the Sunni heartlands to the Jordanian border had already proven thoroughly dangerous. Aid and news organisations had stopped using it after numerous brushes with armed men – bandits or insurgents, people weren't quite sure what to call them – who robbed and sometimes killed passers-by. The convoy passed Abu Ghraib, where American guards had already taken over Saddam's notorious prison, and over the Fallujah cloverleaf.

By late October, with the onset of Ramadan, something crazy had started in Iraq. The killing was soaring, as if open season had been declared on the invaders. Back in August there had been ten to fifteen attacks a day on Coalition forces across Iraq. By the end of October it had doubled, and by late November the shooting, mortars and car bombs would be running at around three times the figure of the summer.

In the weeks that A Squadron had been in Iraq there had been a distinct change in what the soldiers called 'atmospherics'. Widespread unrest in Sunni areas – an insurrection, in fact – had broken out against the Americans. There had also been some spectacular attacks using huge truck bombs: the Jordanian embassy in Baghdad had been blown up on 7 August; twelve days later the United Nations compound had been flattened and their special envoy to Iraq among the twenty-two people killed; and on 29 August Ayatollah Mohammed Baqer Hakim, a senior Shia cleric, had been the victim of another massive blast. The hallmark of all three attacks was the use of what the Americans called 'V-bids' or VBIEDs – Vehicle-Borne Improvised Explosive Devices, driven by suicide attackers against highly symbolic targets, which cause large numbers of casualties. In the case of the bomb that killed Ayatollah Hakim at the Shia spiritual centre of Najaf, more than ninety had been killed.

As the mercury of political killing had soared in autumn 2003, the Americans and their allies had struggled to understand it. There were so many different strands of violence that the intelligence analysts sent to Baghdad, few of whom had much experience of the Arab world, could not untangle them. The Bush Administration's desire to force this mayhem into an ideological template had its own consequences. The orthodoxy coming down from the Office of the Secretary of Defence was that the violence must either be a product of Ba'athist 'dead-enders' trying to regain power or was being perpetrated by foreigners, fuelled up on Osama bin Laden's international jihadism. Many in the Administration believed that Iraq fitted into the Global War on Terror, seeing the country as a great prize in the contest between the US – which was trying to turn it into a modern Middle Eastern democracy – and al-Qaeda, which could not allow this to happen. Some did disagree with this orthodoxy, for example General John Abizaid, head of Central Command, who had ruffled feathers in Washington in July 2003 by calling the situation a 'classical guerrilla war', but the idea that the violence resulted from a widespread Iraqi rejection of the invasion still rankled with Donald Rumsfeld and many others. Consequently, the tasking of critical intelligence assets and, through them, of Coalition special operations forces was closely linked to Administration ideology.

The special ops people had been steadily rounding up the former Ba'athists in the pack of cards. Late in July, Saddam's sons Uday and Qusay had been cornered and killed: the owner of the Mosul house in which they were hiding had sold them out for the reward money. Many of the intelligence people had, however, started to wonder whether rounding up the old leadership was going to get them out of trouble. Instead of the secular old Ba'athists, they worried about the new face of international Islamic militancy. Might they even be doing the jihadists a favour by removing the natural local leadership in many Sunni areas, creating a vacuum? Their answer was to pursue 'transnational terrorists' or foreign fighters at the same time as the Ba'athists. But if thousands of Muslims were heeding Osama bin Laden or al-Qaeda number two Ayman al-Zawahiri's appeal to wage jihad in Iraq against the infidels, then there was a shortage of actionable intelligence about what might be done to stop it. Delta Force had glimpsed this threat in the north, during its early confrontation with Ansar al-Islam, but months had gone by without hard leads. This Halloween, the American agencies had turned up something fresh – a tip about what they might find in Ramadi.

Meeting their colleagues from Delta in a laying-up point outside the city, the SAS received a briefing. The Americans were in pursuit of an important Sudanese jihadist believed to be facilitating the arrival of Islamic militants into Iraq and operating from a safe house in Ramadi. His work had required contact with brothers in other countries and the Americans had homed in on a satellite phone that he used. The operation, codenamed ABALONE, involved a series of assaults on a strip of dwellings on the fringes of Ramadi. The street faced onto open ground and it was across this sand that the main SAS assault would be delivered. Ramadi was already sufficiently dangerous that this operation might produce widespread resistance, so the local US unit, a mechanised infantry battalion normally based in Germany, had assigned a platoon of Bradleys to support the attack. The Bradley is a tracked and turreted heavy armoured vehicle – though many laymen assume it is a tank. It can carry infantry though, and its main weapon, a 25mm cannon, is much lighter than that of a tank.

So, on the evening of 31 October A Squadron prepared to assault a compound near the city, having turned up in Land Rovers and with the small number of night-vision goggles allocated to them. Fortunately the Americans were in support. The Bradleys and some of the Delta operators had gone into an 'overwatch' position, exploiting their vehicle-mounted weapons and night-vision equipment to observe what was going on at the target, and ready to give supporting fire from long range if it was needed.

Meanwhile, Major *Baker*, the OC of A Squadron, gave orders for the assault of two houses. Tall, fair-haired and bluff, *Baker* was respected by his blades as the kind of boss who kept his own ego in the background – his character fitted well with A Squadron's image of itself. One of his call-signs, A20, would hit the first house, while A10 would hit the second. Delta had a couple of target buildings too. A20 entered without incident. A10, led by Captain *Morris*, a young commander who had only been with his troop a few months, prepared to force an entry into their compound. Like many of the larger houses in Iraq, it had high metal gates behind which were a main residence and some smaller structures. Other teams were ready both to block anyone trying to flee and to reinforce the assault as A10 and A20 went in.

SAS soldiers practise house assaults a great deal – it is one of the basic drills that they repeat ad nauseam. Live fire exercises in the 'Killing House' at their UK training area are performed so frequently that each man will know his place as the first trooper goes through a door and will be able to fire without hesitation at any threat they encounter but spare the innocent. During their time in Iraq, A Squadron had already performed several assaults on buildings or compounds with smooth precision. That night, though, things would be different.

When the SAS men burst through the gates of the compound they were greeted with a hail of fire from the windows of the building to their front. An RPG 7 rocket was fired straight at them, and assault rifles opened up too. Within seconds, all the members of A10 had been hit. *Morris*, who had taken a bullet in the backside, turned tail and hobbled out as fast as he could. Every SAS trooper is trained in battlefield first aid and as the captain dropped into cover his men went to work, surveying the wounds to him and the others. Major *Baker*, meanwhile, gathered several men and moved to the roof of a building further down the street, from which they could fire into the target compound.

After a head count he realised that two of A10's men were probably still inside the target. His concern for them meant he could not simply ask Delta and the Bradleys to open up with everything they had. Instead he asked a couple of his men to approach the gate to see whether they could spot their missing comrades.

Inside that yard lay Corporal Ian Plank, blood pumping out of a bullet wound to his face. He couldn't be reached for medical treatment, but in any case it was already too late. Nearby, Corporal *Saltash* was too badly hurt to get himself out. He had dragged himself into cover and lay just a few feet from the windows, where he could hear the insurgents. He scraped away at the sand with his hands to make himself a little lower in the ground then, fighting the pain of his wound, removed the magazines and grenades from his chest rig, laying them in front of him ready for immediate use. The darkness and the layout of the buildings meant that the OC and others firing from the nearby roof could not see the wounded SAS soldier.

Saltash would later tell his mates that he could hear the people inside praying together, seemingly 'they knew they were going to die'. But the wounded SAS corporal did not know whether the jihadists would find him first.

Spotting *Saltash*, his two mates – a sergeant and a trooper – made an immediate decision to rush into the compound and get him. Some might have argued it was too dangerous given what had happened to everyone who had gone through the gates before, but they ran in nevertheless. Perhaps those inside were still praying because as the rescuers ran in nothing happened. But their luck only lasted a few seconds longer. As they hauled *Saltash* to his feet an AK-47 opened up from one of the windows. The two rescuers dragged *Saltash* from the compound with bullets flying all around them and somehow none sustained further injury. The SAS trooper involved in rescuing *Saltash* would serve three tours in Iraq, gain promotion to corporal and become one of the most highly decorated men in the regiment.

With his men accounted for, Major *Baker* had to consider the bigger picture. There was fire coming from A10's target and another as yet uncleared building. Conferring with the Americans, *Baker*'s men prosecuted an assault on their third house of the night, while Delta was given the task of hitting Captain

Morris's original target. The Bradleys opened up with their 25mm cannon and TOW anti-tank missiles, pummelling the house before Delta delivered its assault.

A Squadron's third assault went in further along the street. Clearing the building room by room they met resistance and killed one man. Four foreign fighters – thought to be Yemeni or Saudi – were taken in this SAS target building.

Inside, the houses were strewn with rubble, spent bullet casings, and bodies. Outside the situation was difficult, with running contacts going on with Iraqi gunmen in the surrounding area. A Squadron's Delta liaison had called up a medevac (medical evacuation) helicopter to lift out the more seriously wounded SAS soldiers.

Judging the difficulty of their situation, the SAS knew they could not dawdle. 'Exploitation', as the search of such an objective is called, would have to be done as swiftly as possible. Major *Baker*'s soldiers were not even sure of how many people they had killed. They were clear about the single fighter in the third compound, but suspected that their own and American fire might have killed as many as a dozen in the compound where Corporal Plank had been killed.

The glimmer of first light had appeared, and the scene of the shoot-out was 'messy and pretty chaotic – it was a bloody dangerous place to be around daylight'. They had not caught their Sudanese target alive. Was he among several people believed to have died in the house initially hit by A10 and then by Delta? What they were sure of was that the SAS had detained four non-Iraqi volunteers. 'There was some excitement about that,' comments one special operator. 'It was early evidence of foreign fighters.'

A Squadron and Delta withdrew, with hard lessons learned from that night's operation. They had lost a man and three more had been wounded. Ian Plank, a Royal Marine from the Special

Boat Service attached to A Squadron, was the UK special forces' first combat fatality of the Iraq campaign. Some of the blades had plenty of experience of raiding houses in Northern Ireland and were hence used to being able to reach their target and prepare for the assault in comparative safety. Ramadi, however, had proven entirely different. The revolt there had produced risks to the attacking troops from small arms, rocket-propelled grenades (RPGs) and roadside bombs before they even got near their objective. The British had felt ill-equipped in this fight, particularly in comparison to their American teammates. They needed more night-vision equipment and armoured vehicles. For Lieutenant-Colonel *Beaufort* running the SAS back in the UK, trying to get more resources for his men from an indifferent MoD, Operation ABALONE became an important part of the briefings he gave that autumn. It highlighted the risks faced by operators on the ground, as well as what was at stake as foreign mujahedeen flocked to the Iraqi battlefield.

Ramadi and Fallujah – urban centres with populations in the hundreds of thousands – had already gained a reputation for fearsome violence. But who was doing it and how could they be targeted? Reporters who braved the dangerous roads to talk to gun-toting figures hiding their faces with keffiyehs heard tell of a popular revolt by Iraqis against a blundering invader. One resistance fighter hinted at the panic shown by the foreigners under attack in these communities, telling the *Boston Globe* 'when we attack the Americans, they start shooting like blind people, in all directions'.

Outrage was so widespread that the fighting men received plenty of local backing. 'We don't like Saddam; he was a dictator,' Osam Fahdawi, a businessman in Fallujah told an American reporter. 'But the Americans, they handcuff us, they put us on the floor in front of our wives and children. It's shameful for us.'

All of this meant that, by late 2003, the Americans could

expect to be attacked pretty much every time they went into town from their Forward Operating Bases or 'Fobs'. A Squadron mounted several missions in the two cities during October and November, often adopting a covert approach by donning local clothes and using civilian cars. But while during the 1991 Gulf War or Operation ROW some had simply put a woollen cloak over their combat rig and wrapped a keffiyeh around their heads, this would not do in the ferment of the Sunni Triangle. Instead local markets were scoured for suitable shirts or trousers, sunglasses were binned and skins often darkened. 'We've had the SAS here a few times,' the American ground commander in Fallujah told me at the time, adding with a knowing wink, 'They're wearing Arab clothes and they look pretty convincing . . . except their watches and boots give them away!'

The SAS's attempt to raise its game was, as the year closed, just a small part of what was going on in Iraq special ops. Britain's presence was dwarfed by the American laydown. The players in that world of classified units, barely acknowledged by the Pentagon, were trying to get a slice of the action in Iraq. There was a marked lack of coherence or purpose in their early operations. However, an officer had been sent to take charge and he would soon make his presence felt at every level of the secret war.

3

THE SOLDIER-MONK

'The first thing that struck me about him was how absurdly young he looked for a general.' Honed by his early morning eight-mile run and a single proper meal each day, Major-General Stanley McChrystal was physically greyhound-like, and his manner projected intellectual intensity. He had been appointed in September to take over the Tier 1 classified force – Joint Special Operations Command. One of McChrystal's JSOC colleagues describes him as 'Jesuit-like, ruthless, brilliant'. Often referred to by his SAS colleagues as 'a soldier-monk', he would prove the single most important figure in the cast of characters who defined the secret war in Iraq.

McChrystal's upbringing was typical of the army brat who follows his father around the world, from one military post to another. That officer fought in Korea and Vietnam. Young

Stanley graduated from the US Military Academy at West Point in 1976, a member of a class full of later generals. Those who know him say McChrystal disliked intensely the bullshit and limited intellectual horizons of that institution. His ability to think outside the box was evident as he climbed the promotion ladder. 'I first worked for him in the Gulf War,' Graeme Lamb recalled, 'and General McChrystal was the fastest, sharpest staff officer I had ever come across.'

After that first Iraq war, McChrystal returned from the staff to a prestige field role commanding a paratroop battalion in the 82nd Airborne Division in the early nineties. He tried to find the right outlet for his fierce intellect while dealing day to day with those who could not match it. 'He doesn't suffer fools gladly,' says a fellow officer from his battalion, adding – apparently without irony – 'which must have made it really hard for him to stay in the army.'

McChrystal's turning point came in the mid-nineties, first as a battalion commander and later as overall head of the 75th Ranger Regiment. On the spectrum of military otherness, the Rangers stand about halfway between the paratrooper battalion he had left and the covert non-conformists of Delta Force. Rangers are used for assault missions, often backing up the Tier 1 special operators. McChrystal thrived in the Rangers, and this produced the glowing reports and testimonials required to take him to higher command.

As a one-star or brigadier-general, the rising talent was given another staff job where he encountered more British officers. One, who worked for McChrystal in Afghanistan in 2002, described with wonder the change wrought in corps headquarters by the soldier-monk. McChrystal did not like the hierarchy of information going up the chain of command from battalion to brigade to division and so on. He preferred 'agile groupings' of people to share it, a McKinsey management science approach of de-layered authority over data. His two hundred staff in Afghanistan used an intranet that permitted all, regardless of rank, to have access to the same information. They worked from a common homepage on their screens and communicated via headsets. It was not a free-for-all, since McChrystal still expected to be in charge, but he wanted to bypass the structures, hierarchies and procedures that he felt stopped the efficient flow of information as well as his people giving their best. The mantra heard repeatedly by a British officer from his American brigadier in Afghanistan would prove central to everything McChrystal did in Iraq: 'you've got to build a network to defeat a network'.

Before arriving in Iraq, the up-and-coming general served briefly at the Pentagon. The byzantine office politics and turf wars there appalled him, and his role in briefing the press on the progress of the Iraq campaign could hardly have sat easily with someone more used to the shadows. People who know McChrystal suggest he disliked the Pentagon almost as much as West Point, but in September 2003 he was able to leave. He returned to the fight leading one of the most prestigious but secret commands open to him.

Heading up Joint Special Operations Command (JSOC), he would face an unenviable challenge. Given the difficulties of operating in places like Ramadi or Baghdad, the task of gathering intelligence about who exactly was behind the rising tide of violence and quelling it in a targeted way – by mounting precision special forces raids – was going to be extremely difficult. For troops such as the SAS or US Tier 1 special ops, results required timely and accurate intelligence, but the methods for gathering secret information were rudimentary to say the least. This shortcoming was to prove critical in the matter of how the elite forces might pick out the foreign fighters swimming in the sea of popular Sunni resentment of the invasion.

McChrystal knew only too well that the campaign against the insurgency had so far produced precious few moments when the intelligence picture was of a really high quality. When the Americans had hit the Ansar al-Islam jihadists in the spring of 2003 they had been directed to their target by allied Kurdish groups, who provided information through their longstanding CIA liaison. This had given the Americans the confidence to know that they were striking a major concentration of foreign fighters. Travelling in the north of Iraq shortly after these events, Arab journalist Zaki Chehab found plenty of evidence of the international militant brotherhood. Sheikh Ali, the leader of a Kurdish Islamist party opposed to the jihadists, told Chehab, 'We know for a fact that they have Arab foreigners with them from Jordan, Palestine and al-Ahwaz [the Arab majority area of Iran].' Finding a jail run by one of the Kurdish *peshmerga*, or militia groups, Chehab, himself a Palestinian, met Mohammed, a countryman from Gaza who had been captured after the US onslaught against Ansar al-Islam in April. Chehab asked the prisoner why he had travelled to Iraq when there were plenty of opportunities for jihad back home. The Palestinian fighter replied, 'They are one and the same enemy, and if we succeed in defeating the US here, it will be the end of the Jewish state.'

What could be found in the Kurdish north, which for years had been outside the control of Saddam's *mukhabarat* (secret police), was to prove elusive elsewhere. Even late in 2003, when Operation ABALONE turned up evidence of foreign fighters, finding actual proof of an internationalist jihadist movement channelling people into Iraq was proving elusive. The CIA and military intelligence had no mature networks of agents outside the Kurdish north. There was no mobile phone network to speak of either. This left the questioning of prisoners as one of the only viable means of intelligence-gathering.

When it came to interrogation, however, basic language barriers and the absence of any proper system for collating the information hamstrung operations. Just entering information from Iraqis, translated into English, onto computers caused difficulties. 'Transliteration was a huge problem,' explains one MI6 veteran of those early days. 'We didn't even have a common way of writing "Mohammed". We literally had no idea who we had in prison.' During those first months, interrogation had provided plenty of leads in chasing down the old Ba'athists, but the jihadists were to prove a far tougher target. Being bundled into prison was a novel and highly unpleasant experience for many of the displaced Iraqi elite who had enjoyed a comfortable life prior to the invasion. Many of the religious militants, on the other hand, had already had experience of detention and torture at the hands of secret police across the Arab world, so they were hardly intimidated by the Americans.

Given the paucity of solid information about who was orchestrating the violence – particularly the car bombings – there were heated debates among the intelligence people. Under the American special operations hierarchy, the best targets were to be prosecuted by units variously referred to as 'Tier 1', 'classified', 'special mission' or 'black' SOF (special operations forces). This differentiated them from the so-called 'white SOF', publicly acknowledged Tier 2 units, such as the US Army special forces groups – or Green Berets – which also operated in the region. The SAS were the British equivalent to the American Tier 1 units. The Pentagon's elite within an elite were grouped together as the Joint Special Operations Command or JSOC. Being at the top of the secret pyramid, JSOC was most interested in the links between foreign fighters in Iraq and the al-Qaeda leadership in Pakistan. Their command, codenamed at that time Task Force 121, was set up in such a way that Delta and other elements of JSOC could be switched between Afghanistan and Iraq as required. They saw it as a joined-up struggle, part of the Bush Administration's War on Terror. British experts – from both MI6 and military intelligence – preferred to stress the home-grown nature of most of the Iraqi resistance. In this barely coded way, those who had been convinced by the White House's justifications for invading Iraq, and those who had not, continued to argue it out.

While McChrystal tried to understand his enemy in order to perfect the means to be used against it, the attempts by Britain's special ops community to get the rising tide of violence in Iraq taken seriously in Whitehall had at last begun to bear fruit. Not long after the Halloween fight in Ramadi, a small detachment of RAF Chinook helicopters arrived at Baghdad International, earmarked to support A Squadron's operations. This was a tangible sign of change in the British setup. Late that November, A Squadron used the choppers in an assault on a remote farm in al-Anbar Province. After A Squadron's men came under fire from insurgents inside, air support was called in to hit the compound. When it was finally cleared, seven dead men, whom the Americans believed to be foreign fighters, were found inside.

In the Green Zone, meanwhile, an operation able to gather and fuse intelligence of different kinds was coming together, often under the aegis of SIS. 'We got serious UK buy-in,' notes one SAS officer. 'The Americans were going to support us but they didn't want us to become a draw on resources.'

During the dying days of A Squadron's four-month deployment, the character of the SAS operation in Iraq was changing once again. It had gone from the invasion and Operation ROW, through the G Squadron tour when it was expected to pursue the bewildering range of missions of Operation PARA-DOXICAL, to finding a new focus as a counterterrorist force operating from the country's capital. Its masters in the UK,

Charles Beaufort and the Director of Special Forces had, as part of the price of convincing other Whitehall players who did not believe in their mission, been forced to place the operation under the control of the Chief of Joint Operations in Northwood – the command centre that runs Britain's world-wide operations – instead of running it on their own.

Some argue that this new arrangement would not have hap-pened had Graeme Lamb still been DSF. In July 2003 he had been promoted to major-general and given command of an armoured division. In his place came Brigadier *Peter Rogers* – who, perhaps, was not inclined to take on the fight so early in his tenure. The change might seem like a dry, bureaucratic distinc-tion, but it was important in defining what happened subsequently. It meant abandoning an element of the independ-ence the SAS enjoyed during the invasion and Operation PARADOXICAL. The free-wheeling days of that summer and autumn, in which G and A squadrons had been joined at the hip to Delta and JSOC, were over. And, as the soldier-monk refined his ideas, it would become more difficult for the SAS to cooper-ate fruitfully with McChrystal. UK special forces lost their distinct chain of command in accepting the 'interference' of offi-cers in Northwood, some of whom were deeply sceptical about the Iraq mission. A few of these figures, even if they understood why the main deployment of British forces in southern Iraq was politically necessary, couldn't see why the SAS had to be in Baghdad at all. One officer who fought this battle of office pol-itics back home recalls that some were asking, 'Is this the SF out on the flank doing their own fucking thing again?' The new DSF, *Peter Rogers*, 'wanted to tread more lightly in Whitehall than Graeme Lamb had. [He] had to put the whole thing on a more sustainable footing, and a joint operation was a sort of loss leader.'

So the SAS got its helicopters and expanded military intelli-gence capability. In return, it gave up some operational independence to the Chief of Joint Operations (CJO) at Northwood and planted the seeds for possible conflict with the classified American operation of JSOC. There were various things that the SAS had not or could not be given as A Squadron was replaced late in 2003. Britain did not at that time have its own Predator drones for live video coverage of targets. It had to rely on limited coverage from Nimrod manned surveillance aircraft, but even that was often unavailable. It did not have its own detainee facilities in Baghdad either. And it was in this area that trouble was brewing for both the British and the new JSOC commander.

This establishment of a 'semi-detached British operation' in Baghdad, under closer supervision from UK-based officers, ran counter to the network that McChrystal wanted to develop. But at that moment the finer points of command structures or UK–US cooperation were hardly at the forefront of most people's minds. For at the time the new JSOC commander arrived and A Squadron mounted its Ramadi operation almost every aspect of the US project in Iraq was going wrong. Lives, and American prestige, were haemorrhaging away.

The Coalition Provisional Authority, set up to run the country until an Iraqi government could be established, had proven inefficient, misplacing billions of dollars while living conditions for ordinary Iraqis collapsed. By late 2003 grandiose plans to fashion a model Middle Eastern democracy were already giving way to an accelerated effort to turn over power to local leaders.

Arabists in the British embassy and MI6 station kept up a caustic running commentary as political, security and presentational mistakes multiplied. 'Have you ever met an Arab who said he wanted democracy?' a senior MI6 officer asked – rhetorically – at the time. 'The Americans were in total denial about the state of the insurgency,' says another British intelligence officer. 'The arrogance and hubris of some of them were breathtaking.'

The aggregate effect of American folly, detainee abuse, poor intelligence and the cautionary influence of those overseeing operations in the UK was, for many months, to have a deadening impact on special forces activities in Iraq. In the south meanwhile, some flattered themselves that the British operation was a model of how things ought to be done.

Down in Basra, the Shia majority still remained broadly welcoming towards the Coalition that had liberated them from Saddam's oppression. The area had been tightly gripped by the *mukharabat*, particularly after the Shia rising following the Gulf War in 1991. Thousands had been tortured and murdered and the southern port, once a hub of regional commerce, deliberately starved of investment. The city British troops had entered was friendly. Soft-skin Land Rovers and rented civilian 'white fleet' vehicles remained a common sight, and troops tried to patrol built-up areas in soft hats rather than helmets. There was plenty of time for sport and officers at the air station could enjoy a beer or bottle of wine at the end of their day's work (and indeed continued to do so until late 2005). The MI6 Chief of Station referred to Basra as 'the sleepy shire by the Shatt al-Arab'.

As time wore on, however, the surge of expectations that greeted the fall of Saddam had gone unmet. There had been some signs of trouble: the killing of the six military police in Majar al-Kabir had been the most shocking, but there had been other incidents too. In the slums on the city's eastern edge, such as at the bazaar christened the Five Mile Market by the soldiers or the Shia Flats (the huge housing development known to locals as the Hayyaniyah), aggro had already become routine. Stones flew, causing the soldiers to attach wire mesh to their Land Rovers, and bullets sometimes came in too.

The Shia political parties with their own armed militias promised to look after the streets. After the assassination of Ayatollah

41

Hakim by car bomb that August, the British made the fateful decision to allow Shia militias to run their own checkpoints, claiming that they needed to do so to prevent car bomb attacks on their offices in the city. Large numbers of these armed party members, particularly from the late Ayatollah's party, were also co-opted straight into the police force. The militia had begun to spread their tentacles through the city – with British agreement.

Major-General Graeme Lamb was by October 2003 back in Iraq commanding Multi-National Division South East. When, during a BBC interview that November, I asked him whether his predecessor's decision to allow the militia to bear arms in the city would buy short-term quiet at the expense of long-term stability, he candidly accepted that only time could answer that question.

SAS and MI6 personnel who visited Basra during those months, and through the following year, talk with despair about the general half-heartedness of the operation, even while Lamb, a man after their own heart, was in charge. One describes a 'critical mass' of complacency in an officer corps formed in Northern Ireland and the Balkans. Others highlight the lack of energy with which intelligence gathering or training the Iraqi police was conducted. 'It was not impressive,' notes one frequent SAS visitor to Basra during the early months. 'The Brits were looking over their shoulder and asking "when can we pack up and go home?"' Another SAS man comments in a similar but more caustic vein, 'They were just doing what we'd done in Kosovo, which was to fuck about and count the days until they went home.'

Given the generally quiet nature of the British patch in southern Iraq at this early stage, officers at MND South East HQ were not too keen on the special forces stirring things up. In any case, the challenge for the SAS squadron and its growing contingent of 'enablers' was how they could make an impact on an increasingly violent situation in the capital. They would struggle throughout 2004 to answer that question. The new British mission and deployment was codenamed Operation CRICHTON, a title that remained in use until 2009 when their stay in Iraq ended. Not long after CRICHTON was agreed in Whitehall, a new codename was agreed for the SF squadron and its supporting team in Baghdad: Task Force Black.

4

BUILDING NETWORKS

During the early weeks of 2004 a band of construction workers plied their trade across central Iraq. They ran big risks, not least because they were installing generators at each of the sites they completed, and generators were extremely valuable in that power-starved country. The work they were doing involved hundreds of sites in Baghdad and would eventually extend to 1300 across the country. In some places they made use of existing structures – such as masts or tall buildings – in others the bright red and white painted towers that they needed were brought in through Kuwait. The workers in question were putting up a mobile phone network.

Several months after the invasion of Iraq, bids had been invited for those who wanted to install the new communications system. At the time of the invasion, the fixed phone system provided around 800,000 lines to the country's 26 million people. Naturally the prevalence of telephones was higher among government officials and their cronies, and naturally also the main government phone nodes had been targeted during the invasion. Mobile phone operators therefore saw a huge opportunity – an open market. Three contractors were eventually chosen, operating in the south, centre and north of the country. In the centre, which included Baghdad, the mobile phone company calling itself Iraqna was ready to begin operations in February 2004.

During the early years of the network it would grow nationally at a rate of more than 100,000 new subscribers per month. The birth of mobile telephony might therefore have been seen as one of the rare success stories of the Coalition Provisional Authority phase of government. Inevitably, though, there were some who saw ways in which mobile phones might be deployed to kill people. Their use as triggering devices for roadside bombs or improvised explosive devices (IEDs) soon became a standard tactic. The phenomenal growth of Iraqna would, in time, provide opportunities for the Coalition to turn the tables on the insurgency, but early in 2004 few had the vision to see this.

For one young American, the new mobile network was to exert a lethal attraction. Nick Berg came to Iraq hoping to make big money erecting phone masts. He was a lone figure in the tide of corporate gold-diggers flooding the country in pursuit of fat construction or security contracts. Moving between cheap Iraqi hotels at a time when executives from the big firms were already shielded by convoys of armed security guards, Berg stood out as a naïve, even suicidal, figure. Both American soldiers and ordinary Iraqis warned him of the dangers. Having left the country in February, he returned in March and was arrested in Mosul by the Iraqi police. He was sprung by American officials in April and told to leave. But Berg did not get out, returning instead to a Baghdad hotel, and soon became the victim of one of the kidnap gangs that flourished in the growing mayhem.

During his captivity predictable charges of spying were levelled against Berg. Anguished pleas from his father, an anti-Bush, anti-war activist, were ignored. His captors probably hardly believed the espionage allegations themselves, instead employing the young American as a prop in their jihadist communications strategy. By May, having outlived his usefulness, Berg was beheaded by black-clad masked figures while a video camera recorded the spectacle. The resulting film, complete with screams as a man with a long knife saws away at the tendon and bone of the hostage's neck, appeared on the internet.

The video started with a caption, 'Abu Musab al-Zarqawi slaughters an American'. A few days later US experts studying the masked figure who wielded the knife confirmed that they thought it was indeed the Jordanian jihadist known by that name. Having reached the age of 37 at this time, Zarqawi had already notched up a formidable pedigree in the Islamist underground. The name itself, literally 'father of Musab the one from Zarqa', was typical of those who preferred to hide their identity – in his case the real name was Ahmad Fadil al-Khalayilah. The product of a tough neighbourhood in the Jordanian town of Zarqa, rumours abounded that he had a reputation as a street criminal, indulging in a life of vice until he found religion. Zarqawi had gone to Afghanistan in 1989 and like many on the 'jihad trail' arrived too late to fight the Soviet Army, struggling instead against the Afghan regime it left behind. Returning to Jordan, Zarqawi spent the nineties in and out of jail on a succession of charges that ranged from possessing weapons to plotting terrorist attacks on tourist attractions.

In 1999 the newly crowned King Abdullah freed terrorist detainees, and having served less than one year of his sentence, Zarqawi soon found his way back to Afghanistan where he trained with al-Qaeda but maintained a semi-detached relationship with it, not formally joining. When the Americans toppled the Taleban, Zarqawi made his way via Iran back to northern Iraq, where he fell in with Ansar al-Islam.

By the time Berg was kidnapped, Zarqawi was already well known to the CIA, MI6 and military intelligence, but nobody quite understood where he belonged in the scheme of things. Westerners referred to the 'Zarqawi group' or 'Zarqawi network'. Arabs who watched the jihadist underground knew that Zarqawi's people often referred to themselves as Al Tawhid Wa Al Jihad – 'Monotheism and Holy War' – but the group's relationship with other militant organisations was unclear. Did Zarqawi run Ansar al-Islam or was his group a subordinate part of it? Nobody was sure. Even among the jihadists, lines delineating these groups defeated almost everyone. Some put the differences down to different theological affiliations, others to disputes about the tactics to be employed in the holy war against the West.

What Zarqawi understood well was that reputation and sensation counted for a great deal on the Arab street. Those wishing to give money to the jihad against Bush were more likely to send it to a militant commander with some public profile. Similarly, the young volunteers arriving from Saudi or Syria would gravitate towards somebody they had heard of. The release of the Berg video and other chilling communiqués at this time were therefore an important part of Zarqawi's strategy of establishing himself and his network. By the strangest of coincidences Berg's short and terrible stay in Iraq was a consequence of one emerging network – a mobile phone one – and he became the victim of another, Zarqawi's. There ought to have been a third network in this picture, that of the Coalition forces and their Iraqi allies, but at this time such an organisation, implying a synergy between different elements able to support each other, was hardly working at all.

*

The early months of 2004 were a busy time for those trying to build intelligence empires in Iraq. Good intelligence was critical to everything that the Coalition was trying to do, but without it special operations forces in particular were impotent. McChrystal's people in JSOC had exploited the best information available to them to round up fugitive Ba'athists, including in mid-December Saddam Hussein himself. While Britain's Task Force Black took part in some of these operations, national pride determined that some targets, like Saddam, were reserved for the Americans, and by early 2004 many of the leading 'deck of cards' figures had been accounted for. The violence was worsening by the week, but hard information on the insurgent networks was still lacking.

With such thin pickings, one SAS officer notes, 'You could wait for ever for the ideal intelligence to come along, but what were you going to do in the meantime? We had to sort of make missions up.' Increasingly, this involved using the regiment's capabilities for surveillance reconnaissance to watch suspects, developing the intelligence picture. This could be done with 'eyes on' – observing from vehicles or buildings – but this was dangerous, as one SAS operator noted: 'In Iraq you're compromised the moment you go on the ground. People had to get their minds away from Ireland.' One solution was to use special cameras and other technology developed by the regiment's Research and Development wing and fielded by its specialist Surveillance Reconnaissance Cell. As techniques developed in Baghdad, the SAS learnt to keep time on the ground to the minimum and to let technology do the rest. An American intelligence officer who watched Task Force Black at work explains:

It was pretty apparent that the lessons they'd learnt in Northern Ireland were being put to good use. They were particularly good at using surveillance cameras. They'd find a place to put them – say on a roof overlooking the target's house – that was imaginative and productive. Our technical guys had a look over some of their gear and were pretty impressed.

The SAS summarised their operational process during the early days in Baghdad as find–fix–finish. Working backwards, the 'finish' part of the equation was the actual raid to take down suspects. The 'fix' involved pinpointing a time and place at which the target could be taken. It was in fixing people that the regiment's surveillance skills proved particularly useful. But the problem for them was that in order to target the right individuals – the 'find' part of the process – its starting point had, in fact, to be spot on. The key to this was obtaining intelligence from spies within insurgent groups, but in Iraq at that time this type of information proved surprisingly hard to gather, let alone share.

Early in 2004 the Coalition helped put the new Iraqi National Intelligence Service on a formal footing. The development of the INIS had been a CIA project and by this time it had a couple of hundred members. Although the anti-Saddam exiled parties were invited to send people to the INIS, it was meant to be a non-political security service. One senior US intelligence officer explains that it was 'intended to be an agency that wasn't motivated by sectarian concerns . . . the INIS didn't depend on the Shiite-led government of Iraq to fund it because the CIA completely funded its operations'.

Although the Coalition adopted a policy of de-Ba'athification with the army and ministries, the CIA played by quite different rules. Senior Coalition figures stated publicly that it would be quite unacceptable to use Saddam's former secret police to fight the insurgency but the Agency had other ideas. They wanted people who knew their business, and they also wanted the CIA to be the channel through which any INIS intelligence was fed to other players. A Shia exile was placed in charge of the INIS but, according to a senior British intelligence officer, 'others who were up there at the high level were all previous *mukhabarat* officers and they were much better than the CIA people sent to mentor them. We would much rather have dealt with the INIS people direct.'

As for the CIA, its establishment in Iraq soon swelled to around 450 personnel. In addition to its big Baghdad station, there were several outstations, including ones in the Kurdish north and in Basra Palace down south. Britain's Secret Intelligence Service, on the other hand, never exceeded fifty people in-country. Even so, claims one MI6 officer, 'we had more Arabists than [the CIA] did'.

The US military, meanwhile, had spawned its own civilian humint organisation, and numerous service ones. The civilians, around a hundred belonging to the Defense Humint Service, had been sent to Iraq to search for Weapons of Mass Destruction but when this proved to be the ultimate 'dry hole' or fruitless mission, had rewritten their job specification to hunt for insurgents. Another agent-running organisation, the Special Counter Intelligence Division (SCID or 'Scid'), brought about ninety operators into the picture. Most of SCID's people were effectively detectives from the investigative services of the US armed forces. In addition to these specialists, rapidly trained Tactical Humint Teams tried to sign up Iraqi spies right across the country. These teams of five or six soldiers were attached to military units and often operated with uniformed US patrols. There were a few dozen THTs by early 2004 but the number would peak a few years later at about 140 cells. Britain had its military equivalents, Field Humint Teams.

Given that there were thousands of CIA, INIS, MI6, Defense Humint, SCID and tactical team officers or operators in action it might be supposed that a steady flow of agent reports would have been informing Coalition operations. But this was far from the case. The quantity certainly increased exponentially during 2004, but as one British officer who had to sift through this reporting in the south wearily records, 'You had tons of agent reports predicting this or that but they were just complete rubbish. Iraqis give you answers they think you want to hear and with the Americans' resources they were producing stacks of worthless humint.' The nuggets of valuable information had to be picked from a slurry of tittle-tattle, embroidery and invention. In addition, to exploit the information required sharing, and in the Baghdad setup of early 2004 few players were any good at that.

The Coalition's chief military intelligence officer, sitting in Camp Slayer (part of the American complex of bases at Baghdad airport) with hundreds of staff, ought to have been able to direct the spying effort. But the CIA jealously guarded its freedom and the Defense Humint Service reported to a boss outside Iraq: the head of a joint task force responsible for hunting down FREs – Former Regime Elements – across Iraq and the wider Middle East. Officers in Baghdad from MI6 or the British military found themselves acting as the go-betweens or facilitators between these battling US agencies. Many American officers resented the CIA's attitude, resources and independence. Their British military colleagues often agreed, one noting, 'The CIA were pretty arrogant. If they were at a meeting the body language and tone used suggested they were way above anybody else there.' Another senior British figure describes the CIA's behaviour towards other agencies as 'catastrophic'.

Had these different espionage organisations operated under one person's direction, their activities could have been properly tasked: the CIA perhaps looking after high-level political intelligence gathering, DH and SCID after certain Iraqi militias and so on. But the theory of unified direction was often honoured more in the breach than practice in Baghdad. In addition to their prickly attitude to cooperation, the agent runners found it harder and harder to get out into the 'Red Zone' – Iraq beyond the confines of the Green Zone – as it was deemed too dangerous. In this situation the CIA was often repackaging INIS reporting and the others scraping about for any credible Iraqi who volunteered his services at a Coalition base. When the humint organisations were so reliant on walk-ins, the scope for them to get scammed or for a single individual to take money from more than one Coalition agency increased considerably. Inevitably, valuable tips were not passed from one organisation to another and there was always the possibility, as the SAS would later discover, that one humint operation would accidentally target the assets of another.

The US troops had managed to develop a basic ground-level sense of life in many neighbourhoods, but then in February and March 2004 this was abruptly lost. The first major troop rotation of the occupation (American units mostly served on operations for one year) was under way. Some of the departing commanders painted a rosy picture of improving security, and it was true that violence had gone down since those shocking weeks of Ramadan in November 2003. February, with 'only' twenty US soldiers killed, was a relatively good month. But what little optimism this crude indicator might have produced was soon dispelled. The insurgency was mutating, taking on a more Islamic flavour, but penetration of the Islamic groups was essentially non-existent. As the veterans went home there was a poor handover to many of the incoming units, leaving them struggling to build a street-level picture.

Faced with this jumble of acronyms, dysfunction, and bureaucratic bloody-mindedness, Major-General McChrystal, a man who lived by the mantra 'you need to build a network to defeat one', decided to create his own. Vital months had been lost while the Pentagon leadership was in denial about the insurgency. By early 2004, it was mutating and McChrystal was one of the few who both understood this and the need to get on top of it. He shut down the special ops facility at Baghdad airport, Camp Nama, establishing a new base at Balad, to the north. Balad was a sprawling air base in which Saddam invested hundreds of millions of dollars, building concrete aircraft shelters and other infrastructure. It became a key logistic and air hub for the US forces. There, McChrystal created a state-of-the-art Joint Operations Centre, where JSOC's war in Iraq would be run day to day by the commander of Delta Force. It was up and running by July 2004. Teams from each of the different intelligence agencies were established at Balad. Once he had started to milk them for information, McChrystal put it all into a JSOC intranet similar to the one he'd created in Afghanistan. It would allow those at the cutting edge of the US counterterrorism effort to share information worldwide. In order to bypass protocol-obsessed embassies or jealous CIA station chiefs in neighbouring countries, McChrystal also established a network of liaison offices run by his own people across the Middle East.

McChrystal's counterterrorist Rome could not be built in a day. It would take much of 2004 to take shape. Many questions were unclear from the outset, not least whether Britain's Task Force Black could be full partners in this secret network. Until they were resolved, the UK element had to carry on in 'a semi-detached way', according to one SAS officer. They could not prosecute the 'full JSOC target set', he adds, but were restricted more to 'arresting old men, the FREs'. Another British officer, a senior figure who served in Baghdad, describes the Former Regime Elements as 'the pissed-off bourgeoisie – they'd lost their meal ticket'. Iraq being Iraq, their anger took violent form. Some – in MI6 in particular – tried to portray the arrest of old Ba'athists as a vital mission that fitted with their attempts to put out feelers to the nationalist insurgency, and a rejection of the

Bush Administration's emphasis on foreign fighters and its global onslaught against al-Qaeda. But this was an intellectually elegant way to justify the reality, which was that Task Force Black was kept away from the most violent or dangerous targets. This situation developed less because McChrystal wanted to shut UK special forces out of his operations and more because of the growing disquiet on the British side about the direction of events in Iraq.

By March 2004 British officers knew that a raft of complaints about US detainee operations was percolating through the Pentagon. Back in the final weeks of 2003 Stuart Herrington, a retired US Army colonel, had gone on an inspection tour of the military intelligence setup in Iraq. Herrington was a quiet legend in US military intelligence – one of the last out of Saigon, and a veteran of the Phoenix Program, America's black offensive against the Viet Cong. Few doors were closed to the Vietnam veteran as he took Humvees and helicopters to see what was going on or, more particularly, going wrong.

Herrington wanted to pay particular attention to Camp Nama, on the western side of Baghdad airport. This had been TF-121, JSOC's main operations centre in Iraq prior to the move to Balad. There were also detention and interrogation facilities. It was to these that prisoners taken by Delta, the Rangers, or indeed the SAS had been brought. Concerns about the fate of prisoners taken by the British were voiced by Ben Griffin, an SAS man who went public after leaving the forces, even appearing at an anti-war rally. The Ministry of Defence denied his claims that British troops had been used to deliver suspects into a regime of abuse. However, those sent to investigate the detainee system – and Colonel Herrington was not the only one dispatched to do so – discovered that, bereft of high-quality agent or technical reporting and anxious to pursue the Ba'athists of the High-Value Target list and al-Qaeda suspects, JSOC had often fallen back on interrogation. In August 2003 the CIA had pulled its officers from Camp Nama. Herrington found his access to Camp Nama blocked, but still managed to find out what was going on.

He put it succinctly in his report to the chief army intelligence officer in Baghdad, noting that Iraqis 'who had been captured by Task Force 121 showed signs of having been mistreated (beaten) by their captors'. The colonel, who regarded humane detainee operations as an important part of winning a counterinsurgency, was shocked by the fact that many of the JSOC officers he spoke to seemed to regard the abuse of prisoners – which ranged from hitting with rifle butts and slapping to shooting them with paint-ball guns – as normal.

In the following months there would be a series of investigations and a total of twenty-nine complaints investigated in relation to Camp Nama. Five were upheld, resulting in disciplinary action against thirty-four soldiers. A number of these incidents happened after McChrystal had taken over command of JSOC. The general's defenders note that during the early months of running his classified operation his stays in Iraq had actually been intermittent: there were JSOC operations across Central Command's area of operations, a broad swath of countries from North Africa, through the Middle East to South Asia. By the spring of 2004, however, McChrystal was making Iraq his top priority and evidently began to deal seriously with the level of abuse there. 'What we did was establish a policy and atmosphere that said that is not what you do, that is not acceptable,' he said later.

In fact, Camp Nama simply represented the tip of a looming public relations disaster for the US military. Herrington also investigated what was going on at Abu Ghraib prison where, by late 2003, some six thousand people swept up by regular units had been confined in poor conditions.

While the kicking in of so many doors and detention of thousands of people exacerbated the Sunni insurrection, many of the generals and brigade commanders directing America's mailed fist apparently knew a little better. They had been schooled in doctrines of overwhelming force, a 'warrior ethos' that dictated they should seek out and destroy their enemy rather than use every operation as a chance to win someone over. But more could have been expected from the special operators, whose ranks included many of the small American military cadre who had operated in the Middle East, or indeed experienced the debacle of Somalia. Their understanding of the need to win hearts and minds made the lapses at Camp Nama all the less forgivable.

One night in February 2004, soldiers from B Squadron readied themselves for an assault. Their targets were the product of an extraordinary intelligence operation that showed the high value of building an international network. Operation ASTON took place alongside a bigger MI6 effort to target 'transnational terrorism', or the jihadist network. Using the SAS on a mission spun up by British intelligence sat well with those who wished to give greater independence to Task Force Black – or to keep a greater distance from the Americans. For their part, McChrystal's people and the US agencies tried to lend a helping hand to the Brits, since they still regarded them as acting for the common good. In the case of Operation ASTON, there was a particular desire to help because the British seemed to be on to something very good. Following the invasion, British intelligence had seen an opportunity. It had been trying for some time to operate against the pipelines feeding volunteers towards al-Qaeda's new front, hoping that if they could follow someone down a rat line into the country it could produce numerous intelligence spin-offs. Now, operatives outside Iraq had picked up some suspects who they believed were intending to travel to the country to join the jihad. As the suspects moved across Iran and into Iraq, they were tracked by British and American agencies. It was vital not to lose track of them, but the British directing ASTON were delighted when their targets turned up in Baghdad. The targets then fell in with a jihadist group. Intelligence about this group was then built up by careful surveillance work. Having refined their operation through watching a specific house in southern Baghdad, the assault was ordered.

As several teams from B Squadron approached the 'Alpha' – target – building they were spotted by locals. Whistles, torchlight and gunshots soon disturbed the night air. The assaulters pressed on, breaking their way into the house. Inside the jihadists opened fire from a distance of a few feet. One of the SAS Team Leaders, Sergeant-Major *Mulberry*, was hit in the face by an AK-47 round but had a lucky escape because it was deflected by his equipment, leaving him with only light injuries. In a short-range firefight as the building was cleared, two men were killed. Both were later assessed to be foreign fighters. Some of the insurgents were captured. One of these proved to be Pakistani and another a Qatari national of Pakistani origin. Coalition intelligence assessed the Pakistanis to be members of Lashkar-e-Taiba or the LeT, a Kashmiri militant group. Operation ASTON was therefore judged a great success: it had shown how the British could develop transnational counterterrorist work. In fact, it was precisely the kind of synergy that Major-General McChrystal was hoping to develop within the wider JSOC network, exposing the rat lines from Syria or Saudi Arabia, but, for reasons that did not become apparent for a few weeks, Operation ASTON was to have a negative effect on UK–US cooperation in Iraq at a time when wider developments in the country put great strain on the Coalition. It would also embroil the UK in legal difficulties over the identity of the two men who had been taken to Bagram. Critically, the difficulties about the UK handing over detainees would build during

2004 as rising levels of violence were causing the Americans to lash out, in turn damaging public support back in Britain.

On 31 March 2004 two SUVs drove around one of the US Marine checkpoints outside Fallujah and into the town. Inside the vehicle were four members of Blackwater, a private security firm that liked to project a badass reputation. They were there to liaise with the local police about the contractor convoy coming into Fallujah the following day, but Blackwater appeared completely ignorant of some important changes that had occurred in the preceding week, and would come to pay for their mistakes.

Four days earlier a JSOC surveillance team had been compromised in the town, shooting its way out of trouble. The US Marines, who had taken control of the area from the 82nd Airborne on 24 March, were drawn into running gun battles with insurgents in the hours that followed. Rather sooner than they'd expected, the Marines found themselves using these firefights to test the strength of the resistance in various neighbourhoods. Then the Blackwater men appeared.

Insurgents, apparently tipped off about the contractors, hit them with RPGs and gunfire. The two vehicles were soon ablaze and the men killed. Two charred bodies were dragged through the streets, spat upon, hacked, trampled and finally hoisted up onto a girder of the old Euphrates bridge. These scenes were recorded and soon playing around the world. Fearing a 'Mogadishu moment' in which national confidence faltered as it had during the *Black Hawk Down* incident in Somalia in 1993, senior US officers promised immediate action. The guilty would be found and punished.

The best laid plans of the Marine commanders, a blueprint for how they intended to eat away at the resistance, were junked. Instead, on 5 April, 2500 Marines and the full panoply of destructive power at their disposal were unleashed on Fallujah: tanks, helicopter gunships and air strikes. TV pictures showed automatic grenade launchers sputtering 40mm rounds into the sides of houses, which burst in showers of shrapnel, but the American troops encountered heavy resistance and in little more than forty-eight hours it became clear that their advance into the town was stalling.

As if this wasn't enough to worry the British watching in Downing Street and the military, the Coalition's problems suddenly multiplied. Under orders from Paul Bremer, the head of the Coalition Provisional Authority, troops moved to arrest a senior member of the Mehdi Army – a Shia militia – and close down its newspaper. This touched off an insurrection by thousands of Shia gunmen loyal to a radical preacher, Muqtada al-Sadr. What became known as the First Sadrist Rising marked the awakening of a sleeping giant of Shia militancy. Although many of the Shia, who were the clear majority of the Iraqi population, did not like al-Sadr's party, support for it would soon spiral upwards if it was seen to be taking on the goliath of the US military, or venting national frustration with the failure of the American project. The Sadrist Rising had grave implications for the British, not least because of the Mehdi Army's strength in Basra, Nasiriyah and other places under the control of the British-led Multi-National Division South East. In the south, large-scale gun battles with the Sadrists marked the definitive end of the honeymoon that many of the British military felt they had enjoyed.

In a few days in April hundreds of people died as the Coalition tried to escape a disaster of its own making: a two-front fight. The Sunni revolt was already well established, with Fallujah as its symbolic centre. By triggering a national rising by a powerful Shia militia the Americans ran the risk of alienating the community that was emerging as dominant in the new Iraq. If there was any silver lining for those watching from Downing Street, it was that international attention focused more on Fallujah than on the crisis facing British troops in the south. Having entered the war feeling the need to stand shoulder to shoulder with the US, even Tony Blair began to doubt the wisdom of being too closely associated with operations like those in Fallujah.

Bremer and his military chiefs knew they could not sustain a confrontation on this scale. On 9 April they ordered a halt to the Fallujah operation and the gunmen on the city's streets proclaimed victory. The violence with the Sadrists was far from over. Heavy fighting involving British troops erupted in al-Amarrah, the capital of Maysan, and the following month US troops confronted the Mehdi Army in its centres of resistance: Sadr City in east Baghdad, and the holy city of Najaf.

If Bremer and his commanders had reeled from this battering, there was one more body blow for them to absorb that April. On the 28th the American television programme *60 Minutes* showed pictures of detainees being abused by American guards at Abu Ghraib. The resulting furore produced a crisis of confidence in the US and yet more damage to the country's reputation in the Middle East. It was at this moment that Zarqawi, sensitive to the propaganda value of the moment, chose to dress Nick Berg in a Guantanamo-style orange jumpsuit for his last video appearance, and said he was being killed in revenge for the abuse of prisoners at the Iraqi jail. The video of Berg's last moments hit the internet just a fortnight after the Abu Ghraib pictures emerged, with the story still running high in the global news agenda.

The combination of these setbacks, as George Bush campaigned for re-election, proved terminal for Bremer and his military chief Lieutenant-General Ricardo Sanchez. By June the latter had been replaced by General George Casey, and Bremer signed off to the Interim Iraqi Government. The US–UK occupation authority, the CPA, vanished. With this change, the military gained a legal fig leaf through an authorising United Nations Security Council resolution sanctioning their operations. The good news – that Coalition forces had a legal mandate – was balanced with a difficult new reality: US and British commanders found themselves in a new world of political management, one in which they increasingly had to take account of what Iraqi politicians wanted. This was to prove particularly difficult for ground-holding commanders like Britain's in Basra, where a testy governor and provincial authority second-guessed their operations.

As for British participation in the Coalition, it was profoundly affected by these simultaneous crises. With growing public hostility to the war, Downing Street could hardly blame the press for ignoring 'all the good news coming out of Iraq' as it had throughout 2003. The blistering fighting experienced in the south, where the British had briefly come close to running out of ammunition, had its effect on many at the divisional headquarters at Basra air station. One colonel told me, 'Since the Sadrist rising, we've basically been looking at our watches and asking "can we go now please?"'

The special forces further north, operating as Task Force Black, took a more aggressive attitude. JSOC's operation had, through its intense secrecy, gained a large measure of exemption from the hostile public scrutiny that now focused on the visible Coalition effort. Task Force Black could see the militant Islamists gaining power by the day in the resistance, and they knew their mates in JSOC were increasingly hard-pressed in the struggle against them. But April's crises had produced intense unease in Whitehall. It made ministers wary about being seen to do too much to back the Americans. What was more, Abu Ghraib had also made them extremely sensitive to the issue of detention. At a time when the need for a coordinated Allied response to these crises was at its peak, the UK started trying to distance itself from its faltering ally. This affected even traditionally intimate areas of cooperation such as special ops. It was to be on the rock of the detention issue that UK special forces operations in Iraq foundered later in 2004.

The Abu Ghraib scandal came not long after British intelligence and Task Force Black discovered what had happened to the two Pakistanis whom they had captured on Operation ASTON. It was standard procedure, on returning to the MSS after an operation, to turn over prisoners to the Americans. It had happened that way since soon after the invasion.

In the case of the suspected Pakistani militants dark rumours soon began to circulate. After being handed over, they had been put on a plane to Afghanistan for interrogation at the US facility at Bagram airbase. By detaining them, the British had played a part in this rendition. Campaigners would later argue that Amanatullah Ali, the Pakistani national, was a Shia who had gone to Iraq on a pilgrimage and who could not, by virtue of his religious confession, have been a member of the Sunni militant group Lashkar-e-Taiba. At the time of writing, more than five years after their arrest, those same campaigners have not yet established the identity of the Qatari national picked up with Ali, such was the secrecy surrounding the Bagram detention facility and its inmates.

Defending their actions, the Americans argued that their interrogators in Iraq did not have the linguistic skills to screen the men so it had to be done elsewhere. Unaware of this, the SAS had passed on the prisoners and London was unhappy. The British told JSOC that they could no longer hand over detainees if they were going to be flown elsewhere. The creation of this 'national caveat', as such restrictions are known in Coalition operations, was not to be the last of 2004, nor was it the most damaging to Task Force Black's relationship with the Americans. The vast majority of those taken were, after all, Iraqis and there was no need to send them to Bagram or a 'black prison' in some other land for interrogation. The events in Fallujah, however, were acting as a catalyst, accelerating the change towards an insurgency dominated by Islamists rather than nationalists. And the way in which the US had chosen to deal with Fallujah was simply feeding this trend.

Throughout the summer of 2004 Fallujah operated as a 'liberated zone' for the Iraqi resistance groups. The CIA's formation of the Fallujah Brigade, a Sunni security force under a former Republican Guard brigadier, in April proved to be a costly and divisive miscalculation. Rather than holding the ring and providing the US with a dignified way out of the confrontation, the brigade's soldiers soon declared for the resistance, either handing over their weapons or signing up with the association of jihadist and nationalist groups that vied for authority in the town.

Fallujah had long been a bastion of conservatism. It revelled in its reputation as a city of two hundred mosques. Perhaps inevitably, when credit was being claimed for halting the US Marines in April increasingly it was the Islamist voices that drowned out the others. As to who was leading this chorus, one intelligence figure remarks, 'All the reporting suggested Zarqawi was in Fallujah.' Armed men walked the streets in the white robes and headdresses of Salafist purists, while in the bazaar, DVDs of Hindi musicals were replaced by snuff movies showing members of the new Iraqi army, or terrified men who identified themselves as spies, being murdered on screen.

According to some who served in Baghdad that summer, the CIA used its new Iraqi partners, the INIS, to provide agents for infiltration into the city. All of the men sent in were apparently tracked down, tortured and killed. Others suggest that this version of events was put around by the Agency because it did not want to admit that it had no human sources in the city. Instead, 'there was 24/7 Predator coverage of Fallujah and a huge amount of movement analysis'. Watching their screens at Balad, the analysts tracked patterns of car movements, pinpointing certain properties as the places where car bombs that ended up in Baghdad originated. JSOC was soon directing the Air Force to drop bombs on these places. The analytical work at Balad also extended to identifying movements of people or vehicles that revealed the 'apparent signature' of Zarqawi's presence.

Several of the British who watched this say they were very uneasy about what was going on. From the Blackwater and Berg incidents onwards, Zarqawi began to grow in importance in US public pronouncements. His elimination replaced the capturing of Saddam as the prime focus of JSOC's daily operations. This played well with the Bush re-election campaign's message about international terrorism, and it also served the Iraqi politicians of the interim government, who liked to blame the country's difficulties on foreigners. Political considerations – US and Iraqi – also meant that the US military could not go back into Fallujah to confront the militants. Everybody understood this would entail a huge battle, and while the politicians shrank from it during the summer the situation inside Fallujah became steadily more extreme, playing into the hands of Zarqawi.

'Fallujah became al-Qaeda's FOB [Forward Operating Base],' says one intelligence officer. Car bombs were being sent out, and hostages brought back in through the security cordon that supposedly surrounded the city. As the US bombing of targets inside became increasingly frequent, scores, perhaps hundreds, of civilians were killed. Many ordinary people chose to flee, seeking safety with relatives. Foreign fighters in search of martyrdom found their way in, and the complexion of an already angry city changed markedly. As the waiting game went on, by September 2004 the number of US dead in Iraq topped one thousand. General Casey's British deputy meanwhile penned a memo for his boss giving seven reasons why an assault on the city could prove counterproductive.

The onslaught against Fallujah was finally launched on 8 November, just after the re-election of President Bush. Operation PHANTOM FURY threw approximately twenty thousand US and Iraqi troops into action. By that time, the Coalition estimated more than 95 per cent of the population had fled, and the number of mujahedeen in the city was thought to be 1200 to 1500.

British political nervousness about the possible scale of the slaughter stopped any direct UK involvement, though the Black Watch was moved up to northern Babil Province in order to relieve a US unit so that it could take part in the operation. They were swiftly targeted by Sunni insurgents, losing five men in their first fortnight on the mission – a sobering taste of what the Americans were up against. Such was the nervousness in Downing Street that serious consideration was given to withdrawing the Black Watch after these incidents. British field commanders preferred to plough on. As for Task Force Black, D Squadron of 22 SAS had initially prepared to take part in the operation.

The blades set off for the short drive west, finding themselves a leaguering-up point in the desert near Fallujah. One of Delta's squadrons had already got stuck into the fight, and D, sometimes described as the most intense of all the squadrons, was itching to join in. Their spirit arose from 'airborne aggression' – the traditional domination of the squadron by members of the Parachute Regiment. At Fallujah many of them might have liked to adopt the traditional Para approach, which went by the acronym FIDO: Fuck It and Drive On. But orders came down the chain of command that they were not to do so. Britain had played another red card in a national caveat. Neither the visible army nor UK special forces were to take part in the assault on Fallujah.

In street-to-street fighting, the US Marines stormed the city. It was a bloody, grim and determined business done with hand grenades, small arms and all the support the Americans could muster. One week later the operation was declared complete. Four thousand artillery rounds, ten thousand mortars and ten tons of bombs had been used on the city. The Americans had lost fifty-one soldiers. The tally of bodies recovered in the city was around two thousand. The military said they were all insurgents, but one British officer who was in Fallujah shortly after PHANTOM FURY speculates that the difference between the intelligence estimate of fighters before the attack and the number of bodies recovered suggests several hundred civilian fatalities. Abu Musab al-Zarqawi was not among the dead. Indeed, Islamist sources suggested he had moved to an area south of Baghdad before the assault commenced.

In the months before the assault the balance of power between him and the al-Qaeda leadership hiding in Pakistan had changed decisively. A letter seized early in the year, which was believed to have been addressed to Ayman al-Zawahiri, the movement's number two, showed the reason why 'head office' was nervous about Zarqawi. In it he had preached hatred of the Shia, describing them as the American's puppets in evicting the Sunnis from power. In June 2004 Zarqawi wrote to Osama bin Laden that 'they [the Shia] have been a sect of treachery and betrayal through all history and all ages', arguing that he would not formally join al-Qaeda unless he was allowed to step up his onslaught on the Shia. Zawahiri and bin Laden apparently feared this nakedly sectarian approach, but events had begun to define their response. 'Zarqawi generated so much success and publicity,' says an intelligence officer, 'that al-Qaeda simply had to anoint him.' In October an Islamist website carried a communiqué stating that Zarqawi had sworn an abaya, or oath of allegiance, to bin Laden. His movement changed its name to 'Organisation for the

Holy War's Base in the land of the Two Rivers' (in Arabic, *Tanzim Qa'idat Al Jihad bil Balad al Rafidayn*), leading to the simplified Coalition designation of the movement as 'al-Qaeda in Iraq' or AQI.

As the Americans became increasingly preoccupied with hunting down the Jordanian leader and his network, British special forces found themselves on the sidelines.

Shortly before the attack on Fallujah, MI6 visited Balad to question a suspected insurgent. The Iraqi was being held in a secret jail called the Temporary Screening Facility (TSF). In keeping with Major-General McChrystal's approach, this place provided the JSOC team of interrogators with their own opportunity to question the people they had captured using the full range of intelligence information coming into Balad. It was not visited by the Red Cross or other humanitarian organisations, and its exceptional sensitivity made it, says one British officer, 'a black prison within a black programme'.

Following the MI6 visit, concerns were raised about the detention conditions there. Another visitor to the TSF told me that 'the cells there were like dog kennels – tiny'. In the first place the wooden cells constructed to hold the prisoners were smaller than stipulated by British standards. There were also worries about the condition of some of the detainees. People in JSOC sometimes refer to the injuries a prisoner can take at the moment of capture, when being overpowered by those he was trying to kill moments before. But were the violent practices Colonel Herrington uncovered at Camp Nama being continued?

As a result of MI6's visit and the concerns raised, Britain communicated another national caveat to JSOC in Iraq: from now on Britain's special forces would only turn its prisoners over to the Americans if there was an undertaking not to send them to Balad.

It can be imagined how this news was received by the CO of Delta Force, and McChrystal himself. The American general was carefully building his network and the British had just tugged out an element of it. 'Inevitably [the decision] caused a degree of tension with McChrystal and his crew at Balad,' says one figure in this drama, with remarkable understatement.

JSOC's people knew that Task Force Black, through Operations ABALONE the previous autumn in Ramadi or 2004's ASTON, the capture of the alleged Pakistani jihadists in Baghdad, had delivered some of the only evidence of how the global al-Qaeda network might be operating in Iraq, but this UK–US cooperation was effectively at an end. One senior American figure told me that they had never consciously shut the British out. But the new British caveat had left JSOC with a stark choice. Given the importance of rapidly exploiting intelligence, they did not want to rely upon the British to capture someone who might know where Zarqawi or some other key figure was hiding, because that precious source of intelligence would be delivered into the neverland of the 'white' detainee system rather than to JSOC's own people.

By the autumn of 2004, roughly one year after Major-General McChrystal had taken over JSOC, British special forces were operating in an increasingly 'semi-detached' way. A consensus had emerged between Brigadier *Peter Rogers* as DSF Lieutenant-Colonel *Beaufort* in command of the SAS, the MI6 station and several senior officers, such as those back at PJHQ in Northwood, that Task Force Black needed to put some distance between itself and the Americans. By building up its humint team, analysts, support from intelligence agencies and means of transport, those who had lost faith in the American approach intended to give Task Force Black the ability to find-fix-finish its own targets. The only problem with this approach was that as SAS operators chatted to their Delta neighbours in the MSS, or the spooks shared a coffee after one of their endless liaison meetings in Camp Slayer, Britain's team in Baghdad started to develop a nagging feeling that it might be fighting the wrong war. Up in Balad, McChrystal and his people were coming up with ideas, technologies and tactics that amounted to nothing less than a revolution in counterterrorism. The first target for this new machine would be al-Qaeda.

5

TARGET AQI

On 20 February 2005 US special operations forces had their chance to kill Abu Musab al-Zarqawi. Acting on intelligence, they had landed by helicopter on a desert road in Anbar Province. The jihadist leader was travelling from Ramadi towards Fallujah. As is usual when throwing up a checkpoint of this kind, a machine-gunner had been placed in position to engage any vehicle that attempted to go straight through.

There are different versions of exactly what happened. According to one, a car thought to contain Zarqawi and a couple of bodyguards saw the unexpected American roadblock, stepped on the gas and ran right through it. The machine-gunner, however, did not feel within his rights under the rules of engagement to open fire.

Another account comes from someone in the world of black

special operations. The JSOC team had the support of a Predator UAV, and officers in Balad were watching the suspect car speeding along the desert road on the live feed. The fact that the car was under 'eyes on' surveillance from the Predator should have given the soldiers another chance, even if the gunner on the ground had faltered at the key moment. But as the JSOC personnel looked on, the image on the screen suddenly started to spin madly. The aircraft had developed a technical fault and the camera mounted beneath it was gyrating out of control. The opportunity had been lost.

This incident was one of several in which the intelligence experts working for McChrystal believed that they had been close but had missed their man. Iraqi forces were even reckoned to have had Zarqawi in their custody near Fallujah at one point before the town was stormed, but had not realised who he was and released him. The SAS had its own brush with Zarqawi early in 2004 when it assaulted a house in Baghdad. After forcing an entry, the blades had swiftly reversed, piling out when an artillery shell attached to detonating cord came bouncing down the stairs. The device did not go off, and the occupants of the building were later overwhelmed and captured. Intelligence subsequently revealed that Zarqawi had left a short time before.

By early 2005 JSOC had a clear focus deriving from Secretary of Defense Donald Rumsfeld's apparent obsession with taking down high-value targets. Major-General McChrystal's command had built a regional laydown, which was designed to allow rapid response to intelligence anywhere that the AQI leader or key associates might be found. At Al Asad airbase in Anbar Province were the Seal Team 6 crew, Task Force Blue, or West. In Tikrit a select team of Rangers was deployed as Task Force Red, or North. The Delta squadron – Task Force Green (Central) – operated out of MSS Fernandez in the Green Zone. Their next-door neighbours, the British Task Force Black, were able to operate in and around Baghdad but with the specific target set or mission of hunting Former Regime Elements.

A series of steps initiated by SAS Commanding Officer *Charles Beaufort* back in the UK had increased Task Force Black's ability to operate as a semi-independent unit. Early in 2005 the SAS supplemented their lightly protected Snatch and unarmoured Land Rovers with M1114s – armour-plated US Humvees. The helicopter fleet was changing too, losing its pair of Chinooks and gaining more Pumas. Intelligence back-up had been boosted by establishing both humint and sigint specialist teams in the task force. Cut off from the intelligence flow about JSOC's 'Black List' of targets – that is, Zarqawi and the AQI leadership – the British humint team had provided most of the initial leads for Task Force Black's raids in the latter part of 2004.

Britain's caveats about delivering prisoners to the JSOC jail in Balad meant that those taken in Task Force Black raids were instead handed over to regular US army units. They usually ended up at the Divisional Internment Facility at Baghdad airport where, by this time, the inter-agency task force hunting old Ba'athists had its main station and could interrogate those whom the British had scooped up. This seemed like a joined-up system; the only problem was that many of the SAS and British intelligence people were beginning to lose faith in the value of their man hunt. The former Ba'athists frogmarched from their homes in the middle of the night were often described as 'old men' by their captors.

Increasingly, the great game in Iraq was the hunt for Zarqawi. The JSOC leaders devoted the best intelligence-gathering people and the lion's share of resources to this aim. But Britain had effectively opted out owing to its concerns about American actions. Members of Task Force Black knew all about what their Delta colleagues were doing through the unofficial grapevine but also through the British liaison teams that still went to Balad, to sit in the Joint Operations Centre, but the resumption of full cooperation was dependent upon work to improve the condition of the prison cells and British inspections of the regime there.

It was against the background of this bureaucratic standoff that an RAF Hercules on its way up to Balad disappeared off the radar on 13 January 2005. An Iraqi group swiftly claimed responsibility for shooting down the aircraft, in which nine British servicemen were killed. The Board of Inquiry would eventually rule that the aircraft's low-level flight profile was too dangerous given the capabilities of the resistance and that the Hercules, once hit, might have been lost because its fuel tanks were not fitted with explosion-suppressant foam (as similar American planes were, and RAF ones eventually would be).

The loss of the aircraft was a blow for G Squadron, then starting its tour of duty in Baghdad, and the rest of Task Force Black. Its members responded by devoting particular energy to tracking down the killers. A long intelligence operation led to raids later that year, which captured some of those responsible, and it demonstrated the growing technological sophistication of the Coalition effort.

At the time of the Hercules crash, an American surveillance aircraft equipped with a highly sophisticated radar called JSTARS (Joint Surveillance Target Attack Radar System) had been orbiting north of Baghdad. Designed during the Cold War to pick up impending Soviet Army tank thrusts, JSTARS maps moving objects on the ground. It could thus be used to detect cars. Information from the aircraft gave analysts an initial lead in pinpointing who might have shot down the C-130.

In other areas, too, technology and intelligence relationships were coalescing. That March, a caller to one of the Coalition telephone tips lines had offered information on the whereabouts of one of Saddam's former apparatchiks. The existence of the phone lines, which were also being used in Basra and other cities, was a British innovation in Iraq, based on long experience in Northern Ireland. In the Baghdad call centre police officers from Britain and Northern Ireland acted as mentors for the entire operation. Those who rang in might give a one-off tip, and they might also prove suitable for cultivation as informers. The phone offered an important way for the humint teams to overcome some of the dangers of working in the Red Zone, but also for the callers to make themselves known without publicly giving themselves away. On such an occasion, a suitable case presented itself and a British policeman monitoring the call wondered where to take it, having found that the main US intelligence agencies were not much interested in the raw material produced by the call centre.

His answer lay with the Special Counter Intelligence Directorate, the American joint service organisation that ran humint operations but was considered by some to rank below the CIA, MI6 or the Defense Humint Service in the Baghdad spooks pecking order. But the SCID people were happy to be opportunistic about their cases, and so picked up the caller's details and got to work.

The Iraqi caller gave information pinpointing the whereabouts of Fadhil Ibrahim al-Mashadani, formerly a senior regional official in the Ba'ath party. He was not one of the top Ba'athists in the deck of cards, but even so there was a $200,000 price on Mashadani's head because of the role he was believed to play in the resistance. Having ascertained that the information was true, SCID took it to Task Force Black. Surveillance experts from G Squadron, joined by a member of the SCID team using helicopter and other technical surveillance, fixed Mashadani's location as a farm to the north-east of the capital.

On 11 April 2005 the SAS went in and lifted their man with

a set-piece house assault. The raid was conducted without opposition. Mashadani was flown back to the MSS, where British intelligence officers conducted an initial interview prior to him being processed into the American detention system. Despite the manner in which he had been swept from his home in the middle of the night, the atmosphere in the interrogation was relaxed and Mashadani, an educated and once privileged man, chatted freely with his British captors. He couldn't fathom why the Coalition was still going after people like him. Didn't they understand that the real threat came from the jihadists who had flooded into Iraq? People at MSS Fernandez had heard similar things from quite a few of those whom they had picked up. But there was something about Mashadani's simple eloquence that caused his message to ripple outwards from that interview room. His words became a topic of discussion for many of those involved with the intelligence effort in Baghdad. 'It's over,' he reportedly told his questioners. The Ba'ath party had lost power and, Mashadani added, they all knew it had no chance of getting it back. There was something about having your own targets rubbish the importance of the mission that pricked the pride of many in Task Force Black. Their rivalry with Delta Force and knowledge of what was going on up at Balad told them that Britain had relegated itself from the counterterrorist premier league. Little by little, Task Force Black tried to address the situation, for example by trying to thrash out the detention issue at Balad, but in truth matters could not come to a head until someone of sufficient stature in the world of special forces chose to argue the issue out with the DSF and others in the UK.

The origins of the Mashadani operation, using a humint source found through the phone tip line and developed by SCID, showed how a sort of free market in intelligence had evolved amid the organisational rivalry of Iraq's intelligence agencies. Since the gathering of humint was not being properly centrally directed, nor its product fully shared, those running Task Force Black started going wherever their instincts took them in order to find a starting point for each new operation. Having begun in Iraq with close ties to MI6 and the CIA, they became more professionally promiscuous, searching for the right informers with the SCID, INIS, Defense Humint Service or agent teams run by US ground-holding units. Instead of the neat organi-gram of intelligence process mapped out by the staff officers, the Baghdad scene represented more of a secret information bazaar on the free-wheeling Middle Eastern model. 'There was a free market in intelligence and therefore you could afford to be entrepreneurial,' comments one member of Task Force Black. On quiet days the Team Leaders, usually staff sergeants or cap-tains, would saunter around the Green Zone dropping in on the different intelligence gatherers, sharing a brew, seeing whether anyone was developing any promising informers and catching up on insurgency gossip. For the most part this approach worked in teeing up missions such as the Mashadani takedown, but it could go spectacularly wrong.

At around the time Task Force Black lifted Mashadani, its people went out on another late-night arrest operation. This time they were hoping for a bigger, more meaningful result. The planned raid came as a result of a long-running operation to find the kidnappers of a foreigner in Baghdad. Tracking some men who had offered their services as intermediaries, the SAS moved in. They lifted *Abu Jamal*, formerly a senior Ba'athist official, and another man. The soldiers' disappointment at not finding the hostage in the same house was tempered by the knowledge that these men were definitely connected to the kidnap gang.

When the Humvees roared back into the MSS and the two detainees were taken inside, things started to go wrong. *Abu Jamal* asked if he could use a secure telephone. His request was granted and before long various SUVs arrived bearing US civilians. The American visitors, like intelligence professionals the world over, wanted to reveal as little as possible about their connection to the two forlorn Iraqis sitting in the British interrogation room. But since the SAS were not inclined to release them without a proper explanation, it was eventually wrung out of the night-time visitors. *Abu Jamal* and his friend were CIA assets. The incident raised many disturbing questions: why were people in the kidnap business under CIA pay? If they were agents taking part in the conspiracy at their handlers' direction, why hadn't they yet produced a tip-off that would allow the hostage to be freed? And, given that the CIA was party to hostage working groups with MI6 and other agencies, why hadn't the Americans done something to prevent the SAS carrying out their raid?

This arrest showed how spectacularly dysfunctional intelligence relationships were, even two years after the Americans got to Baghdad. Little wonder that McChrystal wanted to build a separate network under his own tight grasp, fusing intelligence and special operations. The business also underlined that the Ba'athist or nationalist resistance was easier to penetrate than the Islamist network, and that in many cases of kidnapping was operating more like a criminal conspiracy than anything else.

Episodes like Mashadani and *Abu Jamal's* arrest did however bring to a head the debates about whether British special forces were really after the right people. There had been dozens of similar episodes in which the 'right' man had been lifted, but with no noticeable effect on the carnage going on around them. Many US ground-holding unit commanders had through 2004 shared the British view that the main threat to future stability came from a widespread Sunni revolt — an authentic Iraqi phenomenon quite different from the mad nihilism of Zarqawi and his ilk. But the currents of the violence were shifting and, belatedly, changing minds in the Green Zone.

When I asked one senior British figure at what point the UK military had decided that al-Qaeda presented a more significant threat than the FREs he replied, 'You imply a clarity that did not exist . . . most of our tools for intelligence analysis were overwhelmed at that time . . . I don't think we ever made a clear choice.' Perhaps, then, it is unwise to use hindsight to talk about tipping points, but it is clear that around the same time that Task Force Black was bringing in Mashadani, events on the ground were causing senior American commanders to rethink.

That same month, April 2005, had started with a complex assault on Abu Ghraib prison involving machine guns, mortars and two car bombs. The Americans reckoned that dozens of insurgents had been involved in a well-coordinated operation, which wounded forty-four of their soldiers as well as twelve prisoners. Eleven days later, insurgents had mounted a sustained attack on a marine base near the Syrian border at al-Husaybah. Up to a hundred men had attacked the marines, launching three vehicle suicide attacks including ones using a fire engine and dump truck rigged with huge amounts of explosive. Calling in air strikes and helicopters to beat off the attack, the Americans had killed around three dozen insurgents. The operation was also attributed to al-Qaeda. On 29 April the movement had staged fourteen car bomb attacks in a single day, most of them in Baghdad. Force Commander General Casey was so disturbed by the capabilities shown in these attacks that he formally upgraded Zarqawi's organisation to be the Coalition's principal enemy in Iraq.

At this point, an underlying tension between Casey and McChrystal came to the surface. McChrystal, says one senior Baghdad figure from that time, was 'resented by the rest of the army because they were gobbling up a very large slice of the available overhead reconnaissance assets'. The JSOC task force, operating from Balad, had successfully cornered a large proportion

SADDAM HUSAYN AL-TIKRITI
President

The Coalition's 'deck of cards' of High-Value Targets featured leading Ba'athists, with Saddam himself at the top. He was taken in an American operation in December 2003. Rex Features

Fourth on the list, Mahmud al-Tikriti was apprehended by G Squadron of the SAS in a joint operation with Delta Force in June 2003. Rex Features

ABID HAMID MAHMUD AL-TIKRITI
Presidential Secretary

(Above left) Richard Williams who, as Commanding Officer of the SAS, made it his mission to raise the effectiveness of Task Force Black.

(Above right) Graeme Lamb, who led UK Special Forces during the invasion of Iraq before commanding Britain's division in Basra and, in 2006, returning as deputy commander of all Coalition troops in Iraq. Rex Features

(Below) Major-General Jonathan Shaw, commander of the British division in Basra during early 2007. Rex Features

Stanley McChrystal, the architect of
Coalition 'black ops' in Iraq. Rex Features

General David Petraeus, principal
architect of the new American counterinsurgency strategy. Rex Features

General George Casey, seated centre, whose rush to turn over security to Iraq forces
may have exacerbated Iraq's crisis of 2006. He is seen here in October 2006, planning
an operation that would take place in Yusufiyah, south of Baghdad, during one of his
unsuccessful attempts to secure the capital. Rex Features

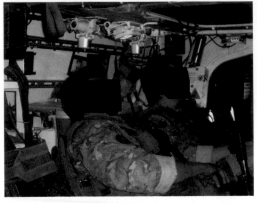

Members of A Squadron sporting 'Crye Kit' camouflage during an operation in 2007.

A typical scene at the MSS helipad in Baghdad as soldiers wait for nightfall and their operation.

A British special forces soldier during a raid on an Iraqi house. He carries a shotgun slung under his left arm, as well as an assault rifle and pistol.

Members of Task Force Knight pictured in an Iraqi living room. It illustrates the element of personal choice in combat clothing. Second from right sports the US version of the 'Fuck al-Qaeda' patch.

(Above) Funeral procession of an unidentified Iraqi in Ramadi, November 2003. The man had been killed in a car-bomb explosion outside the home of a leading tribal sheikh. AFP/Getty Images

(Right) Iraqis burn a flag during a protest against US and British troops in Iraq, April 2004. AFP/Getty Images

(Below) A British military vehicle drives past the wreckage of a taxi at the site of an explosion in Basra, one of three almost simultaneous attacks on police stations in the city on 21 April 2004. AFP/Getty Images

US soldiers frisk Iraqis at a checkpoint in Ramadi.
AFP/Getty Images

The aftermath of a car-bomb explosion in the Doura district of southern Baghdad, September 2005.
AFP/Getty Images

An image from a video posted in the internet by the militant group of Abu Massab al-Zarqawi, Organisation for the Holy War's Base in the Land of the Two Rivers. Masked gunmen stand behind five members of the Iraqi National Guard before their execution, January 2005.
AFP/Getty Images

Iraqi detainees hooded and ready for transport. The way the US processed such captives proved a sensitive issue with both their British and Iraqi allies. This operation, in November 2003, happened at a time when so many Sunnis were being arrested that detainee facilities such as Abu Ghraib were overwhelmed.
Rex Features

The two members of the HATHOR detachment locked up in the Jamiat police station during the incident of September 2005. Both show signs of having been beaten.

Equipment seized from the HATHOR detachment's car displayed by the Iraqi police. It includes an assault rifle, Minimi light machine gun and an anti-tank rocket, as well as communications gear.

Tony Blair pictured with members of G Squadron in Baghdad early in 2005. The Prime Minister took a particular interest in UK special forces operations and was usually briefed on them during his visits.

of the Intelligence Surveillance and Reconnaissance platforms in its hunt for Zarqawi. This meant not only control of Predator UAVs, which every commander wanted desperately, but other technical means such as satellites and aircraft used to intercept and locate mobile telephones. By May 2005 the number of Iraqis using cellular phones had grown to around 1.75 million. Mobiles were becoming a vital intelligence source. Just the details of a call between two numbers could be the start of an operation. What the spooks called nodal analysis could be used to map the relationship between different people and their phones. Once the pattern was better understood, the handset itself could work as a locator beacon. However, JSOC almost monopolised the means of harnessing this information.

The tension between JSOC and the rest of the US military would doubtless have been more easily managed if al-Qaeda had been rolled up with the speed that the Ba'athist deck of cards was lifted. But although there was some progress – for example the arrest in January 2005 of the master bomber believed to be behind the UN and other spectacular vehicle bombings of 2003 – attacks against police stations, recruiting offices or markets just seemed to carry on increasing in number and lethality. One at the end of February, in the largely Shia town of Hilla, south of Baghdad, had claimed 114 lives. To some watchers, the JSOC response of striking, often with bombing, wherever they found a trace of the AQI leadership seemed to smack of desperation. For the American ground-holding commanders – running brigades or battalions in relentlessly violent places like Ramadi or Baquba – the steady toll of young men or women blown apart by the insurgents provoked its own questions about why JSOC, with such a big slice of vital intelligence-gathering assets, was not doing more to help them.

Casey had instituted a morning meeting that united all senior commanders, staff and intelligence people in Iraq via a Video

Tele-Conference or VTC. The meeting, the Battlefield Update Assessment, had its own acronym, BUA – or 'Boo-ah' in head-quarters speak. Once the main news of the day was processed, a smaller, highly classified meeting known as the Huddle took place to discuss sensitive matters. One attendee recalls the atmos-phere: 'The hunt for Zarqawi was paramount. It was mentioned every morning in the BUA and in the Huddle in the mistaken belief that if you got him the insurgency would collapse.'

As pressure increased on JSOC from Casey and others wanting results, McChrystal began to shift the emphasis of his operation in Iraq. Since his target had become that of the entire Coalition force, he needed to do more to take on the local militant net-works that were killing and maiming so many US troops. Many hard-pressed commanders had formed the idea that JSOC was there to take down Zarqawi and a handful of his associates – in short, that they were playing a game of high Pentagon politics that consumed huge resources but was failing to deliver. McChrystal responded by exploiting the growing information flow from drones and cell phones to target the entire al-Qaeda network from top to bottom, but with particular focus on those in between. 'The aim was to go after the middle of their net-work,' McChrystal would later reveal, 'in a regular army, their senior non-commissioned officers. We tried to cause the network to collapse.' The changes were of vital importance, not just because they would bring about dramatic shifts in the secret war but also because they brought to a head various UK special forces issues. McChrystal's new approach required the British to rethink why they were mounting covert operations in Iraq, triggering bitter battles between those responsible.

McChrystal sought to mollify Casey that summer with special operations in support of a broad military effort to interdict the Sunni militant rat lines from the western borders of Iraq to Baghdad. The JSOC commander codenamed this effort Operation

SNAKE EYES. It involved synchronising raids by Seal Team 6 or Delta Force to those of the ground-holding army and marine units up the Euphrates valley. From May to October regular US ground forces fought a series of at least fourteen major operations, each involving more than a thousand troops, along the course of this key watercourse from places such as al-Qaim, close to the Syrian frontier, down through Haditha and Hit, through Ramadi and Fallujah to Abu Ghraib on the outskirts of Baghdad. The battlefield ranged from remote farms fringed with date palms to the suburbs of major cities. The Americans characterised these places as stopovers on the infiltration route of foreign fighters from the Jordanian or Syrian frontiers to the capital. What the ordinary grunts found in many of these communities were well-organised paramilitary groups armed with everything from small arms to mortars or surface-to-air missiles, who manoeuvred against them.

During one of the early operations, a single platoon of US Marines had suffered 60 per cent casualties in five days. Attacking a house in Ubaydi, a small town in western Anbar Province, two men were killed and five wounded. In the words of an embedded reporter, 'It took twelve hours and five assaults by the squad – plus grenades, bombing by an F/A-18 attack plane, tank rounds and rockets at twenty yards – to kill the insurgents and permit recovery of the dead Marines' bodies.' A couple of days later, survivors of that fight were in their vehicle when it was hit by an IED, killing another four and wounding ten. Their parent battalion suffered forty-eight fatalities and more than 120 wounded during a seven-month tour.

As these operations went ahead during the summer of 2005, JSOC mounted dozens of takedowns against suspected local players or middle managers in the guerrilla organisation. These actions exposed McChrystal's men to determined heavily armed opposition that often stood and fought rather than retreating in classic guerrilla fashion. In many places the fighting started with small arms and grenades but soon escalated to strafing runs by helicopters and air strikes.

As Delta Force operators stormed a house in al-Qaim on 17 June, the deadly drama played out on big plasma screens in a hall on the edge of Balad airbase. There, JSOC had built its main operations centre in Iraq. Its centrepiece was a basketball-court-sized control room, the Joint Operations Centre (JOC). Here, during the course of 2004 and early 2005, the technology, people and ideas at the heart of JSOC's war had coalesced. Three large screens at one end of the hall relayed live pictures from different operations, as well as other information that desk officers needed to know. Facing the big plasmas were desks for all of the main sections involved: operations, intelligence, aviation, medical and so on. A 'Jag' or Judge Advocate General, a military lawyer, was always on hand to rule over the legality of proposed operations. Each of these specialist desks had its own array of screens on which officers could bring up information from orbiting drones, their own computers or the JSOC intranet. At busy times there would be scores of staff at work in this darkened cockpit of technology and violence.

People who worked in the JOC sometimes referred to it as the Death Star because of the sense that 'you could just reach out with a finger, as it were, and eliminate somebody'. Others who watched live the white splash of five-hundred-pound bombs on image-intensifier cameras referred to the screens up above them as 'Kill TV'. For many, industrial metaphors were more appropriate to the relentless process of changing shifts, nightly raids and ceaseless target development work. They called the JOC 'the factory' or 'the shop floor'. McChrystal himself often described his whole setup in Iraq as 'the machine'. Around the main area, with its feeling of mission control, were a number of discrete offices. The liaison team from the National Security Agency, the huge US eavesdropping operation, had a private room. The commander of Delta Force ran the battle in the JOC but had his own space too. The task force running this secret campaign chewed through codenames with dizzying speed, often discarding them when they became compromised in the press, going from TF-20, to TF 6-26 then TF-121: by this time, the main operation run by the CO of Delta was TF-145. Major-General McChrystal had offices in a nearby building and while he spent about half of his year in Iraq, was not in day-to-day operational control of the forces there. McChrystal and his people had however worked up doctrines that meant the campaign being fought in the JOC was in itself a quiet revolution.

The JSOC commander and his staff were, by the first half of 2005, putting forward three concepts that were central to much of what followed: they advocated 24/7 aerial surveillance of certain critical targets – a concept referred to as 'the Unblinking Eye'; black operations were to increase sharply in tempo or frequency, something made possible in part by the growing Iraqi uptake of mobile phones; and the emphasis of operations was crystallised into 'F3EA' – find-fix-finish-exploit-analyse. Some argued that finding the bad guy, fixing where he was in space and time, then finishing him had been the essence of their man-hunting techniques even before they arrived in Iraq. But McChrystal's particular emphasis on the exploitation and analysis of each raid meant that intelligence gathering became the point of each strike.

At this time, JSOC's intelligence operation was run by an army colonel, Mike Flynn. The colonel, whose dark hair and prominent nose gave him a passing resemblance to the Hollywood actor Roy Scheider, was one of McChrystal's key ideas men. Flynn and his boss constantly sparked off each other, and such was the intellectual level of their debate that the rest of the staff often struggled to keep up with them. Flynn and two colleagues later gave an unclassified insight into their work in an article published in a US military magazine in 2008. Explaining why JSOC needed to monopolise so many of the best Coalition information-gathering aircraft, Flynn wrote, 'intelligence, surveillance and reconnaissance are most effective against low-contrast enemies when *massed* . . . the purpose of this long dwell airborne stakeout is to apply multisensor observation 24/7 to achieve a greater understanding of how the enemy's network operates by building a pattern of life analysis'. The prolonged siege of Fallujah, and mishaps like the Predator's camera going awry on the Zarqawi stakeout, had taught Flynn that anything up to three aircraft needed to be concentrated simultaneously against a target or network.

Flynn explicitly rejected the idea of fairness in allocating these precious intelligence-gathering assets. This meant not only telling the wider army that it would have to make do with its poorer share, but also moving the drones or other important technologies between the different task forces controlled from Balad. The commander who could work up the most promising case – be it the Delta squadron man, the leader of Seal Team 6, or whoever else – would get huge back-up. Flynn wrote, 'Massing implies focus and priority. Selected parts of the enemy's network receive focus, which should be unwavering for a specified time . . . enemy actions are not easily predictable. Without prediction the next best thing is redundancy and saturation.'

Where this Unblinking Eye was maintained, relationships could be mapped between individuals, their meetings or vehicles being followed from the sky. As JSOC got better and better at this, airborne sensors could be used to lock on to mobile phones carried by these suspects, and earlier recordings examined after a car bomb had gone off could be used to trace an explosives-laden vehicle as it left a suspect house. Little wonder that one visiting

US general described the system they created as 'magic'.

Flynn defined the Unblinking Eye as 'long-dwell, persistent surveillance directed against known and suspected terrorist sites and individuals'. Those working in the JOC knew it had other definitions too. McChrystal's ideas about everyone sharing the same intelligence picture were designed to prevent a 'blink' as one agency or target developer handed the information to someone who had to act on it. The SAS lifting CIA asset *Abu Jamal* was a spectacular blink; more often it was a case of a target individual or network being forgotten or mislaid by poor communication. In the JOC at Balad they aimed to eliminate such slips.

JSOC wanted simultaneous coverage of a target by up to three drones – yet early in 2004 all of the other Coalition units operating in Iraq had to share two Predators between them. By 2007 the US commanders would have twelve Predators and eighteen of the smaller Shadow drones, and JSOC a large ration of its own. But in the summer of 2005 these tensions about the black operation's use of special resources had prompted Operation SNAKE EYES.

The June Delta operation in al-Qaim, for example, was carried out in support of nearby US Marine battalions, which meant hitting further down the al-Qaeda food chain. Even if Zarqawi himself was smart enough not to use a mobile phone, many of his subordinates were busy chatting away. But however disciplined the user was in conversation, the handset could still become a means to locate a man in the anonymous sprawl of a city or indeed in a remote village.

In May, the Delta squadron at MSS Fernandez had deployed west to back up Task Force Blue in the Euphrates valley. They soon became engaged in a series of blistering close-range battles with Sunni militants. Many of the special operators were shocked by the numbers, sophistication and intensity of attacks they faced.

Within a few weeks three Delta operators had been killed in western Iraq. The first Delta fatality since 2003, Sergeant First Class Steven Langmack fell on 31 May during an operation near the Syrian border. In the second incident – that operation on 17 June – two had died while assaulting a house not far from where Langmack had died, at al-Qaim. The two fatalities, Master Sergeants Michael McNulty and Robert Horrigan, were seasoned Delta operators. Horrigan was in fact on virtually his last mission before leaving the army. The Americans had begun their assault oblivious to the fact that a trap had been set. A bunker had been built inside the building, and when the Delta men blew their way in the defenders were waiting unscathed in their strongpoint. After two of the Delta attackers had been killed, the remaining men withdrew and dropped a bomb on the house.

With Delta squadrons fielding only thirty to forty operators, it did not take long before the deaths and injuries seriously limited their capability. In June, McChrystal formally asked *Peter Rogers* whether UK special forces might be able to assist. Apparently citing ongoing British concerns about the Balad detention facilities and other operational issues such as rules of engagement, *Rogers* declined. The Americans flew in a second squadron of Delta Force and pressed on. But the American request had lit a fuse, a simmering conflict between *Rogers* and the newly installed commander of the SAS that would cause an explosion later that summer. The new boss at Hereford was Richard Williams. As a major he had frequently been in Baghdad during the spring and summer of 2003, before being posted away from the SAS on another job. Promoted to lieutenant-colonel, Williams became an outspoken advocate of those within the regiment who believed that they were wasting their time chasing the 'old men' of the Ba'athist target set and needed to do whatever was necessary to assist their brothers in Delta in a time of crisis. While the UK–US stand-off continued, and relations between Williams and *Rogers* worsened, those on the ground tried to deal with daily crises in the best way they could.

On 23 July, the duty squadron in Baghdad would find itself in the thick of it. JSOC had developed intelligence on the type of al-Qaeda target that the US operators would normally have guarded jealously. They were so heavily committed out west, and the information was so urgent, that they had no choice but to give it to Task Force Black in Baghdad. So, with little time to argue about it with the DSF back in London, the British were to get a taste of the fight against al-Qaeda.

The mission was codenamed Operation MARLBOROUGH. It resulted from urgent intelligence that a multiple suicide bombing was about to be launched from a house in southern Baghdad. The unit on duty at the time was M Squadron of the Royal Marines Special Boat Service. This was the second of just two tours in Baghdad by the Royal Marines special operators, and it was due to last just three months. But it was their duty, that sultry evening, to prosecute the kind of al-Qaeda target that the rotating special forces squadrons had been longing for.

Some members of G Squadron had stayed behind to help the marines, but the bulk of the force that assembled that night for the mission was from the SBS. There had been a great deal of tension between the two British special operations units – some of it soothed away with banter – albeit hard-edged – but much of it still festering. M Squadron was the SBS element that had been mauled in northern Iraq back in 2003, losing most of its vehicles and much other equipment. The SAS men did not consider them up to the job, referring to them as 'Tier 2 SF'. Plans to double the size of the SBS at this time had caused further ill-feeling because many recruits from the joint selection process run for UK special forces had been siphoned into the new SBS squadrons. The marines' special unit was not at that time deeply committed to Afghanistan and its commanders insisted they gain operational exposure in Task Force Black.

The SAS–SBS rivalry is deeply rooted and essentially tribal. Many of those who played supporting roles in Task Force Black actually preferred the marines' approach, arguing they displayed less macho swagger and greater thoughtfulness than the SAS blades. C Squadron of the SBS had served in Baghdad in 2004, gaining a reputation for being remarkably leisurely about its business. It had mounted twenty-two raids during a four-month tour, compared, say, to A Squadron of the SAS's eighty-five missions during its 2003 deployment. The slow pace of operations set by C Squadron had reflected many factors, not least that the time had marked a low point in overall US–UK special forces cooperation. Nevertheless that tour provided ammunition for the SBS's critics. But what happened that night in July 2005, on Operation MARLBOROUGH, should have been enough to silence the sceptics at Hereford.

The commandos had arrived close to their Alpha (the target house) with a combination of Humvees and Pumas. The Americans were also closely involved. A detachment of Task Force Red, the Rangers, was acting as a back-up force, and the ground-holding unit had furnished some M1 tanks because of the dangers of the neighbourhood in question. A couple of technical experts from the US special ops community were there too, as custodians of the sensitive technology that had allowed the al-Qaeda cell to be pinpointed, and to act as liaison. Overhead, Task Force Black had Pumas carrying snipers in case the people inside the Alpha tried to launch an attack. An orbiting command and control aircraft was also aloft to help direct the operation.

When the SBS men moved up on foot to hit the target compound a man wearing a suicide vest came running towards them. He detonated the bomb too early to kill the crouching commandos, but one of the Pumas was so low – less than a hundred feet above them – that the explosion caused the aircraft to lose control. It lofted upwards on a cushion of blast and then, for a split second, the troop-carrying helicopter dropped like a stone. Against the odds, given their low altitude, the pilot managed to recover the situation, the twin engines screaming as he piled on the power to pull his Puma up. Having come within a few feet of smashing into the Baghdad rooftops the machine roared up into the night air. Whatever expletives might have been flying in the passenger cabin, they were not given time to dwell on their experience. One of the airborne platforms watching the Alpha had picked up on its image-intensifying camera a man leaving the back of the building and running for it.

The Puma swung around to give the sniper a shot. The SBS man fixed the target in his telescopic sights and opened fire, killing the militant. A second suicide bomber had been stopped.

It was time for the house itself to be stormed. Bursting into the main building of the compound, the SBS began room clearing. As they went, another man wearing a bomb vest ran down a corridor towards them. One of the SBS Team Leaders, a senior NCO, opened fire at close range, cutting him down. Nobody was quite sure whether he had died before he had a chance to press the button or whether his device had revealed itself as faulty – and nobody at that moment wanted to look too closely at the slumped body. As the teams worked their way through the rooms they did so with growing trepidation. There were explosives or other components of bomb vests scattered in different parts of the building. Throwing grenades into rooms or firing indiscriminately might cause a disaster. They withdrew, confident that their tally of three dead bombers represented the total threat and left the place to bomb disposal experts.

With Operation MARLBOROUGH over the SBS was commended, having had a taste of the kind of violence facing Delta as it prosecuted its operations against AQI. The Puma pilot who had saved his ship was decorated for this feat of bravery and airmanship. What the events of 23 July rammed home more clearly than any intelligence briefing could have done was that a world of difference existed between the type of FRE arrest work to which Task Force Black had been relegated and the intensely violent fight taking place against al-Qaeda.

Back in the UK, at the Pontrilas training area, near Hereford, the special forces were conducting one of their gruelling selection courses. The same basic challenge of mental and physical endurance awaited those who wanted to join the SAS, SBS, or the new Special Reconnaissance Regiment. These units, along with the two Territorial Army SAS regiments and special forces signal regiment, all came under direction of *Peter Rogers* as Director of Special Forces. In addition, a battalion of paratroopers were also being placed under his command, having re-rolled to become the Special Forces Support Group. Due to the expanding size of this empire, *Rogers* had been promoted to major-general.

Rogers, an Oxford graduate, had started his career in the Parachute Regiment before serving as a troop commander in the SAS and leading a squadron in the SBS. He was lofty of stature and attitude: highly intelligent, he knew exactly what he wanted to do with his directorate. Few in the SAS whom I spoke to in writing this book have a kind word to say about *Rogers*. Another senior officer, who assisted in his promotion, describes *Rogers* ruefully as 'very cerebral, a cold fish. My conversations with him were never easy. I can't imagine that he got on well with soldiers.'

A self-confessed fan of the DSF from an intelligence background counters that *Rogers* understood the workings of the secret world very well. As for the man's sometimes abrasive style, 'He is an antagoniser by nature. He will meet you and try to unsettle you. As soon as he is with you, he is testing you – it's conversational reconnaissance by fire.' Certainly, *Rogers* liked to surprise or wrong-foot people, another critic describing him as 'a yoga-practising special forces type'.

Meeting Stan McChrystal in Washington that summer, things had not gone well. The Americans were already disappointed by the UK's refusing their June request for Task Force Black's support. When McChrystal had explained to *Rogers* what he was trying to achieve by ratcheting up the tempo of operations, so that the suicide bombing cells were hit every night, *Rogers* had queried whether this 'industrial counterterrorism' could work. The term 'industrial counterterrorism' ended up being used approvingly by many in special operations to describe the McChrystal approach – but *Rogers* had not meant it as a compliment.

Richard Williams, meanwhile, had built a great relationship with McChrystal. The Commanding Officer of the regular SAS, boundlessly energetic and among the most aggressive field commanders in anyone's army, had come to look upon McChrystal with intense admiration. The American's long stints in Iraq dealing with every aspect of his command, his personal presence on many raids – despite holding a two-star general's rank – and his missionary certainty that his new concepts for fighting a war could win success had all won Williams over, say those who watched them work together.

In Balad or Baghdad and elsewhere Williams and McChrystal would chew over how they could get the SAS fighting alongside Delta as a fully integrated member of the team. The SAS commander had been convinced by those working in Task Force Black that the FRE mission was a complete waste of his people. So they went through the checklist: Britain was worried about the JSOC prison at Balad (the TSF). Work had been done to rebuild the cells so that they met British-approved standards – but it would take time and several visits by British officials for this to be confirmed. If the UK was concerned about mistreatment of detainees there, why not contribute an on-site interrogation team to ensure that there was no foul play? *Rogers* had also declined to adopt US rules in calling in air strikes or artillery fire (he considered them too loose), but surely there was a way around this too?

Williams's advocacy of this closer relationship with the Americans was, says someone well briefed on the arguments with DSF, 'the last straw'. The Director of Special Forces had a long list of grievances: *Rogers* felt the SAS commander was an obstacle to his plans to 'rebalance' special forces between Iraq and Afghanistan, with Hereford giving up its role in the latter country to the SBS; and the DSF also felt that Williams was cold-shouldering the newest member of the family, the Special Reconnaissance Regiment. But it was increasingly strident advocacy on the Iraq mission that caused *Rogers* to act. He summoned Williams to see him during selection at Pontrilas, and told the SAS commander that he was recommending his transfer. News of this bombshell soon spread through the senior ranks of the army. Some COs are occasionally removed, but for the head of the regular army's SAS to be stood down was unprecedented.

Rogers took his case to General Sir Mike Jackson, Chief of the General Staff, or head of the army, and other senior officers. It did not take the DSF long to discover that his plan did not command widespread support. *Rogers* cited the personality clashes between himself and Williams, and the generals told their Director of Special Forces that he would have to get along. 'Jackson took soundings,' recalls one observer of those fateful days in the Ministry of Defence. 'This was early days in Williams's command. If you fired him, you had to have a convincing replacement who was better and we didn't.'

At an army cricket match that September the two men made

their uneasy peace. Williams agreed to abandon long-standing SAS objections to giving up deployments in Afghanistan. That would become the SBS's war (at least until the Iraq deployment was wound up). The SAS would specialise in Iraq. Williams backtracked on rebalancing; *Rogers* on his attempt to get rid of his subordinate. But having placed the SAS's operational eggs in the Iraqi basket, the resolution of outstanding differences with JSOC became all the more important. Events on the ground underlined that too.

On 25 August Delta Force had suffered another costly reverse in the Upper Euphrates. Three of its seasoned operators and one Ranger had been killed when their vehicle was blown up. This brought to six the number of Delta operators killed in three months. Many others had been badly wounded. McChrystal could not have needed the SAS's help more.

Asking one senior US figure connected with these issues about this difficult time, he referred to Williams as 'a superb commander; very gracious, very forthcoming, we shared a lot of briefings. Whenever he asked for something we found ourselves able to deliver.' What did the same American make of *Rogers*? He would say only, 'At the field level the [UK–US] relationship is almost seamless. The higher up you go, people get involved in all sorts of foolishness.'

Despite these tensions, the American side of the relationship remained ready to help the SAS, even if the Brits could not reciprocate fully. Just how far JSOC would go to do this would be illustrated by events unfolding on the streets of Basra.

6

THE JAMIAT

Early in the morning there is still some relief from the suffocating, heavy heat of a Basra summer's day. Even in September the thermometer regularly tops 50° Celsius, but in the still half-light, as the bakers prepare their *samoun* and carters start hefting produce to shops that are not yet open, there are hours when it is a few degrees cooler. In this early morning scene, cars driven by British operators moved easily through the light traffic. Out of sight in their battered wagons were automatic weapons, anti-tank rockets and sophisticated communications equipment. The soldiers themselves had darkened their skins and wore cheap, locally bought shirts over their T-shirts. Their features were hardly local and a couple even had blue eyes, but from a distance they could pass. Their lives depended on their skill at blending in. The SAS was on the ground in Basra and on that morning, 19

September 2005, the cars' occupants comprised the regiment's entire presence in the city.

'They were building a pattern-of-life picture,' recalls one colleague. Their target was an Iraqi police officer called Captain Jafar. He was one of the men who ran the Serious Crimes Unit, an outfit that Basrawi bazaar rumour linked with all manner of vice, corruption and brutality. Among British soldiers and police trying to mentor the IPS, the joke was that Jafar's squad had not yet realised they were meant to prevent serious crime, rather than perpetrate it. The cars made their way through Old Basra, south-west on the Zubayr road before turning north-wards to the place where their target worked, the Jamiat police station. This compound sat in the eastern part of the city where the sprawling estates of the Hayyaniyah and Jamiat, areas where there was strong support for radical militias, abutted the city centre.

The man in command of the surveillance that morning was Staff Sergeant *Campbell*, who was also OC of the regiment's residual presence in Basra, codenamed Operation HATHOR. With him in his car was Lance Corporal *Griffiths*. In a different vehicle were other men. The only further member of the HATHOR detachment on that particular morning, a signaller rather than a badged member of the SAS, was back at Basra Palace, monitoring the progress of the mission.

Campbell was a highly experienced operator, decorated for his work in Northern Ireland, who had served with the regiment's Surveillance Reconnaissance Cell, the in-house centre of know-ledge and training in the dark arts of seeing without being seen. Placed in charge of the small HATHOR detachment, *Campbell* had a bewildering array of tasks and masters.

One role was supporting the operations of the Secret Intelligence Service. HATHOR protected case officers who were meeting their sources in the city and brought agents in to meet their handlers, as well as mounting surveillance operations to develop the information those spies provided. It was a difficult job that had, for example, resulted in one member of the HATHOR detachment briefly being charged with murder after pursuing and killing an Iraqi after a shooting incident when the troops were in the city with their MI6 counterparts.

Much of the detachment's job consisted of target development: operations designed to validate intelligence, 'finding and fixing' the targets for strike operations, including those involving the deployment to Basra of Task Force Black reinforcements from Baghdad. On 19 September HATHOR was actually developing a picture for another player, the 'green army', the visible force of around 8500 who were, at that time, trying to hold the ring in an increasingly lawless southern Iraq.

British army commanders in the city had at last determined that Captain Jafar should be arrested. However, the army did not think it should be done at the Jamiat police station. Some in the SAS later suggested that this was because the chain of command did not want the embarrassment of admitting that the IPS, Britain's gangplank out of Basra, was rotten. There can also be little doubt that trying to arrest Jafar from the headquarters of the Serious Crimes Unit could easily touch off a firefight, in which British soldiers might kill their nominal allies in the Iraqi police. So HATHOR's mission was intended to prepare that arrest somewhere away from the Jamiat. They needed to find Jafar's home or some other convenient point. The task was one with a highly specific objective for, as one experienced SAS operator in Basra notes, serials like that on 19 September 'were always done for actionable intelligence because of the risks involved in going out'. On this occasion the risks were to prove disastrous, not only for the men involved but for the whole British effort in Iraq.

*

By the late summer of 2005 the tentacles of militia power had spread through much of Basrawi life. Some, such as the Badr Brigade, had actually been allowed to act openly by the British since mid-2003. Others, such as Muqtada al-Sadr's Jaish al Mehdi, existed in a never-never land where, despite 2004's spasms of extreme violence, they had to be shown limited tolerance in order to help attempts to build political support for the embattled Iraqi government. In the southern city at the confluence of Iraq's two great rivers, this acceptance of the militias' power had disastrous effects for the police and wider community.

The consequences of militia assertiveness and British acquiescence were best catalogued by a New Yorker called Steve Vincent. He set himself up at the Marbid Hotel in the city centre at a time when almost none of the British journalists considered it safe to do so. Vincent's blog and articles written in the middle months of 2005 described a city in which young women at the university were beaten or killed for dressing immodestly, bitter political rivalries between militias were played out within a penetrated police force, and where British mentors often chose to look the other way. A small wiry reporter who had set aside his writing on the Greenwich Village art scene after 9/11, Vincent became increasingly impassioned about how the people of Basra, in particular its women, had been abandoned to what he called 'Islamo-fascism'. In 'Switched Off in Basra', a fateful dispatch printed by the *New York Times* on 31 July, Vincent observed:

> An Iraqi police lieutenant . . . confirmed to me the widespread rumors that a few police officers are perpetrating many of the hundreds of assassinations . . . that take place in Basra each month . . . meanwhile, the British stand above the growing turmoil, refusing to challenge the Islamists' claim on the hearts and minds of police officers. This detachment angers many Basrans. 'The British know what's

happening but they are asleep, pretending they can simply establish security and leave behind democracy,' said the police lieutenant who had told me of the assassinations.

Vincent was particularly angered by the fact that, in training and arming the police while doing little to challenge the growth of militia power within its ranks, 'the British are in effect strengthening the hand of Shiite organisations'.

The power of these truths was such that somebody decided to act. A couple of days after the *New York Times* piece appeared, Vincent and his female interpreter Nouriya Itais were stopped on one of the city's main streets in full view of the early evening crowd. The armed men who took them were dressed as police-men, and bundled the pair into a police car. After cruising around, beating them and calling Itais 'a whore and a pig' for being with an American, their hands were tied. They were then thrown out onto the street and shot. Itais survived, but Steve Vincent became the first American journalist to be killed cover-ing the insurgency in Iraq. For the *New York Times*, it was naturally a big story. The paper's stringer in Basra, a 38-year-old father of three named Fakher Haider, filed several reports on what had happened, capturing local feeling that Vincent had been murdered because he had exposed the ugly nexus of Shia extremism, criminality and infiltration of the police. On the day that the HATHOR detachment began its ill-fated mission against Captain Jafar, Fakher Haider was murdered.

It had taken Staff Sergeant *Campbell* and his team just a few hours to complete their task. One colleague comments that 'the incident happened when the serial was finished and the guys felt they couldn't get any more of value'. But as they drove towards one of the main thoroughfares to the east of Basra, everything unravelled.

Iraqi police had spotted the surveillance. Tension was running high because a few days earlier a leading member of Jaish al-Mehdi had been arrested during a large British army strike operation. Whether or not the militia's supporters in police uniform realised there was a connection between the surveillance cars out that morning and the earlier arrest, HATHOR had in fact helped prepare it. A Squadron had only returned to Baghdad a couple of days earlier, following that raid. But on the morning of 19 September, the special forces soldiers on the ground were bereft of their SAS colleagues' support.

The IPS set up a checkpoint and stopped the car containing *Campbell* and Lance Corporal *Griffiths*. Moving in to pull them out, there was a brief firefight. The SAS shot at least one policeman and drove off. With Iraqi police vehicles in pursuit, they radioed Basra Palace, informing the signaller that there had been a contact. But their car was no souped-up wolf in sheep's clothing – it was a cheaply bought Iraqi banger. 'There was a point where they felt they couldn't outpace the pursuers,' notes one SAS soldier. 'They wanted to try and talk their way out of it.' They laid down their weapons and got out of the car and the Iraqi police bundled the British soldiers into their own vehicles. Two SAS men were in the bag.

At the Joint Operations Centre in Balad, it was breakfast time. Key people worked nights, when the raids went in. During the early part of daytime those players were usually asleep and lesser mortals manned the shop floor in the quieter hours. Then the call from Basra came. Someone was sent to wake Colonel *James Grist* who, as CO of Delta Force, ran the JSOC operation in Iraq. People began to filter in and the place began to crackle with the tension of an unexpected operational situation. The British liaison team, intelligence people, psychological operations (psyops) staff, all began to move about the JOC with focus and purpose.

Grist was soon on the scene and briefed by the specialists represented in the JOC. Decisions were taken swiftly. A Predator was scrambled from its base at Baghdad, but the propeller-driven drone was built for endurance not speed: it would take two and a half hours to reach Basra. It was clear that *Campbell* and *Griffiths* might have to be rescued. Colonel *Grist* offered British commanders the services of a squadron of Delta. This was a gesture of American solidarity that would be remembered within the SAS long afterwards, but Task Force Black wanted to get its own people on site as soon as it could.

At the MSS in Baghdad, there was a buzz of activity. Some twenty members of A Squadron, a platoon of British paratroopers from the recently deployed Special Forces Support Group, four signallers and a medic – more than fifty men in all – packed their kit, readied their weapons and headed out to the airport. There, an RAF Hercules was prepared for action. Within a few hours of the incident in Basra both the Hercules and the Predator were in the air and heading south.

At the headquarters of Multi-National Division South East at Basra airport, the scene was quite different. There, officious notices were stuck to the coffee tables telling soldiers to clear up their mess, and in the airy hallway forces public relations posters proclaimed Anglo-Iraqi friendship. These realities, of a mission bound by rules and politics, were to define the staff's response to the apprehension of the two British soldiers.

Off the hallway, behind doors with combination locks, were the offices of both the divisional and the brigade commanders. The more senior of the two officers, a major-general, was meant to handle the big picture, liaising with the Iraqis or Americans as well as up the national chain of command to Permanent Joint Headquarters back at Northwood. On this day, though, the general was out of the country. The commander of 12 Brigade, Brigadier John Lorimer, an able officer formerly of the

Parachute Regiment, was there and in charge of formulating a response.

After *Campbell* and *Griffiths* had been taken away by the Iraqi police, their movements had been followed. The car carrying the other members of HATHOR detachment had remained briefly on the scene without being spotted by the Iraqis. They tracked their colleagues to the Jamiat, then raced off to get more soldiers from a Quick Reaction Force at Basra Palace.

As this information was fed back, two communications systems were in operation. The HATHOR detachment signaller was constantly in touch with Balad, and was also relaying situation reports to the green army. This single soldier stood at the centre of the information as the first phase of the crisis developed. And while troops and MI6 people at the Palace all began making preparations, they needed definite guidance about what to do.

It was not long before the Predator tasked by the JOC appeared over Basra, relaying live pictures back to Balad. The British division did not at that time have the necessary equipment to downlink these pictures. They relied instead on a Sea King helicopter equipped with a television surveillance system known as Broadsword. Since the pictures from Broadsword could not be watched in Balad or most British locations in Basra city, the system's operator on board the Sea King, a member of the army's Brigade Reconnaissance Force, became, like the special forces signaller at the Palace, another key figure, a thread by which the two captured men's lives dangled. For if the SAS prisoners' whereabouts was lost, their lives might soon be forfeited too.

Inside the Jamiat, things were going badly for *Campbell* and *Griffiths*. They had been beaten up during capture and stripped of their equipment. The men were filmed and the pictures released to the world media. They were described as spies apprehended on their way to carrying out a terrorist attack. Across the Hayyaniyah and the other baking bastions of the Shia militias, word spread of the sensational capture.

Not long after the Predator had arrived on station, different images grabbed the attention of everyone watching. The blood-ied captives in the Jamiat were shown, as were the weapons, radio and other equipment taken from their car. The political sensitivity of the incident had just increased exponentially.

At the airport, Major *Chappell*, the OC of A Squadron, arrived in Lorimer's office. He had not returned to Baghdad with the rest of his squadron following the arrest operation a few days before and, hearing of the Jamiat crisis, he had gone to urge swiftness upon the brigade commander. The SAS wanted its men out as quickly as possible, but they were also worried that the TV images and charges of spying or terrorism levelled against them meant a show trial or some even more summary form of Iraqi justice was on the cards.

Lorimer's hands had been tied by PJHQ, which advised him not to take any step that might inflame the situation. He did, however, send a negotiating team to the Jamiat and put a cordon of British infantry around it, aiming to block the main routes to and from the compound.

On that same September day, dozens of SAS soldiers, their fam-ilies and friends had gathered near the regiment's base at Hereford for the consecration of a new special forces graveyard. The regiment had long buried its fallen at St Martin's, a nearby church. The churchyard was running out of space so the regi-ment had decided to create its own burial place.

Few outfits in the British army devote less energy to spit and polish than the SAS, but this was one of those occasions when padres, ladies in hats and soldiers in spotless uniform were min-gling. When the time came for the ceremonial unveiling, the serenity of the occasion was disrupted by mobile phone calls and text messages.

Such is the nature of the special forces grapevine that communications from Iraq started coming through to officers and senior NCOs in their service dress. The place was soon alive with rumours. What were the army going to do to get *Campbell* and *Griffiths* out? Not much, many members of the regiment concluded.

At PJHQ, consternation at the early TV pictures of the two captured men was followed by shock as shots appeared of the soldiers forming the cordon around the Jamiat coming under attack from angry crowds. Rumour had spread around the Hayyaniyah with dizzying speed, leading thousands of militant inhabitants onto the streets. Rioting broke out, with petrol bombs and bullets — both real and rubber — traded. As Molotov cocktails hit a Warrior armoured vehicle, Sergeant George Long of the Staffordshire Regiment tumbled out of his turret, ablaze with burning petrol. The images of him rolling off the vehicle were for many viewers in Britain the clearest possible indication that they should not accept government assurances that everything was going to plan in southern Iraq.

The British embassy's response to this emergency was to use its official channels to request the men's release. An order to this effect was issued by the Iraqi Interior Ministry, but duly ignored by the officers at the Jamiat. Remarkably, according to a number of people involved in the day's drama, neither the British embassy nor the divisional HQ at Basra nor PJHQ in Britain saw fit to inform the Coalition — that is, the American — command about what was going on. Despite the appearance of alarming TV images throughout the day, the British division in Basra had not asked General Casey, the top commander in Baghdad, what it should do or even informed him as to how they might rescue the men. One senior British officer reflects, 'The whole command relationship broke down because nobody, officially, told the Americans what was going on, although of course they knew through JSOC.'

By mid-afternoon the SAS, through Major *Chappell* at the Basra end and Lieutenant-Colonel Williams in the UK, were pressing hard for a rescue operation. It was at this point that they paid dearly for the command arrangements put in place two years earlier, under which SAS operations in Iraq were run through the Chief of Joint Operations at Northwood. Nobody, however, could be found in authority to approve the mission. Major *Chappell* could not get through to the CJO's mobile phone. It later went around the SAS that the senior officer had switched it off because he was playing golf.

The special ops people in Iraq knew that the police inside the Jamiat were preparing to withstand an attack. Men were being brought in with rocket-propelled grenades, and warned about a possible British helicopter assault. Given the mayhem in the streets outside, those holding *Campbell* and *Griffiths* might well have been wondering whether their prisoners were too hot to handle. They had withstood the pressure from a British negotiator and their own interior ministry to release the captives, but at length, with difficulties multiplying for them, the police decided that it would be better if the men were not in their custody.

At the airport, after hours of consideration, and with little meaningful guidance from the UK, Brigadier Lorimer authorised an attack on the Jamiat. It would be spearheaded by Challenger tanks and Warriors. In his initial orders he gave no authority for the troops to enter any other building or compound.

At this time, the Iraqis decided to move *Campbell* and *Griffiths*. Knowing that there were 'eyes in the sky' above the compound, they put dishdashas (long Arab shirts that come down to the ankle) on the prisoners, and threw blankets over their heads as

side. It was a forlorn
ight be seen by one
ced into the waiting

he streets around the
the helicopter up
ng elsewhere, trying
ged in running gun
scuffle in the court-
l off, the American
ing depended upon
King, relaying ver-
d below.
quadron to tailor its
its members com-
tskirts of the city, a
began their assault
their two comrades
he Jamiat to a house
not far away, they altered their plan accordingly. A couple of blades would go with the green army armour to the Jamiat, while the main ground assault force would hit the house where *Campbell* and *Griffiths* were being held. Those involved in the events of 19 September 2005 still debate whether this second part of this plan, the house assault, was ever specifically authorised by Brigadier Lorimer.

There is disagreement too about whether the SAS had reason to believe its men were about to be executed. Intercepted communications, however, revealed that *Campbell* and *Griffiths* had been transferred to a radical fringe group called Iraqi Hezbollah. If the militants were abandoning the constraints forced upon them by keeping the men in police custody, it was certainly not a good sign.

*

At 9 p.m., the order was given for the armoured column to move in. Warriors and Challengers sped past the crowds near the Jamiat, while A Squadron's assault force moved towards its own target.

Brigadier Lorimer's armour burst into the police station, driving over cars and a couple of flimsy temporary buildings for good measure. The Iraqi police condemned it as vandalism and wanton destruction. One of the tank drivers later told friends it was the best evening of his life.

When the blades hit the house to which their comrades had been tracked by the Broadsword, it was eerily quiet. They blew in doors and windows and stormed the place only to find 'the guys had been left there in a locked room. So the assault went in without resistance.' The squadron would later speculate that neighbourhood 'dickers' or lookouts had warned those in the house, who made good their escape. There was relief all round as the troops involved in the mission returned to base. But the reckoning for the Jamiat was just beginning.

It was immediately obvious that the Iraqi political figures in the city, who stood to benefit from humiliating the British, would be livid. Mohammed al-Waeli, Governor of Basra Province, described the assault on the Jamiat as 'barbarous'. His relationship with the British army was already difficult – one senior officer in Basra, describing Mr Waeli to me a few weeks after the incident, termed him 'a crook and a bastard'. But once the name-calling died down there was a big problem. The Governor ordered his police force to end all cooperation with the British.

The Jamiat affair demonstrated more clearly than ever that the Basra police needed more mentoring and supervision, not less. Yet in the weeks afterwards British soldiers who turned up at Iraqi police stations in order to inspect them or mount joint patrols were often turned away or even threatened. Sometimes they succeeded in browbeating a few officers out on to the streets they moved them to vehicles in the yard outside. It was a forlorn hope for the SAS men to think that they might be seen by one of the orbiting aircraft. But as they were forced into the waiting vehicles a struggle broke out.

With the amount of trouble going on in the streets around the Jamiat, the solitary Broadsword operator in the helicopter up above the city might easily have been looking elsewhere, trying to help some of the soldiers who were engaged in running gun battles with the Shia militia. But he saw the scuffle in the courtyard and zoomed in. As the vehicles moved off, the American Predator was not on station and so everything depended upon the man hunched over his screen in the Sea King, relaying verbally what he could see to those who listened below.

Each new piece of intelligence caused A Squadron to tailor its rescue plan. Having arrived at Basra airport, its members commandeered some vehicles and went to the outskirts of the city, a couple of miles from the Jamiat, where they began their assault preparations. When word reached them that their two comrades had been taken through the cordon around the Jamiat to a house not far away, they altered their plan accordingly. A couple of blades would go with the green army armour to the Jamiat, while the main ground assault force would hit the house where *Campbell* and *Griffiths* were being held. Those involved in the events of 19 September 2005 still debate whether this second part of this plan, the house assault, was ever specifically authorised by Brigadier Lorimer.

There is disagreement too about whether the SAS had reason to believe its men were about to be executed. Intercepted communications, however, revealed that *Campbell* and *Griffiths* had been transferred to a radical fringe group called Iraqi Hezbollah. If the militants were abandoning the constraints forced upon them by keeping the men in police custody, it was certainly not a good sign.

*

At 9 p.m., the order was given for the armoured column to move in. Warriors and Challengers sped past the crowds near the Jamiat, while A Squadron's assault force moved towards its own target.

Brigadier Lorimer's armour burst into the police station, driving over cars and a couple of flimsy temporary buildings for good measure. The Iraqi police condemned it as vandalism and wanton destruction. One of the tank drivers later told friends it was the best evening of his life.

When the blades hit the house to which their comrades had been tracked by the Broadsword, it was eerily quiet. They blew in doors and windows and stormed the place only to find 'the guys had been left there in a locked room. So the assault went in without resistance.' The squadron would later speculate that neighbourhood 'dickers' or lookouts had warned those in the house, who made good their escape. There was relief all round as the troops involved in the mission returned to base. But the reckoning for the Jamiat was just beginning.

It was immediately obvious that the Iraqi political figures in the city, who stood to benefit from humiliating the British, would be livid. Mohammed al-Waeli, Governor of Basra Province, described the assault on the Jamiat as 'barbarous'. His relationship with the British army was already difficult – one senior officer in Basra, describing Mr Waeli to me a few weeks after the incident, termed him 'a crook and a bastard'. But once the name calling died down there was a big problem. The Governor ordered his police force to end all cooperation with the British.

The Jamiat affair demonstrated more clearly than ever that the Basra police needed more mentoring and supervision, not less. Yet in the weeks afterwards British soldiers who turned up at Iraqi police stations in order to inspect them or mount joint patrols were often turned away or even threatened. Sometimes they succeeded in browbeating a few officers out on to the streets

106

with them. The IPS in the city had become a focus of overt conflict instead of the people who would help the British out of Iraq. In Whitehall they still believed ardently in a 'conditions-based withdrawal' where security improvements would allow Britain to turn its four provinces to Provincial Iraqi Control ('Pic'), allowing their troops to move into the background or, in the jargon of the time, 'operational overwatch'. Following the Jamiat incident, the path to improved security, Pic and operational overwatch seemed to have reached a dead end.

British officers did not only feel the wrath of Governor Waeli. During the next day's Huddle, just after his morning Video Tele-Conference, General Casey took his British deputy commanding general to task. This rebuke, witnessed by several senior figures in the Coalition military setup, 'left a bad taste'.

In the hours after the storming of the Jamiat, when the entire British effort in Iraq seemed to be tottering, senior officers and ministers were noticeable by their absence from broadcast media in the UK. The capture of the HATHOR men and subsequent assault on the police station had generated a torrent of comment. It fell to Brigadier Lorimer to appear on BBC Radio 4's *Today* programme to justify his actions.

'I became more concerned about the safety of the two soldiers after we received information that they had been handed over to militia elements. As a result I took the difficult decision to order entry to the Jamiat police station,' said the brigadier, adding that 'by taking this action we were able to confirm that the soldiers were no longer being held by the IPS. An operation was then mounted to rescue them from a house in Basra.'

Even this version reflected the difficulty of the position that Whitehall and PJHQ had placed the brigadier in. Those involved are quite clear: the SAS house assault was planned before the Jamiat raid but executed at the same time. Some even characterise the attack on the police compound as no more than a diversion. But the brigadier's words reflected the bureaucratic state of play on 19 September – he had been authorised only to move against the police station itself, as outlined in his initial orders. Later, John Reid, the Secretary of State for Defence issued a statement backing the troops. But officers who had taken part in the events spoke with great anger about the way their brigadier had been left as the solitary voice justifying their actions, while those in Whitehall silently made their assessment of the political damage.

Issues of media handling should not have mattered too much, given the successful outcome, but they revealed deeper truths. These events caused bitterness in the SAS. At Hereford, in the hours before the rescue, there had been dark rumblings that the entire regiment should go on strike if their colleagues were not brought out – or rather that they should refuse to operate in Iraq if the government was going to be so weak. As one member reflects, 'The incident brought out a huge number of issues: the infiltration of the IPS by the Iranian Revolutionary Guards, and the lack of will on the UK's part to name but two.' As for the Americans, he adds, they reflected that the apparent lack of British determination to confront that infiltration of the police or even save their own men were explicable 'as part of their [the British] stubborn move to operational overwatch'.

It was this feeling, flagged up explicitly by Steve Vincent in his last column from Basra, that the British were, by their inaction, actually making things worse in the city, that gained currency in the American military. From General Casey downwards, there was a suspicion that the British were so determined to get out as soon as they could that the increasingly ugly ground realities of southern Iraq could not be allowed to get in the way.

As far as A Squadron was concerned, many were quite happy to leave the mess down south to the green army. The HATHOR detachment remained in place, mainly supporting MI6, but a commitment of only a few blades was an acceptable price to maintain this relationship. The rest of Task Force Black could return to its focus of developing operations in and around Baghdad, where the 'forward-leaning American approach' was more to their liking.

There was, though, a reckoning even within the SAS about the Jamiat. Some were beginning to feel that the surveillance reconnaissance skills that had for so long set them apart, earning the esteem of the Americans, might no longer be possible in such dangerous environments. If even Staff Sergeant *Campbell*, a denizen of the Surveillance Reconnaissance Cell, had been compromised and captured, what future was there for such operations? And if surveillance reconnaissance was a busted flush, could the regiment find new missions?

There was one last reckoning from the Jamiat; it was political. On 5 October a group of diplomatic correspondents filed into the press briefing room at the Foreign Office in London. It was a regular event, being conducted on background terms. The journalists would refer to their briefer only as 'a senior British official', or in other similarly roundabout ways. Their speaker that morning was William Patey, the British Ambassador to Iraq who was on one of his regular trips home because of the presence in London of Iraq's President.

As the meeting got under way it became clear that Patey, normally careful in his diplo-speak, had some very blunt things to say about what was happening in southern Iraq, and in particular about Iran's role in creating this situation. He reflected on the Iranian nuclear issue, and the election in June 2005 of a tough, ideological new President, Mahmud Ahmedinejad. He alleged that Iran was supplying insurgent groups in Iraq with sophisticated new bombs that had already claimed the lives of eight soldiers and two civilian security guards, and said the Iranians might be 'sending a message' about the nuclear issue. They might also be acting to frustrate Britain's objectives, Patey commented: 'If Iran wants to tie down the coalition in Iraq, then that is consistent with supplying insurgent groups.'

This accusation brought terse – and predictable – denials from the foreign ministry in Tehran. But the Ambassador had let the genie out of the bottle, and the following day the Prime Minister joined the fray when asked at a Downing Street news conference with the visiting Iraqi President about the alleged help being given to insurgents by Iran.

'There have been new explosive devices used – not just against British troops but elsewhere in Iraq,' said Tony Blair. 'The particular nature of those devices lead us either to Iranian elements or to Hezbollah . . . however, we can't be sure of this.'

This statement from Blair put the issue significantly higher up the international agenda, and the Americans soon followed suit with their own condemnation. But, as the Prime Minister had hinted, there was a lack of clarity about the intelligence concerned. By making public an issue that was then being hotly debated in secret by the professionals, Blair may simply have been venting his frustrations, albeit at the risk of embroiling himself in further controversy involving the words 'Iraq' and 'intelligence'.

Explosively Formed Projectiles or EFPs had been in use since 2004. The bombs, which look a little like large tin cans with a concave face pointed towards the target, are manufactured in such a way that this front piece of metal is flipped into a metal bolt by the explosive behind it – a transformation that takes place with such speed and energy that the resulting bolt or projectile can pierce almost any armour.

In May 2004, intelligence experts believed, the first British victim of these devices was claimed when an EFP detonated in

Maysan Province. Iraqi border guards operating in the area seized some smugglers with unexploded EFPs near the Iranian border not long afterwards. In June 2005 a British bomb disposal officer successfully defused an array of ten EFPs, allowing experts to make a detailed study of the devices. They were impressed not just by the manufacture of the bombs, which required high production tolerances, but by the infrared device used to trigger them. The bombs were similar to ones used against the Israelis by Hezbollah in southern Lebanon.

American J2 officers in Baghdad were soon connecting the dots. They were losing soldiers to a sudden spate of EFPs in Baghdad. They had human intelligence that Iran was not just supplying bombs but training Iraqi insurgents in how to use them. One of the British intelligence officers who was party to those discussions in Iraq felt a distinct sense of déjà vu, a worry that information was being stove-piped or selected to reach a particular conclusion. 'The Americans couldn't get their mind around the idea that these things might be produced in Baghdad, in someone's back yard,' he says. 'It had to be another country as far as they were concerned.'

During these discussions, the MI6 station expressed doubt about the credibility of the idea that Iran was directly supplying the insurgents or using Hezbollah know-how to raise the game of the Mehdi Army or other Iraqi insurgent groups. The service simply did not believe that the intelligence proved such suppositions. Views were split though within British military intelligence, as some saw the new roadside bombings as acts beyond the competence of typical Iraqi insurgents.

The individual bombings had generated less media attention or soul-searching than the Jamiat. In the wake of that incident, both the Ambassador and Prime Minister decided to blame Britain's troubles, at least in part, on Iran. Given the ongoing arguments about the intelligence concerned, they were taking a significant risk. Despite this, the *Sun* and other newspapers soon adopted a narrative that the Iranians were behind the death of 'our boys'.

For the SAS or soldiers conducting strike operations in southern Iraq, it was already obvious that Iran and its Revolutionary Guards Corps provided some kind of inspiration for the insurgents. They could see the posters and pamphlets; the growing threat from roadside bombs was eroding previous assumptions that the south was much safer than the areas patrolled by the Americans. But public accusations of Iran at the highest level changed the nature of this confrontation. It was, without doubt, political escalation at a time when many of those running operations in Iraq would have preferred not to have gone in search of new enemies.

Further north, violence was stepping up relentlessly. The Sunni insurgency was mutating in an alarmingly sectarian way. With Sunni and Shia murdering one another in growing numbers, as well as campaigning against foreign forces, the chance of the Coalition getting a lid on the violence seemed increasingly remote. But beneath this tide of violence there were important developments and the SAS would be at the centre of them.

7

BEYOND BLACK

In the weeks following the Jamiat incident, operational pressure caused by an ever-rising tide of violence, and a change in personnel brought an important shift to Task Force Black. These developments unfolded against the backdrop of a new hostage drama that was to prove far more protracted than the late unpleasantness in Basra.

On 26 November 2005 a car was stopped by masked gunmen in the university area of Baghdad. Inside were four members of an organisation called the Christian Peacemaker Teams. The university quarter had been a distinctly desirable suburb during Saddam's time, being home to his smooth-tongued minister Tariq Aziz among others. But from the moment of the US Marines' advance into this sector in March 2003, it had been the scene of trouble, the Americans fighting running gun battles lasting days with *fedayeen* around the campus. The green, open nature of the place afforded plenty of hiding places for criminals and gunmen. As communal relations worsened, it also became a seam for Shia–Sunni violence. Early in 2005, gunmen had kidnapped an Italian journalist close to the same mosque where the Christian Peacemaker Team was intercepted.

That November, the kidnappers were able to take their prize without hindrance from either militias or the security forces. In the car were Tom Fox, an American, and Canadians Tom Loney and Harmeet Singh Sooden, as well as a Briton, Norman Kember. The gunmen simply pulled the driver and interpreter out of the westerners' car and jumped into their seats.

Four days after the abduction, al-Jazeera aired a tape of the hostages and a communiqué from a group calling itself the Swords of Righteousness Brigade. During the first days of December the pressure was ratcheted up with a second then third video, the latter showing Fox and Kember in orange jumpsuits.

Kember, a 74-year-old retired professor and conscientious objector, had gone to Iraq as an ardent opponent of the US-led invasion. His decision to do so ignited heated public debate between those who admired his courage and others who felt he was a well-intentioned fool for putting himself in such danger. As Kember and his three comrades were bundled into their assailants' vehicle, they were to become a major operational priority for the very forces whose presence they opposed. The complexities of the case deepened when Moazzem Beg, the freed British Guantanamo inmate, and the security detainee Abu Qutada, Osama bin Laden's so-called Ambassador in Europe, joined in the appeals for Kember's release. As these vociferous opponents of President Bush and his War on Terror spoke, the subtext of their appeals to the kidnappers – essentially 'you got the wrong guys' – fell on deaf ears. The SAS, meanwhile, responded to the crisis in its own fashion.

At the time of Norman Kember's abduction, the regime of British special forces operations in Iraq was going through significant change. A Squadron finished its four-month tour and was replaced by B Squadron. As part of the rebalancing between theatres decreed by Major-General *Peter Rogers*, Director of Special Forces, the use in Afghanistan of one troop from the Iraq-tour squadron was halted. Afghanistan was to be the responsibility of the Royal Marines elite force, the Special Boat Service.

There would therefore be a reinforcement to B Squadron as it tried to hold the ring, meeting operational commitments around Baghdad and in the south. In practice this meant a squadron gaining up to a dozen soldiers, not a vast number, but the move enjoyed widespread approval since every man counted. Another change, although it remained rumour until officially confirmed the following March, was that B Squadron and its successors would serve six- rather than four-month tours. This was a harder sell for the blades, in that the stresses of tours with JSOC were such that Delta kept its squadrons in country for half that time – just ninety days. The longer SAS tours were principally the idea of Lieutenant-Colonel Williams, their Commanding Officer, who felt that the men would benefit from greater familiarity with the Iraqi scene and its operational peculiarities. The six-month stints also meant, as each squadron was followed by three others, a longer period at home or on less arduous duties between tours.

For the Commanding Officer of the SAS, this period at the end of 2005 and early the following year marked the fulfilment of his plans to integrate Task Force Black's operations far more closely with the Americans. It is in terms of this critical change that fine detail about tours and numbers needs to be seen, for

Williams was determined to raise the effectiveness of his men. When chiding regimental comrades about the effectiveness of Task Force Black, he had mocked it as 'Task Force Slack'. Like any executive preparing for a relaunch, he welcomed some rebranding too. In the wake of the Jamiat incident the name Task Force Black had been published in the press, so it was replaced with a new one: Task Force Knight. In both name and mission the moment had arrived to go beyond black.

Williams was helped by the fact that *Peter Rogers* moved on from the Directorate of Special Forces at the end of 2005. Their personal relationship had often been ugly, and having survived the general's attempt to get rid of him the passing of *Rogers* removed a brake on Williams's freedom of action. Some of the more tangible issues that had prevented this happening sooner, such as conditions in the Temporary Screening Facility, the special ops jail at Balad, had also been cleared up by the end of 2005.

The key benefits to closer integration with JSOC were increased flows of intelligence, particularly that gathered from a growing operation to intercept mobile phones, as well as the backing of American aircraft and so-called ISR or Intelligence Surveillance and Reconnaissance assets. The change had already been felt during the latter part of A Squadron's time. Technology was playing a bigger role. This change did not reflect some drying up of humint or spies – far from it. Rather, it showed what happened when the NSA, America's electronic eavesdropping organisation, switched even a fraction of its huge resources to helping the British.

During the Jamiat incident, the British had experienced a little of that nice warm feeling that came from getting closer to JSOC. Colonel *Grist* had swiftly sent a Predator to help, as well as tasking the NSA to intercept dozens of mobile phones in Basra. There had even been the offer of a Delta squadron to rescue them.

In the series of incremental changes that were made by the SAS at this time, the one that signalled most clearly their changed role occurred in mid-January 2006. It was then that the regiment began Operation TRACTION, its secret upgrade in the world of JSOC. Under TRACTION, the SAS deployed Task Group Headquarters (TGHQ) to Balad, where it could be joined at the hip with the American effort. As violence and missions soared, Williams himself would be there with TGHQ to direct the British side of covert operations in Iraq. It is a measure of the seriousness of TRACTION that this was the first deployment of TGHQ in Iraq since it had left shortly after the 2003 invasion. Williams thus followed Major-General Stan McChrystal's model of spending much of the year in Iraq, personally overseeing what went on. Just as McChrystal did not run the day to-day battle – a task that fell to *Grist* and his JOC nerve centre – so Williams left the execution of SAS operations to his in-country squadron commander, the OC of Task Force Knight at the time.

The presence of Williams and TGHQ lasted only a few weeks, as the hunt for Norman Kember neared its climax, but other aspects of TRACTION were intended to be enduring. Britain upgraded its involvement at the JOC. Although representatives of the intelligence agencies had already been used as part of the British liaison team at Balad, from early 2006 more senior representatives were sent, and aimed for a constant presence. Through this, the British gained the ability to channel far more intelligence to their strike force (Task Force Knight), so raising the pace of their operations. McChrystal was naturally delighted at the prospect of the British boosting their involvement to the 'industrial' scale established by American special operations units. But this was not just being done to allow the British to do more chasing of Former Regime Elements. McChrystal and Williams would get what they had wanted for months: the new target set that was to give the SAS a pivotal role in the fight against Sunni militant groups, and in particular al-Qaeda in Iraq (AQI).

All of this rearranging of the special ops furniture evidently took place in great secrecy, at a time when the public in both the US and UK were growing increasingly alarmed by developments in Iraq. It also happened as JSOC's arch-enemy was taking initiatives of its own.

By a dark coincidence, at the same time as the SAS launched Op TRACTION, Abu Musab al-Zarqawi, the al-Qaeda leader, was recasting his own command. A jihadist website carried news on 15 January that six Sunni resistance groups had formed the Mujahedeen Shura Council. These were not nationalistic factions like the 1920s Brigades but rather cells that embraced the Salafist ideology of AQI. Zarqawi, through the formation of this Council, was preparing the way to reap the rewards of growing chaos in Iraq. He wanted to declare a Sunni state or caliphate in the west of the country that would be run along strict religious principles. He believed this required growing violence, against the Shia as well as the Coalition and, if necessary, against Sunnis who supported the government or the more secular Ba'athist resistance factions.

In the communiqué announcing the formation of the Council, al-Qaeda's spokesman said it would 'manage the struggle to ward off the invading infidels and their apostate stooges'. It also alluded to intra-Sunni tensions, saying the Council would help in 'determining a clear position towards developments and incidents so that people can see things clearly'. Intelligence analysts in Baghdad debated whether these arguments within the resistance had been exacerbated by US operations in the Euphrates the previous year. There had been reports of tensions between the Iraqi tribes in that area and foreign fighters or 'outsiders' whom they resented. Some saw the formation of the Shura Council as a way of giving al-Qaeda's image a more Iraqi face. Many who joined in the debates at Camp Slayer or in the CIA station drew larger conclusions. The British had often questioned the central importance that the Americans assigned to Zarqawi. But was the formation of this new resistance front, with Zarqawi pulling its strings, a sign that US intelligence had been right all along, or simply a self-fulfilling prophecy? Had the US, by putting a $25 million bounty on Zarqawi's head, as well as referring to him constantly, turned him into the central figure in the movement?

Whatever the underlying realities of Zarqawi's status, his organisation had by this time become the target of a large-scale JSOC campaign. Attempts by the jihadists to broaden their organisation were mirrored by Stan McChrystal's launch of a JSOC operation codenamed DAHIR. This marked a new attempt to settle the ill will between the special operators and the visible American ground forces by locking together their campaign plans. JSOC would broaden its takedowns from operations chasing the AQI leadership, mounting more against middle-level players pinpointed by the ground-holding units. They in turn would give more support to McChrystal's people. The intelligence fusion techniques pioneered at Balad would be copied by the US Army and Marine divisions, and they would get greater access to precious assets such as drones. Some of those in Baghdad at the time have characterised Operation DAHIR as the subordination of large parts of the US military effort in Iraq to McChrystal's plan to defeat AQI. One observer comments that, at this period, with General Casey trying in the face of rising violence to cling to his plans to drawdown US forces, 'McChrystal *was* the offensive strategy'. Others insist that the US Marines in Anbar never lost their offensive spirit.

Since McChrystal's people appeared to provide the best and possibly the only chance for the Coalition to take the offensive against Zarqawi's network, his empire grew. The four special ops units operating under the aegis of Delta's CO at Balad (Blue or West, Green or Central, Red or North, and the UK's Knight in Baghdad) were joined by a fifth, designated Task Force East. JSOC received all manner of supporting units under command too – for example a National Guard Black Hawk helicopter squadron to shuttle the growing numbers of prisoners around. When all of the supporting players in JSOC's cast were included it numbered more than five thousand people across the region controlled by Central Command. As if to underscore the growing importance of his empire, McChrystal received his third star, being promoted to lieutenant-general in February 2006.

Britain's relationship with this special operations juggernaut was still complicated. The obstacles to Task Force Knight operating against the al-Qaeda target set had been removed, much to the Americans' delight. At the same time, during early 2006, much of their effort was actually being directed towards finding Norman Kember. In the meantime, the enemy did not stand still. On 22 February, it became clear that Zarqawi had stolen a march – not just on JSOC or the SAS, but on the entire Coalition and Iraqi government campaign.

It was 6.44 a.m. in Samarra, a city sixty-five miles north of Baghdad. Samarra is a predominantly Sunni city, although it is also home to a sacred Shia shrine, the Golden Mosque. That day, in the lull between dawn prayers and the city reaching the peak of its morning rush, the mosque was subjected to a complex attack. The first bomb brought down one of the compound's distinctive minarets.

Major Jeremy Lewis, an American officer who was briefing a joint patrol at a nearby Iraqi security base, turned around to register the scene: 'All of a sudden, the mosque just explodes.' As the smoke cleared it became evident the dome itself had been shattered. Lewis reflected, 'Every last one of us said this was the beginning of the civil war in Iraq.'

It was later reported that nobody – none of the bystanders or security guards, at least – was killed in the attack. But through this symbolic act of violence against their Shia neighbours, Sunni fanatics caused an effect that countless marketplace massacres or murderous abductions had failed to achieve. The characterisation of what followed as civil war was in itself the subject of intense political argument. But it was clear soon enough that the bombing had been what US generals call a 'game changer', and that the effects felt by people in communities across the country were truly horrific.

The Mehdi Army, posing as protector of the Shia community, took vengeance against pockets of Sunni AQI, its Shura Council allies and even some of the 'nationalist' parties answered them back. Bodies turned up in rivers by the dozen, were dumped on Baghdad street corners in Khadamiya or Doura, entire villages in the Upper Euphrates and Diyala were wiped out or driven away. In the weeks that followed, humanitarian agencies estimated the number leaving their homes at fifty thousand per month. Those who did not flee hid behind shuttered windows or locked doors.

In many neighbourhoods masked men appeared, manning roadblocks formed by felling palm trees or collecting burnt-out cars. It was a spontaneous move by citizens trying to stop sectarian abductions.

As this terrifying juggernaut of violence careered into action, Iraq's fledgling security forces appeared to be part of the problem. Sunni complaints against the Interior Ministry and its paramilitary forces portrayed them as Shia death squads. With sectarian factions trading charges, the country stood without a government. Elections in mid-December 2005, praised by many because of widespread Sunni participation, had resulted in a long, painful negotiation to form a coalition. During the early months of 2006, therefore, the violence exploited a political vacuum. Indeed, some of the Coalition diplomats and spooks even thought that groups such as Muqtada al-Sadr's Mehdi Army escalated their killing as a means of trying to influence the political negotiations for a national-unity government. It seemed as if the whole project of Iraqi elections, democracy and security operations was imploding.

It might be imagined that Task Force Knight's first priority would have been the apprehension of sectarian death squads who were killing hundreds of people each week. But Whitehall stressed that the main concern was to find Norman Kember and the other Christian missionaries. One person who sat in the ops room at the MSS, watching daily Video Tele-Conferences remembers 'constant pressure from London and PJHQ on the Kember issue. I recall in particular the Chief of Defence Staff [at that time General Sir Michael Walker] emphasising the importance of this on more than one occasion.'

From a short time before the Samarra bombing these efforts were moved into a higher gear. A team involving intelligence agencies, the embassy and the SAS began to work the case so intensively that, in the words of one SAS officer, 'Our whole squadron was focused on trying to find Kember.' This search was codenamed Operation LIGHTWATER. In addition to the blades from B Squadron, a small detachment of Canadian special forces and intelligence experts joined the team, since two of the hostages were Canadian. There was apparently little resentment in JSOC at the priority given to this hunt because, of course, in soldier turned Quaker activist Tom Fox there was an American angle to the kidnapping too. Indeed, the Operation LIGHT-WATER team benefited from a great deal of American technical intelligence in their hunt.

Life for the four hostages soon assumed a pattern that alternated between fear at what might come (for example after Fox and Kember were filmed in orange jumpsuits), the tedium of spending up to twelve hours a day chained up in their room and gratitude for some small acts of kindness on the part of their guards. They had given the captives a cake on Christmas Day and an Arabic DVD about Jesus. They had also allowed the hostages to have pencils and paper, although Kember, bereft of his reading glasses, could not write. Instead he sketched snakes and ladders as a sort of map of his ordeal – one day up, another down.

Early on it became clear that the guards had taken against Fox in particular. He was American, of course, but had been carrying papers showing he was a former soldier too. He had probably hoped these might help him at the city's numerous security checkpoints but the kidnappers found them, and their antipathy towards the American increased as a result.

For the kidnap gang, holding the foreigners for a long time carried its own risks. Perhaps by late February they had begun to feel the first effects of Operation LIGHTWATER, since doors were being kicked and arrests among their associates made. At times it seemed like a war of videos: one showing Kember appeared on 7 December, followed two days later by an influential appeal on the hostages' behalf by Moazzem Beg. With each new communication, the gang were taking risks, as a video, call or e-mail could be traced back to them or their friends.

The hostage-takers had demanded that the Iraqi and US authorities release all prisoners, but this was never likely to be agreed to. At times it was speculated that appeals to the Gulf States to help solve the crisis were thinly veiled demands for ransom. Like many kidnappers they seemed uncertain how to use their human capital to best effect, but throughout endeavoured to get the best possible propaganda value from them. On the 7 December tape, for example, Kember told the camera:

I'm a Christian peacemaker. I'm a friend of Iraq. I have been opposed to this war, Mr Blair's war, since the very beginning. I ask of him now, and the British government, to do all that they can to work for my release and the release of the Iraqi people from oppression.

When a fifth video was released on 7 March, the Foreign Office expressed concern that it showed the two Canadians and Kember but not Tom Fox. Three days later their fears were confirmed.

8

THE KEMBER OUTCOME

In the dim early light of a Friday morning, 10 March 2006, people in Dawoudi could make out something by the railway line. On the rubbish-strewn ground, where feral dogs rooted around, a body had been dumped. Sectarian killing had not yet arrived on a grand scale in this mixed suburb of Baghdad, so the discovery was a shocking thing. Although the man was dressed in an Arab dishdasha, he was a westerner. His hands were tied, cuts and bruises were visible on his head and body. The police later speculated that he had been tortured before he was shot.

Surveying the scene, one local commented that whoever had carried out the murder would 'distort the reputation of Iraq'. The body was that of Tom Fox.

Hearing the news, Norman Kember's friend, fellow peace activist Bruce Kent, concluded that the Christian Peacemaker

Team hostages were going to be killed one by one. Those in Task Force Knight who hunted the kidnappers drew exactly the same conclusion. The pressure to find Fox's three surviving comrades could not have been more intense.

It cannot be said that the odds of success were high. By this time around two hundred foreigners had been kidnapped in Iraq. They ranged from Italian security guards to Egyptian telecoms engineers and Turkish drivers. In some cases the nationality of the victim coincided with a military member of the Coalition, so the kidnappers appealed for that country's withdrawal. Many other victims came from countries without troops in Iraq.

By March 2006 most of those two hundred had been released, often upon payment of ransoms. The sense that kidnapping was essentially a business activity was reinforced by the even larger numbers of Iraqis who had been ransomed since the fall of Saddam. But while many took their captives for money, there was an ideological angle too; if your prize was American or British the greatest return could come from selling them on to extremists.

For British hostages, with their government's refusal to pay ransoms, the chances of survival were bleak. Ken Bigley had been beheaded on videotape the previous year. Margaret Hassan, a British aid worker struggling for years to alleviate poverty in the country and who had married an Iraqi, was killed by her kidnappers with a couple of shots to the head. Norman Kember's fate appeared to have been sealed. But what few people outside the world of special operations understood was the degree to which the balance of advantage between them and the insurgents was changing.

The Operation LIGHTWATER team had, by the time of Tom Fox's death, already mounted many raids in pursuit of intelligence.

They had homed in on their targets through a variety of methods. There were suspicions about who might be holding the hostages, and possible intermediaries presented themselves. Some clues emerged through scrutiny of the hostage videos and the surveillance of websites. The latter method, for example, suggested that the Swords of Righteousness Brigade that posted the videos might be an offshoot of the Army of Islam, or a cover name for it. The group was not part of the Zarqawi-sponsored Mujahedeen Shura Council of jihadist parties, nor did it line up with the mainstream Ba'athists, but sat somewhere between in the spectrum of extremism. The website discovery led intelligence specialists to focus on Army of Islam players.

Once pursuing subjects of interest, the special operators could make use of advances in the exploitation of mobile phone traffic. According to those involved in intelligence work, the NSA had been recording the details of all calls made in Iraq for many months. This did not mean that they had the content of these millions of conversations, but could refer to dialling details of all calls made and received.

This brought dramatic changes to the intelligence business. If, for example, a cell phone was seized in a raid on a bomb maker's house, this new tool allowed analysts to map all of the calls made on it during previous months. Using these same techniques, the Operation LIGHTWATER team could generate a computer picture of suspects and their contacts that looked, on the classified video screens, like a spider's web.

Raids could then be mounted, often having pinpointed the suspect's whereabouts by mobile phone. In former times, the special operators would have liked to have known much more before conducting their raids, but pressure from London to find Kember combined with the sense that time was running out made Task Force Knight operate during the early months of 2006 at the speed, and without the time spent on deliberate preparation, that Lieutenant-Colonel Williams had long wanted. Whereas squadrons in 2004 had mounted a couple of raids each week, by March 2006, under the pressure of Operation LIGHT-WATER, B Squadron was doing them almost every night. 'In Northern Ireland you spent loads of time doing intelligence development,' says one SAS officer, commenting that by 2006 'in Iraq everything became a fighting patrol. The purpose of our strikes was to produce intelligence.'

Within the squadron a handful of young officers and senior NCOs (usually a total of four captains, sergeants or staff sergeants) were designated Team Leaders. It was their responsibility to plan these operations. 'We were out every night, but every day you were preparing to go out,' recalls a one-time Team Leader. 'You were in a constant state of preparation and anticipation.' This involved working up a 'target pack' on someone who appeared in the intelligence analysts' web of contacts. The Team Leader and intelligence people would discuss the most promising possible targets for a raid, with the SAS man then going away to look at where that person might be apprehended as well as the tactics this might require. These questions might include, for example, whether the person should better be stopped in their car or arrested at home; whether a ground assault force carried in by vehicles or a helicopter assault force would be more suitable, and so on.

During the raid, suspects would be questioned, phones or computers seized. It had also become clear, as TF Knight's operations intensified, that what they termed Tactical Questioning – interrogating the man who had just been arrested quickly on the spot or nearby – often yielded results. 'The shock of capture makes it very important to exploit that moment, and to do it on the spot,' says one veteran of such raids. Another, when I asked about operations to find Norman Kember, told me, 'Individuals were exploited to get to him –

both by putting them under duress and not.' And it was by putting somebody 'under duress' that the key break came, those sources agree. Those who have run special forces operations are anxious to deny that 'duress' consisted of something that went beyond exploiting the detainee's initial disorientation once in custody.

It was during the early hours of 23 March, nearly a fortnight after the discovery of Tom Fox's body, that a team from B Squadron mounted yet another LIGHTWATER raid. Even the codename for that night's assault, Operation NEY 3, indicated the relentless and repetitive nature of this search. Their target was a house in Mishahda, an area around twenty miles north-west of central Baghdad. One of the leaders of the raid was Sergeant-Major *Mulberry*, the veteran NCO who had had a lucky escape when hit by a bullet in Baghdad two years earlier.

Having burst into the building, the SAS men found two men they were looking for. One of them, *Abu Laith*, clearly knew something about the kidnappers. Under pressure – people who know about the operation reject the use of such words as 'beating' and 'torture' – *Abu Laith* began to talk. He knew where Norman Kember and the two Canadians were being held.

For the SAS Team Leader on the ground and his commander, the OC of Task Force Knight, this stunning disclosure posed an immediate question: what should they do next?

The answer to that question was defined by the need for speed, the desire to avoid being drawn into an ambush and the need to protect the life of the hostages. As members of B Squadron looked on, the hostage-takers were telephoned and put in the picture. The SAS were on the way to the house. Their warning: 'How about you disappear and we won't come after you.'

Just before 8 a.m. a ground assault force from B Squadron hit a house in western Baghdad, hardly more than a mile from the Green Zone. They cleared it room by room, finding no insurgents. Video shot by the troops shows the moments after they burst in on the hostages. Kember is in a checked jacket, the same one that he was wearing in one of his captors' videos. Perhaps unsurprisingly given his age, he looks quite bewildered. Harmeet Singh Sooden, the youngest of the captives, is wearing a beanie hat and a smile of intense relief.

The hostages were ushered out of the house, down its front path to the gate where a Bradley armoured vehicle was waiting with its rear passenger ramp down. The blades of B Squadron mounted up in their Humvees in euphoric mood. One SAS man at the wheel of his truck turns to the camera and jokes that this must be worth an MBE at the very least. Across Coalition HQs from Baghdad to Balad there was enormous relief that they had beaten the kidnappers. The three freed men were driven the short distance to the Green Zone, where they received medical checks and were able to call their families.

After 118 days of captivity many had concluded that the 74-year-old hostage must be close to death. But the application of new intelligence techniques and a relentless special forces operation had thwarted what might have seemed grimly inevitable. Even today few people realise the scale of the secret search.

During the weeks of Operation LIGHTWATER, fifty buildings had been raided. British special forces of Task Force Knight conducted forty-four of these door-kicking operations, the remainder were done by other Coalition operators. During the course of these fifty operations, forty-seven people were detained. Only four of the operations were termed 'dry holes', places that were not productive of any useful information. All of this development of intelligence, Tactical Questioning of suspects, taking of risks and burning of money had been required to lead them to *Abu Laith*, the one man capable of telling them where the hostages had been hidden.

As they removed him from the scene of his incarceration the soldiers found it hard to get any response from Kember. One of them says, '[He] was the most frustrating individual I have ever met in my life. From the point of lifting him he didn't address one word to us.' Back in Britain the story that Kember had refused to thank his saviours quickly gained currency. The soldier involved notes, 'The following day the Ambassador wheeled him over to our house and Kember finally said, if I remember his actual words, "Thanks for saving my life."'

The ironies of an arch opponent of the war being rescued by the SAS were not lost on anyone. In the hours following Kember's release, pent-up tensions about why the Christian group had been in Baghdad, the resources used to secure the three surviving hostages' release and the apparent lack of thanks led to a minor onslaught against Kember in the press. Even General Sir Mike Jackson, Chief of the General Staff, was publicly critical. How much more pointed might the debate have been if the freed hostages had been aware of the use of 'duress' applied to prisoners in order to find them?

Abu Laith's rapid interrogation in the house where he was captured revealed a growing practice. One intelligence officer comments that JSOC's prison was by this point 'squeaky clean', with CCTV surveillance and many other checks. Because of this, 'most complaints that came from the Red Cross originated from what happened on site' – that is, when a prisoner was captured. Among officers involved in special ops there seemed to be a recognition that the violent circumstances of many takedowns produced opportunities for their operators to question the prisoner before putting him on a helicopter to the MSS or Balad.

Upon his return to the UK on 25 March, Norman Kember

made a statement at the airport in which he thanked the embassy staff and told reporters that they really ought to be interviewing 'the ordinary people of Iraq'. He concluded, 'I now need to reflect on my experience – was I foolhardy or rational?' The blades watching the news channels back at MSS Fernandez had their own pithy answer to that one.

In responding to Task Force Knight's coup the Coalition tried to exploit a rare positive story. Major-General Rick Lynch, the briefer at Multi-National Force Headquarters, wanted to use the success to hit back after so many months of stories about abuse of Iraqi prisoners, telling reporters, 'The key point is it was intelligence-led. It was information provided by a detainee.' Lynch, in line with standard procedures, did not specifically praise the SAS but referred to 'Coalition forces'. In London they wanted a little more national credit. Jack Straw, then Foreign Secretary, told the press he was 'absolutely delighted' by the news and that 'British forces were involved in this operation. It follows weeks and weeks of very careful work by our military and coalition personnel in Iraq and many civilians as well.'

On 7 November 2006, Iraqi police arrested men alleged to have carried out the kidnapping. Norman Kember, faithful to his principles, insisted that he would not give evidence against them.

Within Task Force Knight and the wider British special forces community, Operation LIGHTWATER was regarded as something of a watershed. B Squadron had achieved the kind of 'op tempo' or pace of action that Lieutenant-General McChrystal demanded of US units in JSOC. And with the Christian Peacemaker Team rescued, there were a wealth of urgent targets against which McChrystal's anti-al-Qaeda task force was itching to use the SAS.

On 23 March, the day of the Kember rescue, a wave of four

car bombs went off just after the SAS's coup. The resulting death of twenty-three Iraqis and serious wounding of forty-eight others did not actually make it a particularly bad day by Baghdad standards. Across Iraq the trend of violence was still steadily upwards. The SIGACTS (significant acts of violence) charts compiled at General Casey's headquarters showed, for example, that in the month of Kember's rescue attacks against Iraqi infrastructure and government targets reached one thousand, and the total for IEDs 850.

Any notion that B Squadron might have earned a few days off after LIGHTWATER was swiftly scotched. The intelligence people were poring over their diagrams showing the networks of al-Qaeda cells that were sending so many bombs into Baghdad. In satellite towns around the capital, like Abu Ghraib, Taji or Yusufiyah, there was a picture of growing complexity of the bombers' organisation. Team leaders began to prepare target packs for those whom analysis of mobile phone traffic could serve up.

As the SAS moved against the AQI target in earnest the scene was set for intense but highly professional competition with Delta Force, their neighbours at MSS Fernandez, which, by coincidence, also had its B Squadron in Baghdad at the time. Having set the broad parameters for their operations Colonel *Grist*, in the JOC at Balad, and his boss Lieutenant-General McChrystal allowed Team Leaders in both squadrons to develop their own plans, pitching for targets 'from the bottom up'. If the SAS plan was more promising they would get the backing and resources of the JOC.

Two and a half weeks after the hostages were freed, the British played host to McChrystal and several other senior US officers at their base near Hereford. The visit was planned as an episode of military diplomacy and relationship-building. It also underlined the fact that McChrystal and his British host, the major-general who had succeeded *Peter Rogers* as Director of Special Forces, had to view events in Iraq as part of the wider special operations effort. Neither of these two officers could divorce what was going on in Baghdad from the regional, or indeed global, perspective. There were different pressures from the two sides of the Atlantic, and the meetings held over two days in Hereford were intended to help resolve those while sealing the understanding they had for Task Force Knight to operate against the full American target set in Iraq.

During the course of General McChrystal's visit there were the inevitable formal briefings. There was also a long hike through the Herefordshire countryside, and then the two days of conversation were rounded off with a dinner at an early Georgian country house. The American visitors were treated to interiors worthy of a Jane Austen novel, views across the manicured deer park as well as a lavish feast: an archetypal English experience. McChrystal, often characterised as an austere soldier-monk who worked almost all the time, rose to the challenge of relaxing with his hosts.

McChrystal had for some time seen the Iraq problem in a regional context. JSOC had established liaison teams in several surrounding countries. 'It was pretty well broadcast that the Saudis were cooperating,' explains one senior American. 'You would pick up a Saudi guy or a Moroccan [in Iraq], feed the information over to them. Then within days, sometimes hours, you got the answers back from them.' The US approach was seen by some British intelligence officers both in terms of the attribution of much of Iraq's bombing to foreign fighters and to the political ideology of the Bush Administration's Global War on Terror or 'G-wot'. Although many of the British believed that the US overestimated both the role of foreign fighters in Iraq and the global nature of al-Qaeda, they conceded there was some value in McChrystal's approach. British intelligence had, after all, mounted Operation ASTON against suspected Pakistani jihadists travelling to Iraq two years earlier.

Any intelligence officer realised the value of being able to confront a suspected foreign fighter in the interrogation room with knowledge of his associates back home or en route for Iraq. The accumulated picture of who was getting into the country, and how, could help to frustrate that jihad trail. At the time of the Hereford meeting Britain agreed to a similar, but far smaller, deployment of regional teams that would follow the US lead in working in neighbouring states. The problem for both McChrystal and the British was that in the places where regional cooperation was needed most – Syria and Iran – it was, respectively, very limited and non-existent.

Still, the adoption of a regional approach was a British step worth toasting. It was just as well for Britain's new Director of Special Forces that the Americans were taking Task Force Knight under their wing because UK concerns increasingly had to centre on Afghanistan.

In the spring of 2006 the British military were deploying more than four thousand troops to southern Afghanistan. Under *Peter Rogers*'s rebalancing of special forces, the Special Boat Service was taking the lead in supporting this new deployment. But, as he had anticipated, the attempt to conduct these two operations at once was going to stretch both his own command and the wider armed forces. UK special forces were only provided with the 'enablers' (for example special secure communications equipment, helicopters and Hercules transports) to support one squadron on operations at a time. Since the Americans at that time still regarded Iraq as very much their first priority, support to the SBS in southern Afghanistan would be limited.

Task Force Knight's growing integration into the JSOC Iraq

campaign was thus coming at just the right time for the British commanders who wondered how on earth they were going to cope in Afghanistan. And, as if on cue, just days after McChrystal and Britain's Director of Special Forces charted their way forward in Hereford, the SAS squadron in Iraq demonstrated its usefulness to the Americans in a most dramatic way.

9

OPERATION LARCHWOOD 4

The scene about the MSS Fernandez landing site that April night in 2006 was one that had already become thoroughly familiar. RAF Pumas had come in from BIAP and their crews were making final checks. 'The guys on standby knew they could be quite relaxed during the daylight,' recalls one crewman assigned to the Task Force Knight helicopter flight. 'They would have an hour or two's warning. But then that might go down to a thirty-minute standby, then a cockpit standby and finally a rotors turning standby.'

In the murk beside the choppers, men formed up nearby, fresh from their quick battle orders. These were usually given in the briefing room of the SAS house, where the marble floors and gilded white sofas reminded the blades of its previous inhabitants. Sergeant-Major *Mulberry* was there, a couple of the troop commanders, two guys with snipers' rifles. It was after 1 a.m. as each man checked his kit: night-vision equipment, radio, magazines for their primary weapon, usually an assault rifle, and a pistol. The blades had formerly worn their handgun or secondary weapon low-slung in leg holsters, but by this time the fashion was for fixing a quick-release holster to the front of the body armour, just beneath the neck. In addition to the standard kit, there would be small personal add-ons. Some men, usually the sergeant-major among them, carried cyalumes, chemical lights that could be used to mark a landing zone or an entry point. One or two men carried shotguns or explosive charges for blowing in doors. Many sported knives too, although the SAS never quite adopted Delta's taste for fearsome fighting daggers.

That night's serial, as the name Operation LARCHWOOD 4 suggests, was a development based upon raids over the previous days. The two B squadrons – SAS and Delta – had been hitting AQI targets in the 'Baghdad belts' – a term used by the Coalition for communities surrounding the capital. There had already been several firefights. On 8 April a raid near the same town they were heading for on this night had killed five insurgents, who the intelligence people claimed were foreign fighters. On 13 April, another two. With each raid, JSOC's intelligence picture of a group of al-Qaeda cells around the capital had evolved.

Yusufiyah, twenty-five kilometres to the south-west of Baghdad, was seething with tension at the time. Fallujah is about twenty kilometres off to the west, Abu Ghraib between the two places. To the east of Yusufiyah is Mahmudiyah and south-east is Latifiyah – the three 'iyahs' marking the points of an area of intense insurgent activity known since late 2003 as the Triangle of Death. By 2006 the violence was going in several different directions. It was an extremely dangerous area for Coalition forces but the presence of many Shia villages had also led to numerous sectarian murders.

During the spring of 2006, there was a series of sweeps by US troops through the area. They had rounded up the usual trophies of Kalashnikovs, mortar rounds and IED materials but had also suffered many casualties at the hands of Sunni insurgents. The vicious war in this part of Iraq had also produced one of the Coalition's most serious lapses, or rather collapses, in military discipline.

Just one month before B Squadron's planned raid, several US soldiers had got drunk on local bootleg whisky at their checkpoint not far from Yusufiyah and deserted their post. They had broken into an Iraqi home and raped and murdered a fourteen-year-old girl named Abeer Qasim Hamza. They killed her parents and five-year-old sister for good measure. At the time of the planned B Squadron mission the implications of these crimes were just beginning to percolate up the US military system, with the first conviction seven months later and several more to follow. Evidently, though, word of what had happened spread very quickly through the community. If the local people or the AQI groups in Yusufiyah needed any further reason to fight the Coalition, revenge for this act could be added.

The target pack worked up by Captain *Ewan*, one of the B Squadron Team Leaders, on the night of 16 April featured one *Abu Atiya*. He was typical of the mid-level al-Qaeda leadership being targeted by JSOC at the time. *Abu Atiya* was classified as the 'Admin Emir' of the AQI cell in Abu Ghraib. He was credited with running the local group's media efforts, such as posting videos of its attacks on Coalition soldiers on the internet. But, as the B Squadron men had heard during their briefings, intelligence also showed that *Abu Atiya* had a role in setting up 'V-bids' or car bombs. Those familiar with the operation say that there was both humint and signals intelligence implicating him in these activities.

A final trigger for the operation was the identification of *Abu*

Atiya's cell phone by electronic means and the production of a grid reference graphic. The GRG took the form of an aerial photo, where the target insurgent-held building or Alpha could be marked up, accompanied by symbols that would be used to denote aspects of the Team Leader's plan as key players were briefed that evening.

In the case of LARCHWOOD 4, the Alpha was a farmhouse on the outskirts of Yusufiyah. To the west were open fields. To the north, an orchard, and east, close to the building itself, a sand berm or bund separated the farmhouse from surrounding fields. Captain *Ewan* plotted L1, the helicopter landing zone for his assault force, to the north-east of the Alpha, where the fruit trees would offer a certain amount of screening. Approaching from this cover, *Ewan* would then lead the assault force of four teams to the Alpha. Once there, they would split into two groups before prosecuting the assault, one blowing its way in from the east, the other from the south. As they did this, SAS snipers would be orbiting in Lynx helicopters in case the targets eluded the assault force. Inside the Alpha, two members of the Apostles, the SAS's Iraqi helpers, would interpret and assist Sensitive Site Exploitation – the search of the building for further intelligence.

Captain *Ewan* would exercise command of the operation on the ground. Although still in his twenties, he was a seasoned SAS officer. The second captain, a less experienced officer, would be given the task of leading one of the assault teams.

Mounting up in the Pumas, the B Squadron men each understood their part in this scheme well. With a bit of luck, they would deliver the 'vinegar stroke', entering the Alpha, taking *Abu Atiya*, and nobody would die. The Pumas dusted off for the short ride to Yusufiyah, and their RV took to the night sky with the rest of the operation.

In addition to the blades of the assault force, the British were also taking with them a platoon of Paras from Task Force Maroon. Americans from 1st Battalion 502nd Infantry – the battalion involved in the Hamza rape charges – had also been assigned to support Operation LARCHWOOD 4. Its function that night was simply to be in reserve as a Quick Reaction Force. The British Paras would be used to block off the area around *Abu Atiya*'s house, preventing either reinforcements arriving or people escaping. The cordon rode that night in Chinook helicopters.

Above the choppers flying through the darkness towards the outskirts of Yusufiyah were three fixed-wing aircraft. A small surveillance aircraft would orbit with night-vision equipment. Two American C-130s were also on station: a command bird coordinating the entire effort and an AC-130 Spectre, a fearsome gunship that could saturate the ground with fire if everything went wrong.

It might be imagined, with this circling fleet of aircraft, that the entire neighbourhood would be up in arms before the first soldier came anywhere near the Alpha. However, as one Team Leader explains, 'By this point the people in Baghdad and some of the surrounding places were thoroughly used to the sound of helicopters at night.'

The Pumas hit L1 just after 2 a.m., and the four assault teams were off in moments, their rides returning to the dark skies. Making their way across the few hundred metres to the assault point, the blades listened to the radio chatter through headphones. Given the violence following the Samarra bombing, even a short walk through the darkness in a mixed community like Yusufiyah had to be undertaken with the utmost care. One SAS man explains, 'Because of sectarian violence people were leaving booby traps and pressure pads to protect their own neighbourhoods – you had to move very carefully.' Once safely in cover within yards of the house, two operators were sent forward to scout its south-east corner.

To the soldiers' delight they found that at the rear of the carport on that side of the building was an open door into the house. They peered in to determine that the place was still, as one might expect in the early hours of the morning, and went back to their waiting comrades.

Pleased that he could enter the Alpha without explosions or commotion, Captain *Ewan* ordered the assault. One team moved swiftly past the parked car, entering the house through the door beside it.

Just seconds later a burst of gunfire rang out. Three of the SAS team had been hit by someone waiting in a corridor of the house.

In moments the team ran back out through the door, helping the worst-wounded members to the cover of the sand berm just to the east of the house. The radio came alive with staccato reports: *Contact!* The call-sign had taken casualties. Fingers probed for bullet wounds; trauma packs were ripped open; the treatment of casualties began. All of them had been able to get out of the place on their own, but a man could be fatally pumping blood from a bullet-ruptured artery into some internal cavity at the same moment that he was celebrating his survival. It was vital to conduct a proper survey of their wounds.

Those inside the house were not content to rest on their initial success. From the upper floor they opened fire in the direction of the berm. One man ran on to the roof and started lobbing grenades at the SAS operators.

At this moment a torrent of options must have entered the mind of Captain *Ewan*. Those above would be straining their ears, awaiting his decision. Could the snipers in the Lynxes get clear shots? Should the Spectre give those inside a taste of its three Gatling guns, each of which could lay down a hundred rounds a second? Or should the air controller on board the command Hercules simply whistle up an F-16 while Captain *Ewan*'s men retired to a safe distance, and just level the whole place with a JDAM?

Those listening out for the Team Leader's Plan B were not kept waiting for long. *Ewan* decided to resume the assault. Their mission was to capture *Abu Atiya* for questioning, and who knew who else might be in the building?

Putting himself at the head of his men, Captain *Ewan* renewed the assault. Approaching the building under covering fire, he and one of the blades lobbed in grenades.

As they went in, though, two more were wounded – one by a bullet and the other by a grenade fragment. To those watching the events unfold on Kill TV back at Balad or in the MSS, the drama had reached its critical stage. Flashes from explosions and zips of tracer stained the night-vision image captured by the aircraft orbiting above. The eagle-eyed spotted someone dart from the rear of the house. Little did they know, watching the battle on video, but this insurgent was wearing a suicide vest as well as carrying grenades and an assault rifle. An aerial sniper and members of Task Force Maroon not far from that western side of the building were ordered to engage him, but the man swiftly took cover under a car parked nearby.

Inside the Alpha, Captain *Ewan*'s men had killed one of the gunmen in the corridor, and then began to go through the house room by room. Another man was shot. In one room, the SAS burst in to find half a dozen terrified women and children cowering in the darkness. They soon discovered that one woman had been killed in the fight, with three others and one child wounded.

Once the rooms were clear, the assault force turned their attention to the building's roof, from which they had taken fire. One of the SAS NCOs, already wounded, told his comrades he would go up the stairs in the middle of the building to clear the roof. Waiting for him was a second man in a suicide vest. As the

NCO reached the door at the top of the staircase, the al-Qaeda man detonated his bomb. There was a further flash across the video screens. The NCO had been blown backwards, down the stairs, by the blast. Although sustaining further injuries, he was able to pick himself up.

Outside, the last man resisting, the one under the car, died without setting off his own suicide device. Located by the surveillance plane, he had been killed by a hail of bullets.

The assault force, pumped full of adrenalin with five members wounded, now had to move to the business at hand. Their primary mission, after all, was to arrest a man in the pursuit of intelligence. Five of the defenders were dead, including two who had been wearing suicide vests. Five men, as well as several women and children, had survived. Working through the Apostles, the SAS quickly established that one of these survivors was *Abu Atiya*. An older man also appeared to be an insurgent. They were cuffed and made ready for the helicopter. The wounded women and child meanwhile were taken to the landing zone for evacuation to the 'Cash' – the 10th Combat Support Hospital – in the Green Zone.

It was now time for Sensitive Site Exploitation. The soldiers moved through the house looking for things of intelligence value. It was a shambles – blood, spent bullet casings and broken glass were trodden underfoot. There were men lying dead in some places. The blades trod gingerly around one of them when they realised that clutched in the dead man's grasp was a grenade with the pin pulled out. Up on the roof, the suicide bomber who had tried to take a British operator with him had been blown to bits, his limbs and head scattered among the other debris.

Despite the carnage, the SAS could not afford to miss anything in the limited time they still had on the ground. In fact they recovered a great deal: weapons including four AK-47s and one that seemed in the torchlight to be an M4 (a 5.56mm assault rifle usually used by Coalition troops); and other possessions that might yield clues. Their mission had been accomplished, albeit with much violence. They had no remit to go on a further house-to-house search of the neighbourhood. The team had neither the time nor the men for that anyway, since dawn would soon be upon them, and given the level of resistance they had experienced that night there was no telling what daytime might bring. Subsequent intelligence suggested though that Abu Musab al-Zarqawi himself was in another building not far away. Once again, Coalition troops had unwittingly come within a whisker of capturing Iraq's most wanted man.

The SAS had already experienced plenty of violence in Iraq. But the ferocity of their reception that night, and the speeding-up of operations that had generated Operation LARCHWOOD 4, were signs of a sea change. Lieutenant-General McChrystal's vision of a relentless cycle of missions, with each revolution producing the intelligence that could fuel the next, was becoming a reality. Under this growing pressure, al-Qaeda in Iraq, as well as some of the other insurgent groups, appeared to have raised their own game. They were prepared to get their retaliation in first against the special operators – or at least to try to. There were suicide bombers ready to go, ambushes set up for helicopters and in some places houses rigged to explode.

Returning to the MSS after LARCHWOOD 4, members of B Squadron felt exhausted and elated in equal measure. They had overcome suicidally determined resistance and, fortunately for them, none of the five men wounded that night was so seriously injured that they would be absent from duty for long. They could have little imagined at that moment how successful their raid would prove to be. They were nearing the end of the SAS's first six-month squadron tour and were collectively almost spent.

Their time in Iraq had been a period of frenetic activity but crucially, given the miserable overall security picture, one of considerable success. They had freed Norman Kember and the two Canadian hostages. They had also demonstrated the faith of their Commanding Officer, Lieutenant-Colonel Richard Williams, that the SAS could operate intensively as an integral part of the black American special operations task force. Given the relative scarcity of resources on the British side, this earned credit with McChrystal and the other key commanders. It should come as no surprise that the OC of B Squadron was decorated for the tour. Captain *Ewan* received a medal for his conduct on Operation LARCHWOOD 4. Many of the squadron's NCOs were decorated or received commendations too. More importantly, although they had experienced many intense firefights and had eleven men wounded during the tour, B Squadron returned home without losing a man.

Daytime on 16 April was too early for the full results of Operation LARCHWOOD 4 to be appreciated. *Abu Atiya* and the other suspect were on their way to Balad. Belongings seized at the house were likewise en route to JSOC's technical experts. One thing already seemed clear to members of B Squadron: the rifle they had captured looked suspiciously like one of those left behind during the ill-fated SBS raid in 2003. There was of course much banter about the SAS having to recover weapons lost by the Royal Marines' 'Tier 2' special operators. But the more significant thing about the gun was that it was the sort of prize weapon that would hardly have been carried by some run-of-the-mill insurgent. Indeed it had appeared in a photograph, propped up against a wall next to Abu-Musab al-Zarqawi.

10

ENDGAME FOR ZARQAWI

It was not long before the product of Operation LARCH-WOOD 4 was being processed at Balad. "The Americans have a hugely greater capacity for forensic analysis,' notes one British senior officer. 'You'd take a guy's computer, suck it of information, squirt it over to somewhere on the east coast of the US and the initial analysis of what was on it would be fed back in time to plan the following night's operation.' In the case of the Yusufiyah seizures, it did not take long for examination to produce some startling discoveries.

When the NSA and JSOC experts went through these seized possessions, they found video of Zarqawi giving political messages and posing with followers in the desert. At this time the only photographs of the Jordanian jihadist in circulation were very dated. Here was fresh footage, showing exactly what he looked like just a short time ago. What was more, in one scene, in which Zarqawi sat inside a building talking politics, the gun leaning on the wall beside him was none other than the former SBS weapon captured by B Squadron a few nights before. It was clear evidence both that the SAS had got Zarqawi's prized possessions and that they might have been very close to the man himself on 16 April.

The American commanders were thrilled with the haul from B Squadron's raid. It seemed to vindicate the long-debated idea that the SAS should be used against the same targets as Delta and effectively be placed under the tactical control of Colonel *Grist*, the American who commanded it. Though, as one of the British officers involved admitted, 'It was a total piece of luck that the minute we switched to al-Qaeda we had a result, a trace of Zarqawi, a total jackpot.'

The detainees from the raid, *Abu Atiya* and the other man, were placed in JSOC's Temporary Screening Facility at Balad. Once transferred, Britain's direct involvement with them ceased. At Balad, the force of contractor-employed or reservist inter-rogators – 'gators' in base slang – got to work, apparently ignorant even of the fact that the SAS had taken them. Author Mark Bowden was allowed access to the team working at Balad at the time. He describes their backgrounds:

> Some were lawyers. Some had advanced degrees. Some called themselves 'reserve bums', because they signed on for tours of duty in various parts of the world for six months to a year, and then took long, exotic vacations before accepting another job. One raced cars when between jobs; another was an avid surfer who between assignments lived on the best beaches in the world; another had earned a law degree while working as a city cop in Arlington, Texas.*

* Mark Bowden, 'The Ploy', *The Atlantic*, May 2007

This disparate bunch conducted its interrogations in a hangar left over from Saddam's time. Ten different interrogation rooms were divided from each other by plywood partitions, and each was kept under CCTV observation. The gators worked their cases in pairs, and since none of them spoke good enough Arabic to grill their man an interpreter was in there too. Interviews could last several hours, and when they were over the prisoners were taken back to their 'boxes' or personal cells in another building nearby.

Since new prisoners were coming in most nights, the capacity of the TSF imposed its own limits on JSOC's interrogation operation. It could only accommodate a couple of dozen prisoners. There was also a time limit, imposed by the US chain of command, because of concerns about charges of detainee abuse and the fact it was a black facility, unregulated by the likes of the International Red Cross. A prisoner could be held for a certain number of days on McChrystal's say-so. Going beyond that for a further period required authorisation from General Casey. If that was not forthcoming, the detainee had to be turned over to a regular jail – usually Abu Ghraib or the Divisional Internment Facility at Baghdad airport. Some suggest that a few of the insurgents seemed to know that if they held out for enough days they would be processed out of there and the pressure would be off. The gators were already under time pressure, but all the more so with the LARCHWOOD 4 detainees since the evidence of Zarqawi uncovered in the raid was so fresh.

As time passed, the gators formed the impression that the second insurgent taken in the Yusufiyah house, an older man, was more important than *Abu Atiya*, the 'Admin Emir' of the Abu Ghraib cell and the original target of B Squadron's operation. In his article about the gators, Bowden assigned the pseudonym *Abu Haydr* to this other player. *Abu Haydr* was a stately figure who successfully parried questioning by *Mary* and *Lenny*, the two interrogators assigned to his case. As days slipped by, tension mounted between the gators and the supervisor about the best way to crack the prisoner.

Nine days after the Yusufiyah raid, Zarqawi took his own bold initiative. He posted a video on a jihadist website. It was an edited version of the material found at the Yusufiyah house. The message was put out under the logo of the Mujahedeen Shura Council, with an accompanying statement by them. In it, the al-Qaeda leader, dressed in loose-fitting black combats, with a black bandana around his head, harangued his followers. His main message was that they had already frustrated American plans to control the country and should fight on. 'Your mujahedeen sons were able to confront the most ferocious of crusader campaigns on a Muslim state,' he told the camera. 'They have stood in the face of this onslaught for three years.'

The release of the video prompted a torrent of analysis and speculation across the Arab media and on the internet. Why had Zarqawi gone public? Was it a sign of weakness, given the recent rumours that he was under pressure from the homegrown Iraqi jihadists? Was showing the Coalition his face suicidal or a sign of bravado intended to reassure his followers?

There was, of course, a subtext to the posting of his message. Whenever Zarqawi might originally have intended to release it, following Task Force Knight's raid in Yusufiyah he had reason to believe that the Coalition knew exactly what he looked like. Zarqawi's image was compromised. Best get the video out under circumstances that he could control.

If Zarqawi was indeed concerned that the captured material might be used against him, then he was right. There were also out-takes from his video sessions captured in Yusufiyah.

The US chose a weekly media briefing in the Green Zone to fire its return salvo in the battle of the videos. On 4 May journalists were shown Zarqawi trying in vain to clear a stoppage from his machine gun. 'So what you saw on the internet was what he wanted the world to see,' said Major-General Rick Lynch. 'What he didn't show you were the clips that I showed, wearing New Balance sneakers with his uniform, surrounded by supposedly competent subordinates who grab the hot barrel of a just-fired machine gun; [you] have a warrior leader, Zarqawi, who doesn't understand how to operate his weapon system and has to rely on his subordinates to clear a weapon stoppage. It makes you wonder.'

Lynch's briefing produced its own debate in the press and blogosphere. Had the Americans really been right to release the material just to make fun of Zarqawi? And if he was so incompetent, why had the US built him up to be its leading enemy in Iraq, with a $25 million bounty on his head? In fact, Lynch had used the video to start a section of briefing in which the American military gave its latest assessment of the campaign against al-Qaeda in Iraq. This *tour d'horizon* proved just as contentious among the special operators and spooks because it revealed much about recent operations against AQI that they would rather have kept secret. British players in this drama also regarded it as a public revelation of ideas about the jihadist campaign, some of which they disagreed with, that would usually have remained highly classified.

Lynch talked about five operations around Baghdad during the preceding weeks (actually conducted by JSOC and including the SAS's LARCHWOOD 4, although he did not describe it in those terms), indicating that they had killed thirty-one foreign fighters. He asserted that 'Ninety per cent of the suicide bombers that Zarqawi employs are foreign fighters', and that therefore the degradation of April and May 2006 operations was taking away Zarqawi's capability to mount suicide bombings in and around Baghdad. He claimed that suicide attacks in Iraq had fallen from seventy-five per month early in 2005 to twenty-five per month at the time of the briefing.

The general went on to describe the attrition of AQI by Coalition operations, revealing that 161 significant players in the organisation had been killed or captured since January 2005. Explaining that 'we believe that Zarqawi and al-Qaeda in Iraq is organised into three tiers', he broke down these losses into eight 'Tier 1' terrorists – those with personal contact with Zarqawi – fifty-seven Tier 2 'leaders in local and regional areas' and ninety-six Tier 3 fighters.

This 4 May presentation caused quiet controversy. Task Force Knight soldiers did not like the mention of its recent operations and considered that the reference to thirty-one foreign fighters killed was utterly speculative. Who was able to establish, for example, whether the man who blew himself to bits on the roof of that house in Yusufiyah was Iraqi or not? Both MI6 and British military intelligence analysts had long been sceptical of claims that most suicide bombers were foreign fighters. As for the classification of al-Qaeda in tiers, this was entirely a feature of the American analytical approach rather than a description of genuine levels within the jihadist organisation. Looking with hindsight at Lynch's seventy-five suicide attacks in 2005 versus twenty-five in 2006, it can only have been possible with the most selective use of the facts, which showed a steady upwards trend in violence during 2006.

Overall, the emphasis given to Zarqawi and the organisation of AQI worried British observers. One British figure holding a senior post in Baghdad at the time of the briefing recalls, 'Zarqawi had become a local bin Laden phenomenon. He was demonised and inflated into a figure rather more significant than he was.'

Although British critics might have punctured some of the hyperbole and trickery of analyses such as the Lynch briefing, their views had their shortcomings too. They were sometimes guilty of being overly negative or cynical. The language used by

Zarqawi in his video, or by the Mujahedeen Shura Council upon its formation, betrayed a concern about the pressure these jihadist groups were under from Coalition operations and from a split in Sunni opinion about the best way ahead for the resistance. Some aspects of Lynch's presentation, such as describing Zarqawi's determination to derail the Iraqi democratic project before a new government could be formed, can be substantiated by resistance communiqués at the time. As for the 161 significant AQI members accounted for between January 2005 and May 2006, this was progress too, given the Coalition's lamentable early performance against the insurgency.

McChrystal's approach of 'industrial counterterrorism' had got under way in earnest. With each new takedown the intelligence picture was becoming clearer. The networks sketched out on computers in Camp Slayer showed an intricate web of relationships. And as interrogators worked on captives like *Abu Haydr*, the fidelity of that intelligence picture improved still further. JSOC's units were getting enough information to mount operations the whole time. But as the squadrons competed with one another this carried its own risks.

The 13 and 14 May fell, in 2006, at the weekend – or at least what the bosses back in the Pentagon and Ministry of Defence regarded as their weekend. In Iraq the only meaningful cycle for the special operators was that of day and night. One visitor to Balad recalls, 'If you arrived there at 9 a.m. it was a wasteland. The raids had gone in at 3 a.m., the prisoners had been brought back at 5 a.m. and everybody had got their heads down. In the afternoon they would start prepping the next operation and it would all start again.'

Task Force Knight's Operation LARCHWOOD 4 was part of an intense series of operations in the Triangle of Death southwest of the capital. Most of these operations were carried out by

Delta and other US forces. Over that May weekend, for example, they took out an entire network in and around Latifiyah. The cell led by Abu Mustafa was held responsible for shooting down an American Apache helicopter early in April, and a welter of other attacks on US forces in the Triangle. On 13 May the Americans had raided four houses used by the Abu Mustafa network. But their pace and exploitation of intelligence from the first raids was such that they intended to go back on Sunday night to hit three more locations. During these operations around Latifiyah fifteen 'suspected al-Qaeda associates' as well as Abu Mustafa himself were killed.

At the same time as they were planning their second wave of raids against the Abu Mustafa group, JSOC's attention turned to a further target several kilometres away, not far from Yusufiyah and the SAS raid of 16 April. It is unclear whether it was yet another arm of the Abu Mustafa network or the result of a separate targeting process. Such was the determination of Delta's B Squadron to get in and take down their suspect that it was decided to strike in mid-afternoon – in broad daylight.

Special ops Black Hawks from Task Force Brown (known publicly as Task Force 160, the JSOC helicopter regiment) carried an assault force of Delta men towards their target. With them was an SAS liaison officer, Captain *Morris*, the man who had been wounded during the regiment's October 2003 battle in Ramadi. The British and American Tier 1 units fostered many formal exchanges and postings with one another, but in Iraq there was often informal liaison too: people who went out on operations to see how their comrades/rivals did things, or even just for the hell of it as an extra shooter. That Sunday, 14 May, other elements of JSOC were backing up the Delta raid in the usual manner, and they would certainly need them.

The Americans' first target building sat among a group of rural dwellings close to a waterway. A line of electricity pylons and a road ran parallel to that water. Delta's landing zone was thus in a pocket of open space near the road, flanked on one side by pylons and on the other by trees. Soon after they landed the Delta men started to take fire from a nearby house.

What followed was a rapidly escalating battle in which, at times, the al-Qaeda defenders of the area seemed to get the upper hand. One SAS man, recounting tales of the raid, says, 'No sooner were they down, than the Indians were all over them!' Hunkered down close to the road, the Delta soldiers came under small-arms and mortar fire. At one point three al-Qaeda fighters – one wearing a suicide vest – jumped into a truck and tried to mount their own attack on the special operators. The vehicle was hit by a hail of bullets and the vest detonated.

The helicopters that had dropped the Delta men circled, their door gunners using mini-guns to fire thousands of rounds into the neighbourhood below, but the assault force commander did not have the option of getting the choppers to pick him up – the firefight was simply too heavy and the landing zone too narrow. An already difficult situation was further complicated as the helicopters started taking heavy machine-gun fire from the ground. Two other machines from Task Force Brown, the small gunships called AH-6 Little Birds, made runs against the insurgents. Iraqi accounts suggest that al-Qaeda also used shoulder-launched surface-to-air missiles against the Americans. Such was the intensity of the ground fire that one of these helicopters was shot down. Despite the attempts of Captain *Morris* and others to save the Little Bird crew, the two men inside died in the wreck.

Even though the fighting was ferocious, Delta succeeded in getting to its target and detaining four people. They also treated three injured women. During a lull in the shooting near dusk they brought in a casevac (casualty evacuation) helicopter to remove these locals but it too came under heavy ground fire as it left. Faced with such resistance after hours of fighting, the Americans hit several targets around their landing zone with air strikes.

The toll from this intense running battle was high. In addition to the shot-down helicopter, British sources suggest that three other machines were forced to land due to serious damage from ground fire. In the course of the fight, small arms, missiles, mortars, heavy machine guns and a suicide bomb had been used against Delta, killing two pilots and wounding five other men. For their part, the Americans said they had killed 'more than twenty-five terrorists'. Resistance sources were to claim a toll of forty fatalities, mostly civilians. One tribal sheikh told the *Washington Post*, 'We spent a long, scary night with our families and children.'

This battle was a bitter lesson for JSOC. The Delta Force B Squadron commander was relieved of his duties after the incident. The unfortunate lieutenant-colonel had also lost three operators in an IED blast on an earlier tour. Whether it was the whiff of Zarqawi's presence in the area or the desire to roll up another AQI network, he had allowed aggression to get the better of him in mounting a daylight raid into a hornets' nest of opposition. One SAS man concludes, 'It all happened because someone got too cocky. It was a watershed because after that everyone went kinetic – they were less inclined to take chances.'

Between the neighbours at MSS Fernandez in the Green Zone such incidents caused serious reflection but also teasing banter. The British could not feel smug, since anyone scoring points from the American side could easily have reminded them of an incident in Basra four months earlier. A convoy of armoured SUVs carrying CIA officers had been hit by an IED on the outskirts of the city. As the incident developed into a complex attack, with Shia militiamen following up with gunfire, a British regular army Quick Reaction Force assigned to back up the CIA if necessary had failed to deploy fast enough. Two American guards were killed and another couple were seriously injured. JSOC people did not in general blame the SAS for this incident; rather, they considered it further evidence, after the Jamiat affair, of the British army's lack of grip in the city. The gap between what Task Force Knight was achieving around the capital and the British army's record in the south was growing ever wider. Underpinning this difference was a fundamental difference in approach, as one distinguished visitor to the Task Force discovered.

Late that May, as the interrogators worked away on the detainees in Balad and the bitter lessons of Delta's raid in Yusufiyah were still being digested, Tony Blair flew into Baghdad. The Prime Minister had visited the SAS before, being photographed with G Squadron on the MSS helipad in 2005. By the time of his May 2006 visit, however, the security situation had acquired a more desperate complexion.

Blair was accompanied by senior officials and the Chief of Defence Staff. His briefers included Lieutenant-Colonel Williams and the then OC of Task Force Knight. More or less all of the key people in defining Britain's Iraq policy, including the lieutenant-general resident in Baghdad, were in that air-conditioned briefing room.

The Prime Minister was shown video from surveillance aircraft of recent strikes, including LARCHWOOD 4. The briefers pointed out the running figures being pursued from one Alpha. They told him about the increasing ferocity of their encounters with al-Qaeda. According to one of those present, Blair was 'gobsmacked' by the briefing. What was scheduled as a one-hour meeting went on for more than twice as long as he asked a series of questions.

For the man centrally identified with Britain's decision to join the invasion of Iraq, this briefing gave him an insight into the active tactics being used to neutralise al-Qaeda at a time when almost all of the news coming out of the country was dire. Perhaps it may even have given him hope. One of the men in the room says that the Prime Minister did not issue directives or attempt to shape the special operations campaign, 'He regarded this as the professional preserve of the people doing it. He wanted a successful outcome to the campaign but he avoided prescriptive advice.'

The message that Blair took away was one of a strategy to defeat al-Qaeda that would be carried out with aggression and commitment. It characterised the SAS operation, but was absent in many of his visits to Basra. In one respect, however, the special operators may have miscalculated. All of the Task Force Knight briefers had that morning chosen to wear a patch that was a 'must have' item in JSOC at the time.

After the previous summer's bitter battles in the Euphrates Valley, American operators had designed a badge that was run up by the tailors' shop at the PX or military supermarket in Balad. It featured the Stars and Stripes with the words 'Fuck al-Qaeda' written across the top. Some British operators had acquired these and they were instantly judged so 'ally' or 'warry' that an order had soon been put in for a version featuring the Union Flag. One eyewitness said that Blair clearly saw these patches during the briefing but refrained from any comment. Some of his party did, however, later ask why the soldiers had worn them. One blade explains, a little self-consciously, 'The guys had been brutalised by this point, many of them had been on hundreds of raids. The badge was about that experience.'

The 'Fuck al-Qaeda' patch also spoke of a US–UK camaraderie that went beyond any rivalry about particular ops. The British had cemented this when they started operations against the al-Qaeda target set. And late in May dramatic events unfolded as word emerged from the screening cells in Balad of a change of heart from their British-captured detainee *Abu Haydr*.

Under the US guidelines for initial holding of prisoners at the Temporary Screening Facility, *Abu Haydr* should have been released by early May. But the evidence of Zarqawi's possessions and the general demeanour of the man made his interrogators reluctant to loosen their grip. They had been given more time. The original team, *Mary* and *Lenny*, had been bypassed by their supervisor *Doc*. He had established a rapport with *Abu Haydr* over the weeks of his captivity, flattering the prisoner on his insights about the Sunni–Shia schism and the American game in Iraq. According to Mark Bowden, who interviewed the gators, the key moment came when *Doc* offered *Abu Haydr* an important role in the future of Iraq: 'There was no sign that the detainee knew he was being played. He nodded sagely. This was the kind of moment gators live for.' *Doc* sought the name of *Abu Haydr*'s senior contact in the organisation.

More days passed and it was around 20 May before *Abu Haydr* finally revealed his bombshell, that he was close to Sheikh al-Rahman, Zarqawi's religious adviser. *Abu Haydr* knew where to find the sheikh and also something of the security routine he adopted when meeting his boss. Thrilled with their success, the gators passed their intelligence to Colonel *Grist* and his team at the Joint Operations Centre.

There are other versions of how the Coalition found Sheikh Rahman – for example that he had already been subject to a long surveillance operation in 2004, or that his whereabouts were revealed by a Jordanian al-Qaeda operative who'd been captured and sent back to his country in the spring of 2006. But multiple sources have confirmed to me the accuracy of Bowden's article on the interrogation.

It seems there was a further aspect of British involvement too, in using Task Force Knight operatives to mark the sheikh's location as surveillance picked him up in Baghdad. They even watched on Kill TV as he drove off in a small blue saloon on the afternoon of 7 June 2006. One observer relates, 'It was handed over to the Americans because they wanted the kill. It was a matter of national pride.' It was more than that for in truth, during these final days, the Americans were firmly in command of the evolving operation. A short way into his journey, Sheikh Rahman switched off his phone, 'but by then that was irrelevant, we had eyes on anyway'. The sheikh was being tracked from a Predator high above the road north from Baghdad towards Baquba.

In the JOC at Balad, the progress of his car was monitored on the plasma screens at the front of the room. As the sense of anticipation built, McChrystal himself joined the audience. The sheikh drove to a remote farmhouse surrounded by date palm groves in Hibhib, a village outside Baquba, reaching it just before 6.15 p.m. A portly man in black appeared to greet Rahman. Those watching at Balad instantly recognised the figure from the video seized by the SAS.

The discussion in the JOC was brief. They had *Abu Haydr*'s intelligence and they had also done much pattern-of-life sur- veillance on Rahman. Then they had glimpsed the man in black. The discussion about releasing one of the two F-16s orbiting in a stack nearby was swift, remarkably so. The aircraft dropped first one five-hundred-pound bomb then another on the house.

US troops from a regular unit nearby were the first on the scene. They recovered Zarqawi from the rubble and restrained him as he tried to get off the stretcher. But whatever fight he had shown in those last moments, Zarqawi was soon dead. Sheikh Rahman, two women and two children were also killed by the American bombs. It didn't take long for JSOC people to make the short flight from Balad to survey the scene. Zarqawi's body was flown back to Balad where Lieutenant-General McChrystal himself went to look at it. The soldier-monk knew he had got his man at last.

Zarqawi's body was packed off for formal identification. Meanwhile, a Sensitive Site Exploitation team went to work, sifting the debris in Hibhib. Based on their initial assessment of the intelligence gathered there, the Americans raided seventeen places in Baghdad that night. It was the following day before the momentous news was announced.

At the morning command conference, the BUA, news was given over the video circuit to commanders watching across the country. One reflects that the mood of the meeting was 'Job well done. Well sighted, well conducted.'

Later that day, the Coalition announced its success to the world. Major-General William Caldwell, the Coalition spokesman, began his briefing with the words, 'Today is a great day in Iraq.' Given the time and money spent hunting Zarqawi, and the many lives snuffed out in that pursuit, the official presentation was sober. Caldwell even acknowledged the analysis of many, including British, colleagues that questioned Zarqawi's centrality. He noted AQI's capability for regeneration and accepted that 'one man's life does not signify an end to an insurgency'.

Speaking from Camp David, President Bush noted that Zarqawi's death would not end the war: 'It's not going to stop the violence but it's going to help a lot.' He also told reporters that he had rung McChrystal to congratulate him. This presidential reference marked the first implicit acknowledgement by an official source that the Pentagon's classified or black Joint Special Operations Command was centrally engaged in Iraq.

There was, as those in Baghdad or Balad congratulated themselves that night, an unanswered question. Zarqawi had put so many thousands into their graves, but where should one be found for him? Ideas such as repatriating the body to Jordan were swiftly dismissed. Iraqi graveyards did not seem suitable since they might become a place of jihadist pilgrimage. The task of implementing a burial plan eventually fell to special operators. The body was taken in the dead of night to a spot on the outskirts of Baghdad and dumped without ceremony in an unmarked grave.

11

THE BATTLE FOR BAGHDAD

It was around seven o'clock on the morning of 10 July 2006 when masked gunmen appeared on the streets of Baghdad's Jihad neighbourhood. They gathered in groups at intersections, forming their own checkpoints. Drivers and passers-by were asked for their ID cards. Any Sunni males among them were taken to a bus where more gunmen were waiting. The neighbourhood, just a short distance from the airport and Coalition military headquarters, was a mixed one, but intercommunal tensions had boiled over. Samarra had its dread effect but the sectarian war in this area had really started the previous night. A suicide bomber had entered a nearby Shia mosque and blown himself up, killing eight worshippers.

The following day the Mehdi Army was out rounding up Sunnis. The bus drove to waste ground where the captives were all shot. By the end of the day local hospitals were reporting that thirty-six dead had been brought in, although the final total may have passed fifty. While the Mehdi Army were busy with their slaughter, two car bombs went off to the east, killing seven in Sadr city. That evening, the Sunni bombers were out again, mounting a double car-bomb attack on a northern Baghdad Shia mosque, killing nineteen and wounding fifty-nine.

Sunday 10 July was a bad day in Baghdad, but not exceptionally so. It did, however, mark the start of five days in which multiple suicide bombings and Shia retaliation claimed more than 150 lives in the city. It was bad enough to cause some Sunni leaders who had joined the long-awaited national unity government to threaten their withdrawal. Militant Sunnis had been trying to goad the Shias into sectarian conflict from soon after the Coalition invasion of Iraq. There had been countless car bombs and suicide attacks, many with this aim. But by the summer of 2006, spurred on by the desecration of Samarra, it was becoming clear just how bad things would get when Shia militias engaged enthusiastically in the cycle of bloodletting. And as the intensity of this slaughter increased so too did its depravity. Those sent to recover bodies dumped in rivers or on dusty street corners noticed more frequently signs of torture. Drills had been used on some victims, electricity or acid on others.

The violence of that summer was especially troubling because to those in command it seemed to make a nonsense of America's grand strategy. Not only had the tardy formation of Nouri al-Maliki's government, sworn in on 20 May, failed to have an effect despite the significant Sunni participation in the process, but new security measures were failing too. At the time of the Jihad murders, Operation TOGETHER FORWARD, also known as the Baghdad Security Plan, was nearly a month old.

For many months, senior British officers had been urging General Casey to make Baghdad the main focus of his operations. It seemed to many of the intelligence analysts that that was precisely what al-Qaeda had intended to do as well. A document seized in the raid near Yusufiyah by Task Force Knight had spelt out the organisation's determination to give attacks on the capital a central role in its plans to undermine the new Iraqi government. For this and other political reasons, the Security Plan was described by the Pentagon as 'Iraqi-led'. It was all in keeping with its message of striving to turn over a growing part of the fight to them. Certainly, more than three-quarters of the sixty-one thousand security forces involved were Iraqi, but the ideas behind TOGETHER FORWARD were entirely American. They wanted to clear neighbourhoods of insurgents one by one before turning them over to Iraqi security forces.

As had often happened during the preceding two years, it fell to British officers with the Multi-National Force headquarters in Baghdad to be the purveyors of negative assessments. Casey nicknamed one UK colonel on the staff 'the gloomy Brit'. During his morning BUA, the American general would often ask, 'Has the gloomy Brit got anything to say this morning?' At this time, a subtext of exchanges between these British staff and the Americans was that the junior partners felt Casey and his people were massaging figures about security incidents or the readiness of Iraqi forces in order to boost optimism. In some cases – for example the senior British officer in Baghdad's 2004 warnings against storming Fallujah – these dissenting opinions were unduly pessimistic.

In the face of such a dire situation, had the British staff in Baghdad not become an irritant to the Americans? Some US military officers certainly say they had. 'They were quite glad to have people around who weren't a great challenge to their authority,' counters one of the British who questioned Casey's assessments of what was being achieved, adding, 'A Brit can challenge them without any implications for their or someone else's career.' At least both sides could agree about the need to make Baghdad the focus of Coalition efforts. It was vital that the security plan succeed.

Clearance operations were already wearily familiar to many of the city's inhabitants: they involved lockdowns, door kicking and the inevitable seizure of weapons. In this new operation, however, local troops were then meant to hold the neighbourhood. Within weeks of TOGETHER FORWARD getting under way it was obvious that it was not working. American commanders accused the Iraqis of failing to provide two promised brigades. Where units did appear, particularly those from the Ministry of the Interior, they were often blamed for making matters worse. Stories abounded of police acting as an arm of the Mehdi Army, using their freedom of movement to enter Sunni areas on murder missions.

It was not as if the foreign forces were setting a shining example either. News of the charges against the American soldiers involved in May's Yusufiyah rape and murder broke. Accusations of setting out to kill people on the notoriously dangerous airport road were also levelled against American private contractors. The reliance on contractors was in itself an admission that the US forces in Baghdad could not achieve the kind of strength required to bring security to a city of five million souls.

What difference was the death of Abu Musab al-Zarqawi making to all this mayhem? It seemed that even those who had hoped his loss might lead to some temporary lull due to infighting or jockeying for position had been disappointed. But JSOC's black war was continuing, intensifying even, and it played out to its own imperatives and timetable, impenetrable to those who were not cleared to know about it – that is, the great majority of soldiers as well as the public who heard only the daily dirge of mourning and body counts.

In May 2006, B Squadron had been replaced in Task Force Knight by D Squadron. The exhausted members of B Squadron had completed the first six-month SAS tour, an effort crowned by the success of rescuing Norman Kember, finding key evidence in the hunt for Zarqawi and earning their boss his gong. Some might have expected D Squadron to be even more aggressive – certainly its reputation within the regiment was as 'the most intense of all the squadrons'. Some put this down to the dominant influence of Paras among its senior non-commissioned officer cadre, others to a tradition that it embodied most clearly the 'green-eyed' aggressive approach of the airborne forces.

The identity and indeed integrity of the different squadrons had, however, been progressively diluted. So many members had gone to specialist groups, such as the Surveillance Reconnaissance Cell, liaison jobs or detachments, that an SAS squadron might have fewer than forty men in Baghdad. In order to maintain the numbers, blades with special skills from other squadrons, or men from the SBS, or operators with the newly formed Special Reconnaissance Regiment might take their place in Task Force Knight.

In Northern Ireland the surveillance outfit known by such cover names as 14 Intelligence Company or JCUNI (Joint Communications Unit Northern Ireland) had attained a legendary reputation for stealth and expertise. They used unmarked cars or observation posts to mount eyes-on and technical surveillance, often finding themselves just feet away from the terrorists they tracked. This unit was expanded during 2004 and 2005 into the Special Reconnaissance Regiment. The idea behind the SRR was not that entire squadrons would rotate through operational theatres but that each one would specialise in a particular role, with sub-units doing tours there. The birth of the SRR was nonetheless far from happy.

Many in the SAS, including Commanding Officers such as *Charles Beaufort* and Richard Williams, were openly sceptical about the value of this new venture. 'You could slink around a council estate in Northern Ireland because guys could blend in,' explains one experienced SAS type. 'They couldn't do that in Baghdad and Kabul.' The new regiment was given Portakabins in the SAS camp at Credenhill while it formed, leading the blades to deride them as 'trailer trash'. They also jokingly referred to the SRR as 'Tier 3 special forces'. After the capture of two of its own men in Basra the SAS was less able to insist its own surveillance skills were superior, but the incident hardly helped the SRR either. Nonetheless, by mid-2006 a handful of SRR operators were operating in Baghdad with Task Force Knight and an SRR officer had taken command of what was known as the 'SpR Det'. This Specialist Reconnaissance Detachment of Task Force Knight made up of a variety of special forces soldiers undertook difficult observation missions on the streets of Baghdad.

Another respect in which these SAS tours were quite different from Northern Ireland was in the power and confidence of junior officers. With just a single troop commander resident in Ireland during the nineties, few officers had been exposed to daily operations and within this setup experienced NCOs often relegated the twenty-something 'Ruperts' to the background. It was still the case in 2006 that a captain commanding a troop or his boss, the major leading a squadron, might spend little more than a year in post. Old sweats like *Mulberry*, who had during his tours of Iraq gone from sergeant to staff sergeant and then sergeant-major, had vastly more experience than his commanders, and often took the role of Team Leader in an assault. In Iraq prospects for officers had changed.

Troop leaders such as Captain *Morris*, hit in Ramadi in 2003, demonstrated their courage time and again leading house assaults. Acting as liaison with US units (as that captain had been doing on Delta's Yusufiyah mission) often allowed an officer to remain in Iraq, continuing to accumulate operational experience. By 2009, after three tours in Iraq and scores of raids, *Morris* had been promoted to major and given command of A Squadron. In the competitive world in which the SAS squadrons operated there was rivalry between Team Leaders – some young officers, others experienced senior NCOs – who vied to set up target packs for bigger and better operations. Liaising with intelligence organisations or absorbing highly technical information put more of an emphasis on brain power. 'The concept is of the strategic soldier,' explains one young officer, 'that you need to have strategic effect, that you have to absorb a complex intelligence picture. You need the intellect and versatility to deal with that.' In Iraq the old class-based battle between Ruperts and old sweats gave way to a more generalised rivalry. Naturally this also existed between squadron leaders, as one followed the next. Not only were they keen to outdo their predecessors, but were used to being given considerable latitude in how that might be done. As D Squadron replaced B this caused considerable tension.

The OC of D Squadron, Major *Lavity*, was a most careful operator who defied any 'green-eyed Para' stereotype that his unit might have built up. He considered his approach to be one of brain rather than brawn. Physically slight, *Lavity* had come to the SAS via the Royal Engineers. Under Lieutenant-Colonel *Beaufort*, *Lavity* had served as the regiment's chief of staff, planning operations around the world. Those who watched him at work in Baghdad say that *Lavity* soon questioned the point of many of JSOC's raids, arguing that they netted only 'pipe-swingers' or low-ranking street life. Perhaps, after watching B Squadron, he had concluded that some high-profile successes were more important.

During the early weeks of D Squadron's tour *Lavity* frequently clashed with his boss, Richard Williams, over the squadron's priorities. Their differences were aired during nightly Video Tele-Conferences (VTCs), as well as by e-mail and face to face, and soon became widely known among both British and American special operators.

Williams had his own doctrine and it was as important in shaping SAS operations in Iraq as anything handed down from JSOC. The CO told his squadron commanders that he expected three things of them: that they conduct an operation every night; that every operation be completed; and that every raid produce intelligence. These dictums fitted very well with Lieutenant-General McChrystal's central idea – that the insurgency could only be overwhelmed by a relentless tempo of operations. Al-Qaeda had to be dismantled faster than it could regenerate itself. In order to maintain this pace of nightly activity, McChrystal sacrificed some target development in the interests of getting the raids themselves to produce intelligence. The Americans were also willing to launch their raids on a single 'trigger' or piece of intelligence. This philosophy played itself out with spectacular consequences in the Triangle of Death during May to July 2006, as one wave of strikes followed another.

There were quite a few on the British side of the operation who shared Major *Lavity*'s unease at launching nightly raids. After all, each Task Force Knight mission carried myriad risks: of losing a helicopter; of soldiers being shot; of hitting the wrong house and pointlessly killing Iraqis. The OC of D Squadron made clear he did not want to run them simply to lift pipe-swingers. The raids might simply be stirring up violence if the quality of those being taken had been sacrificed in the interests of quantity. He articulated what some felt was the distinctive British approach. 'We generally wanted two or even three indicators on a target, which was different to the Americans,' comments one British intelligence officer.

Both McChrystal and Williams, it seems, felt there was a danger of Task Force Knight falling back into a slower and more deliberate pace of operations after the fireworks of B Squadron's tour, almost a return to the old 'Task Force Slack' approach. When Williams put pressure on *Lavity* during the nightly VTC there was a wider audience in the special ops community watching the circuit. Eventually, after some bruising public airing of differences, D Squadron maintained the rate of operations. Those who disliked Williams considered that his pressure on squadron commanders formed part of a scheme of personal aggrandisement with McChrystal and the Americans.

The scope for discrete British operations in Baghdad was in any case decreasing. Sectarian strife created its own limits for Task Force Knight's operations. Surveillance reconnaissance in cars by members of the SpR Detachment was largely a thing of the past: there were simply too many checkpoints, official and militia, on the city's streets. The ability to gather distinctive British intelligence through agent networks was also limited. Both SIS and the Defence Humint Unit Detachment (also called the Field Humint Team) had already curtailed their missions due to the dangers involved. Their agents were still operating, but with less supervision – and therefore it was less likely that operations could be run solely on the basis of their information. It was a case of accepting American technical intelligence, often based on mobile phones, or losing one's ability to operate, say some who were there.

Just as the dire security situation and personalities involved brought argument to the running of Britain's secret campaign, so matters concerning the overt effort came to a head during the summer of 2006. Much depended upon the views of the generals holding the two key British positions, that of General Casey's deputy, a lieutenant-general or three-star also referred to as the Senior British Military Representative in Iraq (SBMR-I), and the commander of Multi-National Division South East, Britain's force in the south. Major-General Richard Shirreff was about to take over the latter post in Basra. On his reconnaissance he had become alarmed by how militia power had grown, hardly checked, in the south, but his attempts to challenge that would not unfold until later that summer.

Meanwhile, Lieutenant-General Rob Fry of the Royal Marines had taken over as SBMR-I in Baghdad that March. Some saw him as a typical 'political general' determined to drive through the British agenda of withdrawal come what may. Fry's predecessor, Nick Houghton, gave a final interview in which he revealed that Britain would start turning over its provinces to Iraqi control that spring and be out of Iraq by the summer of 2008. 'A military transition over two years has a reasonable chance of avoiding the pitfalls of overstaying our welcome,' he said, 'but gives us the best opportunity of consolidating the Iraqi security forces.' Speaking about the Samarra bombing, Houghton commented that it had 'not in any way altered the plan and its potential time-scale. The degree of restraint in the face of huge provocation was reassuring.'

Such words caused alarm among senior US officers. British leaders mouthed the American message that the withdrawal had to be 'conditions-based', but just how bad did things have to get for the UK to reconsider their plan? Up until around this time – July 2006 – there were also plenty in the US chain of command who saw their duty as driving towards withdrawal, whatever horrors were being perpetrated on the streets. But as the Baghdad Security Plan began to falter serious questions were being asked from the Green Zone to the White House about junking Plan A and finding a new way to deal with the worsening situation. It cannot be said that a new idea had crystallised, and General

Casey stuck doggedly to his strategy of turning over the fight to the Iraqis. Senior officers and Washington policymakers were using the failure of the Baghdad Security Plan to open the debate about what needed to be done, and whether Casey was the right man to do it.

Rob Fry, an intellectual Royal Marine, absorbed these discussions in Iraq, undergoing what one observer termed a 'Damascene conversion'. The general was unpopular within the SAS, having in his previous postings questioned the early special operations campaign in Iraq and been one of those UK-based officers whom the blades deemed to have moved too slowly when the Jamiat incident happened. Fry began to question the mantra he had previously believed, of moving to 'operational overwatch'. The situation was one of the utmost seriousness. The Coalition was staring defeat in the face. Was Britain willing to do anything about it? UK domestic politics made it impossible for the British army to reverse and reinforce itself in Basra. It might even be impossible to abandon the withdrawal plan set out by his predecessor, so Fry concluded that they would have to bring something else to the party. It was vital that Task Force Knight keep up its contribution to the main effort, the battle for Baghdad.

In addition, Generals Casey and Fry agreed that the British team in the capital should spearhead F-SEC, or Force Strategic Engagement Cell. The intelligence people could join in this new effort to turn the Sunni community against the jihadists.

So Task Force Knight and the Strategic Engagement Cell were to become more important at a time when security was deteriorating rapidly and Whitehall wanted to stick to its withdrawal plans. Those who believed Britain should fight on could only try to stand in the way of the stampede for the exit. At this turning point, a handful of British soldiers effectively lost faith in their national plan, sharing the growing realisation among the

American military that more force might be necessary before any drawdown could be resumed. These included not only one or two senior officers, but many of the blades in Task Force Knight. One British general who visited Baghdad in the early summer of 2006 gave me a stark example of the tensions at play:

> The sergeant-major of the SAS squadron approached me and suggested we have a word in the garden. We pulled up a couple of chairs and then, as if pre-arranged, a couple of other senior NCOs appeared from various corners, as if by magic, to join us. They had a message and it was soon clear what it was. 'The Americans say we've given up, that we don't want to fight any more. Is that true, boss?' It was a good question. And it wasn't easy for me to answer.

As they spoke, beyond the manicured gardens of the Green Zone the murder and violence seemed to be unstoppable. Hundreds of thousands of Baghdadis had fled to Jordan or Syria.

By late July US senior officers, concluding that Operation TOGETHER FORWARD had failed, were setting in train plans to launch a new security drive for the capital using a higher proportion of US troops. But, given the dire nature of the national security situation and the apparent desire by those at the top of the Pentagon not to commit more troops to an increasingly unpopular war, nobody was quite sure how Baghdad Security Plan Mark II might work.

During the violent weeks following Zarqawi's death, the atmosphere of the shop floor at the JOC in Balad remained one of intense focus. Responding to the haul of intelligence from the scene of his killing and from other sites raided in Baghdad, the Coalition had mounted 450 raids in little more than a week – operations on a scale far beyond the resources of JSOC and its small group of secret task forces. At the core of these raids was JSOC's approach of attempting to exploit the killing of Zarqawi. A senior British officer who encountered General McChrystal frequently during these months noted that 'he was . . . one of the coolest assessors of the situation, despite being involved in the hurlyburly he had a detached intellectual view of the overall picture'. McChrystal's instinct was that, despite the failure of Zarqawi's death to improve the surrounding Iraqi mayhem, and despite the faltering of the wider US military effort, JSOC was still doing the right thing.

'We sensed that al-Qaeda was going to implode,' McChrystal later told a journalist. 'We were watching it, and feeling it and seeing it.'

The reasons behind him forming such views lie in part in the secret intelligence picture to which the JSOC commander and a select few were privy. They had known about tensions in the Sunni resistance since the latter part of 2005. There was the letter from al-Qaeda leader Atiyah Abdel Rahman, thought to be hiding in the Pakistani tribal areas, criticising Zarqawi for stirring up sectarian hatred with the Shia. Atiyah had also argued that Zarqawi's 2005 bombing of hotels in the Jordanian capital was a mistake. A great deal of intelligence supported the view that many Sunnis were heartily sick of al-Qaeda's extremism. Other al-Qaeda assessments seized during the raids following Zarqawi's death had shown the movement knew that the passing of months might be working against them because of the speed with which new Iraqi units were being trained. One read, 'Time is now beginning to be of service to the American forces and harmful to the resistance.'

These scraps of information were obviously subject to differing interpretation, and there were still some who, working away in their air-conditioned headquarters during the summer of 2006, believed that events were working against the Americans and not for them. The costs of the war were enormous and public support declining. Nonetheless, McChrystal maintained his belief that it was possible to dismantle the AQI infrastructure faster than it could regenerate itself.

The question of who might be right was about to be answered, at least in part. It was to happen not in Baghdad, which everyone agreed had become the central battle of the insurgency, but to the west, in al-Anbar.

12

THE AWAKENING

On 17 August 2006 a Marine Corps colonel named Peter Devlin fired off a secret assessment entitled 'State of the Insurgency in al-Anbar'. His job, as the top intelligence officer for the US force operating in the west of Iraq, meant that he was party to the most sensitive information at his country's disposal. His first paragraph concluded, 'The social and political situation has deteriorated to such a point that MNF and ISF are no longer capable of defeating the insurgency in al-Anbar.' The colonel's stark judgement shocked many, and was promptly leaked to the press, feeding a sense in Washington that President Bush's great project in Iraq had been defeated.

Who, then, had won? 'AQI is the dominant organisation of influence in al-Anbar, surpassing nationalist insurgents, the Iraqi government and MNF in its ability to control the day to day life of the average Sunni,' wrote Devlin. But if he was party to much of the same intelligence reporting as Lieutenant-General Stan McChrystal, how had they reached such different conclusions about the ability of Coalition forces to prevail against al-Qaeda?

At the time of his report, and despite British encouragement to shift the focus of US operations to Baghdad, al-Anbar Province was still the most difficult and bloody part of Iraq for US forces. In August 2006, for example, thirty-two of the seventy Americans who lost their lives across the whole of Iraq perished in Anbar – twice as many as were lost in the greater Baghdad area. Al-Qaeda cells that mounted bombing attacks into the capital from towns like Abu Ghraib or Yusufiyah in fact relied upon a secure line of communication through Anbar, and the organisation viewed the province as central to its project of declaring a caliphate. Between February and August 2006, violent attacks in Anbar increased by 57 per cent.

For anybody trying to secure it, the province presented a host of challenges. Its main cities, Fallujah and Ramadi were, like the US bases, islands of population in a sea of desert. The backstreets of the provincial capital, Ramadi, were probably the toughest urban environment that any Coalition troops faced in Iraq. As for the human geography, there were stark contrasts between the civic divisions of districts or ministries so important to soldiers with a western mindset and the tribal identities that defined so many Anbaris.

Since 2004's crescendo of violence in Fallujah, the centre of militant resistance had been displaced to Ramadi. American intelligence estimated that around five thousand al-Qaeda fighters lurked among the city's population of four hundred thousand. American patrols into the city were usually attacked, and the local resistance groups were reckoned to be setting eight IEDs per day for them. A systematic campaign of assassination against those who sided with the Baghdad government had by mid-

2006 left the province almost without leadership. As for the police, it illustrated well the hollowness of many of the statistics about Iraqi forces reeled off by Coalition spokesmen. The city had posts for 3386, of which only 420 were filled and most of them did not turn up for work. On a normal day, there were around a hundred police on duty in Ramadi.

On 18 June the Americans had launched a concerted attempt to 'retake' Ramadi. A new commander, Colonel Sean MacFarland of the 1st Brigade Combat Team of the Germany-based 1st Armoured Division, had come in with a bold plan to wrest control from the militants. He intended to establish combat outposts across the city in order to challenge AQI. Their fighters picked up the gauntlet and Ramadi was soon the scene of intense daily firefights in which the Americans, with their Predator drones, armour and Humvees, were pitted against snipers, road-side bombs and suicide bombers driving trucks full of high explosive. MacFarland's 1st Brigade Combat Team was equipped for heavy armoured warfare on the plains of Germany, fielding Abrams tanks and Bradley infantry fighting vehicles – the most heavily protected types in the US inventory. Bitter experience had however shown that even this level of armoured protection was not always adequate when faced with a hail of RPGs or huge IEDs buried under the roads in Anbar.

The intensity of the combat can be judged by two medal cit-ations for US Navy commandos killed at the time. They belonged to Seal Team 3, a special operations force used to stiffen Iraqi troops in the fighting. One was killed on 2 August after evacuating a wounded team-mate during fighting that involved dozens of insurgents and American tanks. Another, Petty Officer 2nd Class Michael Monsoor, was nominated for his country's highest bravery award after falling on 29 September. Monsoor's citation for the Medal of Honor noted that the 25-year-old special operator had been in a rooftop position with three other American commandos and eight Iraqi soldiers during operations in Ramadi. They were providing sniper cover to American troops fighting their way through the city. Monsoor's position became a target for the insurgents, who first fired an RPG at it before closing in with small arms. One threw a grenade onto the rooftop. According to an internet source, 'Monsoor yelled "Grenade!" and dropped on top of the grenade prior to it exploding. Monsoor's body shielded the others from the brunt of the fragmentation blast and two other SEALs were only wounded by the remaining blast.'

That Seal team operating in Ramadi was part of the Tier 2 effort, bolstering local Iraqi forces, rather than McChrystal's Tier 1 JSOC. It had a stake in the battle in the form of Task Force Blue, based at al-Asad airbase. Like Green, the Delta operators, the Seals from Task Force Blue mounted takedown operations against al-Qaeda targets on the basis of high-level intelligence. Neither Blue nor Britain's Task Force Knight, which rarely ventured into Anbar, were to have much of a part to play in MacFarland's plan for Ramadi. For, alongside the visible axis of his advance – the city's main thoroughfares, such as Route Michigan – was his operation based on social lines – his plan to turn the tribes. Many had tried and failed to enlist the support of Anbari tribal sheikhs but the effort was about to produce dramatic results. Like many a success, this one has many fathers – or those who would claim credit – but the British role in this secret business is little understood.

The origins of the Force Strategic Engagement Cell lay in instructions given by General Casey to Lieutenant-General Rob Fry in May 2006. This task fell to the British in part because the Deputy Commanding General swept up all sorts of other business on behalf of his US Army boss. The cell was a working group of several officers, led by the British military but including the Americans and closely involving the CIA as well as MI6. Its business, as 'strategic' implied, was the turning of key power brokers. Placing this effort under British leadership may also have been an attempt by the American general to insulate himself from responsibility if it all went wrong. A senior member of one of the civilian intelligence agencies involved in the effort to turn tribes into new militias notes, 'Casey's concern was that would be unacceptable in Washington and could be interpreted in Iraq as a sign of weakness.' The US military was very nervous about arming such militias, but not so the CIA. One of the Brits involved insists that 'the CIA contribution was absolutely pivotal'. The Agency not only pinpointed targets for cultivation, based on its long work in this area since the invasion, but was ready to arm Sunnis in a way that gave the US military shudders of anxiety.

From its earliest days in the country, the CIA had tried to woo the tribes. These efforts had yielded little for a variety of reasons. The 2004 Fallujah operation poisoned a good deal of rural opinion in Anbar. It also, in the shape of the Fallujah Brigade formed from former Ba'athists in November 2004, temporarily discredited the option of arming local Sunni militias. They had simply gone over to the insurgency. During 2005 the bitter fights in the Upper Euphrates had opened rifts, particularly between local communities and foreign fighters, but al-Qaeda had been so successful in killing or driving away any community leader who stood up against them that contacts remained tentative.

During May and June Fry received a couple of important delegations at his office in the Green Zone. The first came from Abu Ghraib and the second from Diyala, a province to the north-east of the capital. The nature of these meetings meant they had to be clandestine. The tribal leaders were picked up in covert vehicles for transport to the Green Zone. After discussions they were returned to a discreet drop-off point. These early discussions proved inconclusive: the sheikhs were polite and emollient, but seemed vague about how many men they might be able to field as militia or when they might actually do it. But around the time of Peter Devlin's memo on the hopelessness of the situation in Anbar, a meeting was arranged with some key people from that troubled province. The CIA Station Chief in Baghdad was instrumental in spotting the individuals, and so was the Iraqi governor. One figure who was party to early discussions hosted by Rob Fry noted, 'The last to become involved were the Anbaris but they had far greater cohesion than the others.' The Coalition and some power brokers from Anbar had taken a good look at one another and it seemed they might be able to do business.

That these Sunni sheikhs were risking their lives in meeting Lieutenant-General Fry or US officers was obvious. An attempt late in 2005 to organise an anti-al-Qaeda front called the Anbar People's Council had produced intense violence. These local dignitaries had helped secure elections in December 2005, but following this, as Devlin wrote in his secret report, 'Faced with this blatant challenge to their hegemony, AQI destroyed the Anbar People's Council . . . through a highly efficient and comprehensive assassination campaign.' To side with the Americans often meant not only death but torture, beheading or the desecration of your body, with the video of these acts going on sale in Ramadi's bazaars.

Sheikh Abu Ali al-Jassim came forward with a pledge to induct his men into the Iraqi police and history seemed to be repeating itself as he was soon targeted by al-Qaeda. They abducted and killed him, hiding his body for four days before telling his relatives where to find it. This violation of the Islamic principles concerning treatment of the dead was a step too far. Ramadi had experienced blistering violence since the fall of Saddam, not least in the security drive launched by MacFarland that June. Countless buildings had been flattened and stray American bullets and bombs had killed hundreds if not thousands by the time that Sheikh Jassim was murdered. Despite this catalogue of horrors and, just like the Samarra bombing, it was al-Qaeda's symbolic act of desecration that proved so powerful.

Over glasses of tea in the diwans of their family compounds, with tissues ready to hand to mop their brows in the crazy heat, the sheikhs talked and their views began to coalesce. *Halas* – enough. Some of them were people whom the CIA, MacFarland's officers or the Strategic Engagement Cell had cultivated, but many were not. On 9 September 2006 they went public.

The newly formed Sahwa al-Anbar or Anbar Awakening embraced twenty different tribes under the chairmanship of Sheikh Sittar abu Risha. A stately figure whose manicured beard and robes gave him an appearance older than his actual age, Sittar's grandfather had been part of the 1920 anti-British rising and his father fought them again in 1941. His reputation in the western part of Ramadi, where he came from, was as a minor sheikh and major smuggler whose influence had grown because of the murder or emigration of more senior figures. Given his family's lineage in the nationalist resistance he was an unlikely partner for the British-run Strategic Engagement Cell, but those involved confirm that is precisely what he became. Less than a month after Peter Devlin's pessimistic memo there had been a change of strategic importance in Iraq's biggest province. The Awakening initially committed 1300 men to the police, but US military records suggest that in the second half of 2006 four thousand or so actually joined in Anbar.

Faced with this counter-revolt, al-Qaeda responded both with agitation and violence. In mid-October it announced the creation of the Islamic State of Iraq, with Ramadi as its capital, but this attempt to fulfil the vision of Abu Musab al-Zarqawi and other jihadists had come far too late. Al-Jazeera and other Arab networks were given pictures showing public celebrations of the formation of the breakaway Sunni state. This venture would involve not just the imposition of strict sharia but also the deliberate dismemberment of the country. Innately conservative Iraqi nationalists such as the sheikhs did not want any part of this – and it wasn't hard for them to convince their people of the futility of following the al-Qaeda lead. On the streets and in villages tit-for-tat violence intensified as vendettas escalated between the jihadists and tribes. At several crucial moments American tanks and aircraft joined the onslaught in defence of their new 'police' allies. The official death toll for Colonel MacFarland's area of operations in Ramadi between June 2006 and February 2007 was 750 insurgents killed (eighty-five US troops died and five hundred were wounded in the same timeframe). This might have been the toll for the 'official' fight, but rumour and dark anecdote surround what happened between those who took sides following the formation of the Anbar Awakening.

During the intense battles of October and November 2006, al-Qaeda was largely eliminated from Ramadi. When I asked one senior Coalition officer how this had happened, he replied without hesitation: 'Sittar and his boys went out and killed them.' Panic began to spread through the insurgent organisation. The foreign fighters in particular stood out, and the Awakening people often knew where to find them. Some suggested that this killing spree was triggered by the murder and beheading of several teenagers belonging to an Awakening tribe. One American lieutenant serving in Ramadi explained:

The mosques in the city went crazy. The imams screamed jihad from the loudspeakers. We went to the roof of the outpost and braced for a major assault. Our interpreter joined us. *Hold on*, he said. *They aren't screaming jihad against us. They are screaming jihad against the insurgents.**

* Thomas E. Ricks, *The Gamble: General David Petraeus and the American Military Adventure in Iraq, 2006–2008* (Allen Lane, 2009)

How far this beheading incident triggered subsequent events remains open to debate. The fact is that an estimated five thousand al-Qaeda in Ramadi disappeared between June 2006 and early 2007. Hundreds fled. Teams of militants turned up in Baghdad and elsewhere during the following weeks. Many others may have melted back into the community, for al-Qaeda had always relied on casual help in the planting of bombs or sniping at patrols. But the suspicion remains that many more than the official 750 met their deaths. Hundreds, possibly thousands, were dispatched by the Awakening and lie in unmarked graves in the desert.

By October Britain had switched its senior officer in Baghdad under the six-monthly rotation that the Americans found so exasperating. In Rob Fry's place came Graeme Lamb, returning to Iraq after his visits as Director of Special Forces and time as commander of the British division in Basra. Lamb had a particular knack for getting on with the American commanders, many of whom he knew from these earlier tours. In company with some of his more strait-laced cousins Lamb even moderated the swearing with which his personal staff was so familiar. As this language suggested, he was a particularly aggressive general whose experience with the SAS and friendship with Stan McChrystal led him to take a particular view of the business started by his predecessor.

Under Lamb the Strategic Engagement Cell stepped up its activities considerably. Meetings with tribal leaders became more frequent. Some were held in the ornate diwan at Maude House, the military residence where the general stayed next to the embassy. Despite this very British-sounding name, the place was fitted out in the style of an Iraqi power broker, the reception room replete with gilt sofas, polished marble floors and chandeliers. Other meetings were held nearby, at the house of Iraq's Deputy Prime Minister in the area known as Little Venice, a section of luxury homes where the artificial waterways had long since gone green and fetid. A few were held in the sheikhs' own homes. Mindful of the duties of the Arab host, when on home ground Graeme Lamb was careful to serve his guests their tea personally.

Lamb soon saw the potential for locking together the tribal strategy and JSOC's industrial counterterrorist drive. One of those present in a meeting recalls an Iraqi potentate, active in the resistance, telling the British general, 'The Iraqis are just sheep. You must find the shepherds.' The sheikhs were excellent sources of intelligence about who was killing whom in their home areas. In some cases, too, the alignment of a particular neighbour or village with the jihadists prevented a friendly leader from declaring for the Awakening. If the local AQI emir could be taken down, in one stroke the militants would suffer a blow in the district, an element of intimidation would be removed and a new sheikh could declare himself in support of the government. Lamb co-opted an SAS major – initially the officer who had led B Squadron during the invasion – into the Strategic Engagement Cell to act as the linkman between his charm and JSOC's harm offensives.

It was at this time, autumn 2006, that a change of language became apparent at Camp Victory and the US Embassy. 'We started using the terms "reconcilable" and "irreconcilable",' recalls one key player. 'This was taking away the simplicity of language of saying "enemy" or "insurgent".' Some Americans credit their British deputy commanding general with this change of emphasis, arguing that it became central to his Awakening strategy. Others claim that the 'irreconcilable' label had been around for a while out west, courtesy of the Marines. Whether or not Lamb coined the term or simply picked it up and ran with it, it started to figure in his e-mail exchanges with his old colleague General David Petraeus. Petraeus had already spent much time in

Iraq, as commander of a division during the invasion and its aftermath, as well as in senior staff jobs. The failure of General Casey's Baghdad Security Plan was causing people in Washington to question his future. Some were already touting Petraeus as his successor.

Although the events that followed soon after Peter Devlin's intelligence assessment might seem to have proven him a man with a singular lack of understanding of the underlying situation, his main failing was one common to a great many other officers at that time: a pessimism born of repeated reverses, notably in the assassination of leaders who tried to support the Coalition. But the colonel had identified the connection between this insecurity and troop strengths in Iraq, arguing extra marines were needed to turn around the situation. Increasingly the understanding that more soldiers were required if the US was to prevail spread among America's military leadership.

13

CHOOSING VICTORY

Late on Saturday 17 July 2006 British troops moved into one of the most hostile neighbourhoods of Basra in pursuit of Sajjad Badr Adal Sayeed, the leader of JAM (Jaish al-Mehdi or the Mehdi Army) in the city. Warriors rumbled in to put in place a cordon while a storming party prepared to enter Sajjad's house. His role and whereabouts had been identified during a lengthy intelligence operation. Having gathered their dossier, the experts referred it to their chain of command for action.

Moving on a kingpin in the militia required a careful military–political judgement. Muqtada al-Sadr, the leader to whom Mehdi Army units in the city owed loyalty, had been drawn into powersharing arrangements with the new Prime Minister, Nouri al-Maliki. But securing a role in the Baghdad power game had little soothing effect on his movement; rather, their attacks on

Coalition troops continued to escalate. Since direct confrontation with the Mehdi Army – the kind of bloodletting seen in al-Amarrah or Sadr City in 2004 – would have been politically damaging to the Maliki government, the Coalition had to go easy on the Shia militia. In its public pronouncements the British army explained the growing rain of rockets on its bases or IEDs against its vehicles as the work of 'rogue elements' or 'splinter groups'. Certainly there were some Iranian-backed militants at work in many attacks, but the simple truth was that thousands of Mehdi Army foot soldiers were engaged in fighting the Coalition despite Muqtada's political manoeuvres, or even perhaps as part of them, in an effort designed to enhance his bargaining position.

As they considered the request to mount a major strike operation against Sajjad, British decision-makers knew there could be difficult repercussions. In the constant rotations of operational leaders within Iraq, however, the planets were aligned for tough action in a way that had rarely been before. There had, for example, been a brief window of opportunity ten months earlier when a significant Mehdi Army leader was arrested and Sajjad unsuccessfully targeted by the SAS. By the summer of 2006 the commander of 20th Armoured Brigade favoured an aggressive approach, as did Fry and Lamb, the senior British officers in Baghdad during that summer and autumn. Most important, the central figure in the UK national setup in the south, the commander of Multi-National Division South East, had decided to send a message to the militia. Cavalry officer Major-General Richard Shirreff had arrived in Basra with a sense that his division had lost the initiative to its enemies, and found it unacceptable that the British army had become so passive in the face of mounting casualties.

Shirreff had been dispatched to Iraq with the words of the Chief of Joint Operations, his military superior in the UK, ringing in his ears: 'We want no displays of military testosterone in

Basra.' The CJO at that time, Lieutenant-General Nick Houghton, was the officer who had preceded Rob Fry in Baghdad and who, prior to departing, had publicly declared plans to get the British Army out of Iraq by the summer of 2008. Shirreff was not interested in machismo, nor in keeping British troops in Iraq indefinitely. He was however determined to allow them to withdraw under conditions of their own making, hopefully having broken the Mehdi Army in Basra first. So he ordered the strike operation against Sajjad.

The British troops that hit his house were men selected from the Brigade Reconnaissance Company, spearheaded by the HATHOR detachment. Although they succeeded in removing Sajjad without major difficulties, Mehdi Army militiamen were soon engaging the strike force cordon with assault rifles and rocket-propelled grenades. Black-clad militants ran through the streets with RPGs on their shoulders or guns in their hands, keen to join in the battle. For two hours exchanges continued between the army and Sajjad's men, during which it was estimated that the Iraqis fired 104 RPGs and thousands of small-arms rounds. Corporal John Cosby, a Team Leader in the Brigade Reconnaissance Force, was killed, as were four Iraqi militiamen.

These battles became typical of the kind of reception that awaited large-scale strike operations in Basra's militia strongholds. While SAS operations around Baghdad also required a cordon it was usually provided by paratroopers of the Special Forces Support Group. In Basra, companies of mechanised infantry in Warrior fighting vehicles had to be employed for the same purpose. This heavy presence could bring hundreds of armed militia onto the streets. Thus while the actual target building would often be entered without violence the reception awaiting a strike force in notorious Basra neighbourhoods like Hayyaniyah, Qibla, and Jumhuriyah was as violent as some of the toughest places the Americans operated.

The Sensitive Site Exploitation at Sajjad's compound produced a host of documents and other leads, triggering another operation in the city three nights later, in which two tons of weapons (mainly rockets and mortar bombs of the type used in the frequent attacks on British bases in the city) were seized. Back home, the Defence Secretary hailed the twin operations as causing 'a very significant deterioration' in the militia's capability. Over the following days Mehdi Army supporters showed their anger with riots and further attacks on British bases.

Under the UK's plans to turn over the south to Iraqi control, Britain had moved to 'operational overwatch' in al-Muthanna Province on 13 July and was due to hand over Dhi Ghar in September. Of the four provinces originally under British control this left Maysan and Basra, both seats of major difficulties. Shirreff wanted to mount a big clear-and-hold operation in Basra that autumn. He christened his plan Operation SALAMANCA in honour of his hero the Duke of Wellington's finest offensive victory. SALAMANCA, as planned, involved several extra battalions of British troops as well as Iraqi reinforcements. It would have thrown many thousands of security forces into battle to 'isolate and destroy' the city's militias. Some British generals back home were alarmed because, as one of Shirreff's staff officers told me at the time, 'it looked like he was going to do a Fallujah'. They denied him the extra troops he was looking for, instead giving him two battalions for a few weeks, citing the need to channel men into the burgeoning Afghanistan operation. The Iraqi government meanwhile refused to support such an ambitious operation because it could bring an open war with Muqtada al-Sadr.

Faced with these obstacles, Shirreff's options were distinctly limited. He would boost the intelligence and special forces capabilities needed to mount more offensive operations; move an armoured battlegroup out of Maysan so it could join in the attempt to clear Basra; and accept Maliki's suggestion that the Basra security drive be given an 'Iraqi face', with an Iraqi general notionally in charge, far more limited aims and the new Arabic-sounding codename Operation SINBAD.

In pushing forward his strike operations, the commander of MND South East found the SAS supportive. Richard Williams had run Shirreff's staff in the Balkans when he was commanding 7 Armoured Brigade. The two men worked well together, unlike some previous high-ups in Basra who had cold-shouldered the SAS. Among the rank and file of the SAS some of the anger resulting from the Jamiat incident before had now dissipated, and they felt duty-bound to help their comrades as the situation deteriorated. As a result of this the SAS presence in Basra was later upgraded from the HATHOR detachment to Task Force Spartan, which was around twice the size. Spartan would be used to develop target intelligence and spearhead strike operations. The addition of several SAS operators might seem trivial in the context of the thousands of troops already involved, but one of the commanders who worked in the city says, 'Those few men were the equivalent of a battalion.'

During Richard Shirreff's command a detachment was also picked from the regular army garrison and given the job of supporting special operations. Armageddon Platoon, as it soon became known, was based at Basra Palace, providing a Quick Reaction Force for the intelligence people.

In pushing ahead with SINBAD, despite all of the limitations placed upon it, the British divisional commander also needed to free up the armoured battlegroup deployed in Maysan Province. By the summer of 2006 their situation had become extremely difficult. Camp Abu Naji, the main British base, south of the provincial capital al-Amarrah, was a constant target of indirect fire attacks, being hit almost every night and sometimes several times. In fact, by this point Camp Abu Naji and Basra Palace were two of the top three most rocketed or mortared bases in the whole of Iraq. Roadside bombs took a steady toll, including soldiers operating the army's heaviest troop carrier, the Warrior. Resupplying this armoured force required frequent convoys of a hundred-plus vehicles from Basra, the protection of which could tie down an entire battalion. While many in the British Army would happily have handed Maysan over to its notoriously independent people, there was great pressure from the Americans to maintain a close watch over the 283 kilometres of the province that bordered Iran. American intelligence was convinced that a large number of the EFP bombs came from Iran via Maysan. In the ripe phraseology of one senior US officer, Maysan Province was 'the sewer where all the shit was coming through'.

Major-General Shirreff's solution was to abandon Camp Abu Naji, withdrawing the armoured battlegroup from the province while keeping a smaller force, using light armour, Land Rovers and other soft-skin vehicles to move around the desert and mount surveillance of the Iranian border. This solution, Operation VIDETTE (named after the cavalry observation outpost lines of Wellington's day), seemed elegant but involved many difficulties. In the first place the Mehdi Army and Badr Brigade militias celebrated the abandonment of the camp as a great propaganda victory, announcing that they had 'kicked out the occupiers'. Thousands converged on Abu Naji to strip the camp of facilities intended for the use of the Iraqi army. Pictures of the resulting scenes caused criticism of the British, both at home and from some Americans.

The solution of mounting patrols along the border was hardly likely to stem any flow of EFPs either. In many areas the frontier presented a moonscape of earthworks from the Iran–Iraq war, where people trying to cross could easily be spotted. In others, such as an official crossing point and on certain waterways in the marshes, the volume of traffic was too large to be monitored effectively. Some even suspected that the new British operation along the border was little more than a demonstration, a ruse designed to impress both Americans and Iranians. If this was the intention it failed. 'There was a lot of frustration from the American organisations as to what we were really doing out there,' remarks one SAS man. British commanders, nervous about what the Americans were thinking, decided to step up special operations in Maysan. The regiment formed a Maysan intelligence fusion cell, mounting many surveillance missions in the desert during the summer of 2006. But these efforts produced little in the way of results.

Having taken these steps in August, the British moved ahead with Operation SINBAD in September and October. In a series of 'pulses', each of Basra city's districts was flooded with troops. With Warriors posted on corners, and frequent street patrols, the militia lay low while the British engaged in a variety of tasks from trying to improve schools to mentoring the police. Given most of the pulses lasted no more than forty-eight hours, the impact of the operation was bound to be limited. The intention was to establish Iraqi army positions in many areas, but by this juncture the soldiers and Iraqi Police Service were in almost open conflict.

A visit to the Farahidi police station during SINBAD brought home the scale of the distrust. Farahidi was one of the difficult 'new' suburbs on the east of the city, close to the Jamiat district and the Hayyaniyah, the hotbed of militia activity. Inside there was tension as the British began biometrically logging officers at the station – the duty commander began shouting that he did not want it filmed. This registration showed how little the British thought of the police, suspecting them of a wide variety of misdemeanours ranging from paybook fraud to involvement in criminal acts using their police uniforms or militia membership. The IPS for their part returned the compliment. While the biometric team worked in one room, an officer outside denounced the British to me, saying that they had promised to leave but only seemed interested in talking about oil. In the station armoury a poster of Ayatollah Khomeini adorned the wall. As we left the patrol came under a hail of stones.

Britain's Chief of Defence Staff later said that the 2006 operation in Basra was 'emasculated' by the Iraqi Prime Minister. Equally, it is clear that Britain would not commit the troops necessary to confront the militias, or indeed to disband large sections of the police, and was fearful of the consequences if it did. And so, with this mutual failure of will, the city slipped deeper into the hands of the gunmen and the British Army's opportunity to leave the inhabitants a reasonable degree of security disappeared. Even so, the strike operations went on, fed by a stream of good intelligence. But the aspirations of the British general in charge to break the power of the militias were not met. Instead strike operations continued with the aim of taking down mortar or IED teams and so trying to reduce British casualties as the army prepared for its exit.

While SINBAD, also known as the Basra Security Plan, unfolded in its halfhearted way, the failure of the Baghdad Security Plan, even in its modified form, was evident by the October of 2006. So began the comings and goings at Camp Victory or the US Embassy compound, of consultants, policy wonks and congressmen. It was evident that the existing strategy upon which Casey had based the entire operation in Iraq, that of turning over security to the Iraqis as swiftly as possible, had, if anything, made the chaos even worse. What was to be done? A high-level panel of Washington's great and good, the Iraq Study Group, began its deliberations. Their eventual recommendations – of beginning a phased US withdrawal, engaging the White House's arch-enemies in Syria and Iran, and putting more effort into training Iraqi forces – formed a sort of counsel of despair.

Behind the scenes, a lower-profile group started to think in very different ways. On 19 September, the retired general Jack Keane briefed Secretary of Defense Donald Rumsfeld on a proposed new strategy for Iraq which involved suspending planned withdrawals and waging an ambitious US-led counterinsurgency campaign on the streets of Iraqi cities. Neither Rumsfeld nor General Casey, who only days before had told Congress that he did not need any more American troops, was ready to accept these ideas. Both men were, however, falling behind the Washington curve, for Jack Keane increasingly had the ear of the White House.

When Keane and some civilian experts[*] eventually published their ideas they called their paper 'Choosing Victory'. It provided a strategic blueprint for what was soon to unfold: the shift to a counterinsurgency strategy and the surge of US troops into Iraq. 'Choosing Victory' charted a way through the apparently hopeless mayhem that the US found itself in. Dividing the spectrum of violent groups it saw that Ba'athists and nationalists (much like those sheikhs already cooperating with the Strategic Engagement Cell) were 'much more likely . . . to become open to negotiation and political persuasion'. If surge troops were used to secure Sunni and mixed neighbourhoods in Baghdad, deterring Shia death squads, then Sunni vigilante or self-defence groups would wither. Strike operations against al-Qaeda and other jihadist groups would have to continue in order to prevent them derailing this process. This defence of certain quarters required more American soldiers – the surge, which was initially estimated at twenty-one thousand and later nearly thirty thousand. It was only once the heat was taken out of the sectarian conflict, and therefore the Shia militias had been deprived of their pretext of operating as a defence force for their community, that the politically charged issue of confronting

* This thinktank was the American Enterprise Institute.

the Shia groups could be tackled. Keane and the others recommended that 'clearing Sadr City is both unwise and unnecessary at this time'.

This strategy, reflecting Keane's consultations both with David Petraeus, the army's leading counterinsurgency thinker, and with General Casey's deputy Ray Odierno, the general running operations in Iraq, was to prove remarkably far-sighted. It secured the backing of a president desperate to avoid defeat and thereby cut the ground from beneath Rumsfeld and Casey. The US adoption of the surge strategy near the end of the year left Britain with great political difficulties. Operation SINBAD underlined what the authors of 'Choosing Victory' knew only too well: that confronting Shia militants was the most difficult thing to do because of their political ties to the Maliki government. Britain could and would play its role in the Baghdad battle through Task Force Knight and the Strategic Engagement Cell, but as far as Basra was concerned the limits of Britain's will to impose a security solution had been exposed. Down in the streets of the Shia Flats, the city was becoming increasingly dangerous for British troops and it fell to small teams of soldiers to retain the initiative.

On a Sunday morning in November a ceremony of remembrance for Britain's fallen was conducted at Basra Palace. Following this, a group of three patrol boats set out, heading north into the Shatt al-Arab waterway. Journeys by the river route were a welcome break from the routine of helicopter and were considered safe. Although there had been a few incidents of the craft taking fire, the trips normally provided a lighthearted distraction for those in the boats.

That day a Field Humint Team (FHT) from the Defence Humint Unit was shuttling north. They were still successful in running agents in the city despite the growing lawlessness. One of their colleagues describes the mission as one of 'ground familiarisation' rather than an agent meet. It was very difficult to go out into the streets but fellow members of the unit say that they had acquired many different techniques for recruiting and meeting their sources. A surprising number of prospective agents simply approached Coalition bases offering information. 'You pay them to get them under control but they usually acted through altruistic reasons,' notes one agent runner. 'They wanted to help Iraq become a better place.'

British FHTs in Iraq were small – usually just a handful of people each in Basra and Baghdad (where they operated under Task Force Knight). Their system of working was informal with the case officer running a particular agent meeting regardless of the rank of those backing him or her up during the encounter. The pace of operations in Basra during late 2006 was such that the team were working flat out. On this Sunday they were on their way to 'the Shatt' – the Shatt al-Arab Hotel, headquarters of the Basra City Battlegroup.

As the boats reached a pontoon bridge in the centre of town they had to hug the western bank for there, underneath the ramp that led down to the bridge, was a channel big enough for them to get through. Each took its turn – the main transport carrying the FHT and its two escorts. It is a place just below the corniche where, in happier times, couples had strolled arm in arm before taking a meal in one of the floating restaurants moored nearby. But wedged into the wall just below the promenade was a huge bomb. As the boats passed through the gap they were being watched and videoed. The bomb detonated just as the main passenger craft passed in front of it. Two soldiers and two Royal Marines manning the boat were killed. Several others were wounded. Among the casualties were members of the Defence Humint Unit.

There were inevitable recriminations after an incident of that kind. If the boats could only get around the pontoon bridge in this one place, why wasn't it kept under fixed technical surveillance or at least searched regularly? The forces' failure to perform such checks or to equip the boats with counter-measures drew criticism at the subsequent inquest. But there were other questions posed by the incident too. Had members of the DHU deliberately been targeted? Did the skill with which the bomb had been used suggest Iranian training or technical involvement?

For British troops in the centre of the city, following the loss of a helicopter six months before and so many roadside bombs, this was just one more indicator of how their enemies could target all forms of transport. The Army, though, had its own ways of taking the initiative and the general onslaught on the Mehdi Army and other gangs continued.

D Squadron had posted Staff Sergeant Jon Hollingsworth at Basra Palace as the Team Leader of its HATHOR detachment. HATHOR had not yet been replaced by the larger Task Force Spartan, so it received regular support from Baghdad. The days in which MI6 had jokingly called Basra the 'sleepy shire by the Shatt al-Arab' were long gone. By late 2006 the tiny detachment was doing target development work on a variety of militia figures as well as spearheading many of the bigger strike operations.

In September HATHOR had been involved in target develop-ment work on an important member of al-Qaeda's international network. Omar al-Faruq was an Iraqi who had become a con-vinced international jihadist. Arrested in Jakarta in 2002, Faruq had been taken from Indonesia to the Bagram detention facility in Afghanistan. There he had been extensively interrogated by the CIA and, having been wrung dry of information, was scheduled for transfer to Guantanamo when he and other al-Qaeda opera-tives managed a daring escape. Faruq had found his way back to Iraq, taking up residence in Basra — a curious choice given the overwhelmingly Shia nature of the city and his association with the militant Sunni underground.

Following an intelligence tip-off the SAS led an operation to storm the house where Faruq was staying. Had Faruq been captured, his return to Bagram or Guantanamo might have posed a difficult question for the British, given their aversion to assisting with renditions. This difficulty was avoided when, according to the British military spokesman, Faruq opened fire on the assault force and was killed. The operation that ran him to ground was an impressive intelligence coup that underlined the value of the HATHOR detachment.

Jon Hollingsworth had the energy, charisma and, above all, physical courage needed for this task, according to those who knew him. Originally from Hull, he had graduated from the 3rd Battalion of the Parachute Regiment to the SAS. He was awarded the Queen's Gallantry Medal for operations in Northern Ireland.

Early in November, shortly before his squadron was due to be replaced, Hollingsworth, then thirty-five years old, had led a raid at the head of his detachment. While clearing a building he had been shot through the neck but had pursued his attacker and killed him. That bullet, which missed his carotid artery by millimetres, took the staff sergeant out of the fight and back to the UK for treatment. Hollingsworth returned to Iraq within days, leaving a citation for the Conspicuous Gallantry Cross behind him in the Hereford paperwork.

On 24 November he met his death, the first member of the task force to fall in action since Corporal Ian Plank in Ramadi three years earlier. Two SAS men, Major Jim Stenner and Sergeant Norman Patterson, had been killed when, driving late at night through the Green Zone in January 2004, their vehicle hit a concrete block. Dozens of men had also been wounded during the years since Plank had been killed, but what many had considered a run of good luck ended with the loss of Staff Sergeant Hollingsworth.

On the night in question, a strike was planned against a block of flats in Basra. It was a difficult mission, at night, in a hostile part of the city against an Alpha crammed with families. There were three assault teams but Hollingsworth, as the HATHOR commander, was in overall charge. Another soldier led the way into the target flat and told the inquest:

There were females with young children in there so there was a lot of screaming and shouting. As we were about to make entry into one room there was a lot of commotion and it seemed like a fridge had been pushed behind the door to barricade it. I was first into that room and saw some males in there and I was calling for John [sic] to back me up because I felt exposed and then [Jon] said 'I need a medic'.

Hollingsworth had been shot. He was evacuated by helicopter to the nearby British military hospital at Shaibah, but died soon afterwards. Mystery surrounded both who had shot him and how they came to do it with a 5.56mm round, the type of bullet used by Coalition weapons. One soldier told the inquest that two men had been seen fleeing the building. Certainly nobody was apprehended in the flat where the assault team were looking for suspects, nor were weapons recovered. SAS colleagues dismissed the idea that Hollingsworth had died in a friendly fire accident: it is certainly true that Iraqi insurgents prized captured British or American weapons as trophies.

One SAS colleague gave Hollingsworth this pithy epitaph: 'CGC! QGM! He was like Bodie from *The Professionals* – he was bound to die in a hail of bullets!' To many of the operators, Hollingsworth personified the green-eyed warrior: completely fearless in battle, someone who exerted an irresistible pull over lesser men. As such, his leadership was sorely missed. Many considered that with the frantic pace at which it had pursued missions in 2006, Task Force Knight's people had been living on borrowed time. Hollingsworth left behind a widow and two boys, one just a baby.

Hollingsworth's repatriation produced a discreet but well-attended SAS funeral at Credenhill Camp. His body had been brought back under escort by members of his squadron, dressed in their assault rig, a pattern that was followed with future losses. Another important precedent was also set: the staff sergeant's widow was invited to a private meeting with Tony Blair at Downing Street. This audience, which Number Ten regarded as a special form of recognition for the dangers faced by the SAS, underlined the Prime Minister's personal interest in and gratitude for their work.

The hectic pace of operations in Basra was set to continue. In December a team from G Squadron was flown down for Operation DOVER. The undercover warfare specialists always reserved a particular zeal for hunting down those who had claimed their colleagues' lives. In the case of DOVER, members of the DHU had managed to recruit a source with intimate knowledge of November's Shatt al-Arab river bombing. The agent located the insurgent cell and leader responsible for carrying out the operation. These people were apprehended after G Squadron stormed a building in northern Basra. Video of the attack and much other intelligence was gathered.

The punishing tempo set by the British divisional and brigade commanders in the city continued with a raid on 22 December which netted Captain Jafar among five other officers in the Iraqi Police Service. He was the man in the Serious Crime Unit under surveillance by the HATHOR detachment in September 2005 when two of its members were captured. This hammering of the Iraqi police culminated three days later, during the early hours of Christmas Day, with a huge raid on the Jamiat police station itself. More than 120 prisoners were released from its cells, many of whom, British army spokesmen claimed, showed signs of torture. Stacks of material including computers and files were taken away from the station before the whole place was blown up by the British.

And what did all of this raiding and killing achieve? As 2006 came to an end General Shirreff's aggressive approach had yielded only partial results. The trend of violence was still climbing upwards. Operation SINBAD had been blunted in its conception by both British and Iraqi doubters. Local support for it, even within the Iraqi army, had faltered early on due to fears that it would precipitate an open contest on the city's streets, unifying the many splinter or radical groups with the Mehdi Army. The British general had at least confronted the issue of police involvement in Basra's death squads, kidnapping and criminal mafias. One of the senior officers most closely associated with Britain's Iraq policy throughout the 2003–8 period later told me, 'In Basra we did not go there to win. We went to create the best conditions we could for withdrawal and that is not winning.' Richard Shirreff presented an honourable exception to this mindset. But the limitations placed upon him by the MoD and Iraqi leaders effectively showed that Britain was incapable of 'choosing victory' in the same way as the United States.

Behind all of these problems faced by soldiers on the streets of Basra was the growing power of the city's militias. Takedown operations could remove key figures but Britain could not produce the kind of operation JSOC was achieving further north, removing entire cells of Sunni extremists night after night. The intelligence effort, pool of specialist forces and, above all, political will were all lacking. Such an approach would have touched off huge gun battles with possible British losses most nights. So while the British could detain leadership figures such as Sajjad Badr and confiscate growing quantities of weaponry, the membership of insurgent groups was so large that empty shoes or caches were soon filled.

The question that people from Balad to Langley or Basra to Hereford asked themselves while these events were unfolding in the latter part of 2006 was whether the Shia extremist threat had reached such a scale that it needed to receive the same treatment as al-Qaeda and other Sunni groups. The issue of Iranian involvement was inextricably linked to this, for if JSOC's tactics were used against the Shia groups they would sooner or later threaten Iranian interests. And how on earth could Balad take on a whole new target set when its people were already straining every sinew against al-Qaeda bombers in Baghdad and elsewhere?

14

THE COMING STORM WITH IRAN

Just after 3.30 a.m. on 11 January 2007 Black Hawks and Little Birds from Task Force Brown swooped across the roofs of Irbil in northern Iraq. The city, distinguished by an ancient walled citadel at its centre, could trace its history back beyond 2000 BC. With its beautiful sites, mountain views and relative peace, Irbil's people were unused to the sounds of American raids. But as the choppers pulled up over a walled compound in a part of the city known as Old Korea that was precisely what was happening. As the area was roused from its slumbers men from Delta Force leapt off the choppers and rushed across the roofs of the building while a ground assault force broke in through the main gates. 'It was a strategic moment,' says one special operator. For the build-ing that Delta was about to force its way into was the Iranian Liaison Office, effectively the country's embassy in that region.

At the Joint Operations Centre in Balad, JSOC's commanders watched on their plasma screens as the Delta men went into the building. For months a debate had gone on, from the White House down to the JOC, about how to prosecute the Iranian target. Even on that night some of the arguments were unresolved. And so, remarkably, the special operators made their own decision, as someone who watched events develop in Irbil points out: 'The general feeling in the JOC was "nobody can make their minds up . . . let's just do it!"'

JSOC had not put themselves out on a limb policy-wise, but there were some difficult matters of interpretation. Since November 2006 a new directive sanctioned by President Bush had allowed US forces in Iraq to kill or capture Iranian nationals if they were engaged in targeting Coalition forces. This change in Washington tied in with wider international developments: Hezbollah's success in the Lebanon war of June 2006, as well as Iran's continued defiance on the nuclear issue. The new mission had its own acronym, CII – Counter Iranian Influence.

Many in Iraq felt action was long overdue. The British had seethed with frustration at the increasingly obvious signs of Iranian involvement in the south. Late in 2006 one officer in Basra told me, 'Iran is at war with us here, killing British soldiers, and nobody seems to care.' The flow of EFP bombs, started in 2004, had been followed by growing human intelligence about the training of Iraqi insurgents in Iran as well as financial backing for attacks on Coalition forces. Finds of mortar rounds or rockets with recent Iranian markings had multiplied. These realities did not just affect the British in the south; MNF commanders knew that, by early 2007, most of the indirect fire attacks on the Green Zone were coming from Sadr City and other Shia areas. US intelligence reckoned that Iranian support for Iraqi insurgents was so extensive that anything up to 150

Members of Task Force Knight showing their eclectic taste in camouflage clothing. The points of light on their helmets are produced by their night-vision equipment.

An AH-6 Little Bird helicopter takes off from the MSS with British troops on board. These special operations helicopters were used for a variety of roles such as transport, observation and fire support.

Another scene at the MSS helipad. The tail of a British Lynx helicopter can be seen on the left.

A soldier at Basra Palace, walking down a protected path made necessary by the frequent rocket and mortar attacks during 2006 and 2007. Rex Features

US Marines wait concealed in a building overlooking a road near Yusufiyah, November 2004. Rex Features

A member of A Squadron pictured with an American special operator in Baghdad in 2007.

By early 2007 and the start of the surge, US helicopters had lost their invulnerability to insurgent fire – several were lost in a few weeks. Rex Features

An Iraqi policeman checks a car at the entry control point to Fallujah, November 2006. Getty Images

A US soldier patrols the site of a car–bomb attack in Baghdad in September 2007. AFP/Getty Images

Norman Kember pictured in a kidnappers' video with orange jumpsuit and the
Swords of Righteousness Brigade's symbol. Rex Features

An early video picturing the four hostages from the Christian Peacemaker Team.
Norman Kember is on the far right, next to Tom Fox, the American who was
murdered by the kidnappers. Rex Features

A series showing British special forces during an early operation to seize a gunman. His weapon can be seen on the ground in one picture. The rudimentary nature of this early operation is shown by the unarmoured Land Rover and the soldiers' basic personal equipment. It also became unusual to see such incidents in daylight. AFP/Getty Images

Doura marketplace in Baghdad, previously thriving but deserted at the height of violence there in April 2007.
Mark Urban

The Combat Outpost in Doura market, where US and Iraqi troops came under daily attack during the surge of early 2007.
Mark Urban

Members of the Sons of Iraq militia group receiving their pay. For a few dollars a day thousands of men, many of them Sunni insurgents, were hired away from the insurgency as part of the Awakening strategy.
Mark Urban

US Marines entering a house near Yusufiyah prior to establishing an observation post. The business of entering Iraqi homes was a daily routine for ground-holding units as well as special forces ones, and a constant source of friction in insurgent strongholds.
Rex Features

members of the Iranian Revolutionary Guard Corps or other special forces were in Iraq at any one time. For several months the Pentagon had kept quiet about its growing losses to the Iranian proxies; commanders knew that public accusations would create a demand for action.

The problem with trying to close down this Iranian operation was that many were afraid of fighting on two fronts at once. Al-Qaeda was far from broken, despite its rout in Ramadi. Nobody wanted to repeat 2004's mistake of triggering a war with the Mehdi Army at the same time as the Fallujah operation. Abu Musab al-Zarqawi had himself sought to embroil the US in a war with Iran as a means of further weakening the superpower. Wouldn't targeting Iranians be doing exactly what he had wanted?

Of one thing they were sure at Balad: it was essential to maintain the pressure of nightly raids against AQI. The Pentagon's solution was to keep the commander of Delta, working through the JOC, in charge of the fight against the Sunni jihadists. At this time this effort (formerly codenamed TF-145) was referred to as Task Force 16. A new command, based around the headquarters of an army special forces group (Tier 2 special ops), was designated Task Force 17 and given the mission of Counter Iranian Influence. TF-17 could, and did, draw on the same Predators or Delta squadron as TF-16. But putting these command arrangements in place was just a small part of the picture. The big question about killing or capturing Iranians was one of political judgement.

In Baghdad on 21 December the US had captured two Iranians it believed were senior officers in the Quds Force, the branch of the Revolutionary Guards that operated in support of Iran's overseas allies. The arrests had produced a hue and cry from Iran, the State Department and some Iraqi leaders. Nine days later the Iranian prisoners had been released.

Three weeks on, the Delta commandos moving through the corridors of the Iranian Liaison Office in Irbil were under pressure to find compelling evidence of Iranian involvement in the insurgency. As they burst into rooms they found staff hurriedly trying to destroy records and, bizarrely, alter their appearance by cutting off hair. The men had fake ID cards and one would later test positive for handling explosives. The Americans were looking for two senior figures from across the border: Mohammed Jafari, the deputy head of Iran's Security Council, and General Minjahar Frouzanda, head of intelligence in the Revolutionary Guards.

The Irbil raid had resulted from human intelligence. The CIA Station in the Kurdish region had learned about the visit of the two top Iranians from one of its agents. The British government did not want Task Force Knight to arrest Iranians and so they could only watch what was about to happen.

However, the 'fixing' of Delta's targets was not all that it might have been. As the raid proceeded, failing to find the two senior officials at the Liaison Office, the Delta team moved swiftly to Irbil airport, a few miles to the north, in case they were trying to escape by plane. There was a tense standoff between the Americans and Kurdish troops. The Delta team was withdrawn, taking five arrested Iranian officials with them, and the recriminations started. The MNF press office in Baghdad put out a release better calculated to soothe ruffled Kurdish feathers than reveal anything of substance: 'Coalition Forces conducting routine security operations in Irbil Jan. 11 detained six individuals suspected of being closely tied to activities targeting Iraqi and Coalition Forces. One individual was released and five remain in custody.'

Iraq's President and Foreign Minister, both Kurds, knew that the operation was anything but routine. They considered the raid to be a humiliating violation of their authority. Some Iraqi

Kurdish officials used a similar line to that adopted by Iran in response to the raid – one that had also been deployed after the 21 December arrests in Baghdad – that the Iranian officials had been there at the invitation of the Iraqi authorities on a mission to improve security cooperation between the two countries. Since the Kurds were the group usually most supportive of America's mission in Iraq, this political blowback was particularly embarrassing. State Department officials were soon asking the army to release the five Iranians. The generals refused, producing a standoff within the US bureaucracy. Admiral William Fallon, running the wider Middle East theatre at Central Command, backed the decision in Baghdad. American commanders wanted Irbil to send a signal and they believed that it had got through, one telling me, 'They realised we were coming after them. The Iranians didn't like doing much dirty work or getting their hands dirty. A lot of them would prefer the Arabs to do the dying.'

TF-17's early operations had netted an intelligence treasure trove. Analysts got to work using the same network mapping and phone record techniques that they were employing against the jihadists. But the evidence of official Iranian sponsorship of insurgent groups posed almost as many questions as it answered. Brigadier Mohsen Chirazi, the Quds Force officer arrested in Baghdad in December, had been found in the compound of Abdul Aziz Hakim, the leader of the Supreme Council for the Islamic Revolution in Iraq. Everyone had long believed that SCIRI and its armed militia, the Badr Brigade, were agents of Iranian influence because the movement had been exiled to Iran during the Saddam era. In fact, much of SCIRI's middle management had grown up in Iran.

Analysis of papers and phones tied to Chirazi and the Irbil raid revealed that the Iranians were assisting a much wider variety of insurgent groups than many might have expected. Indeed, the

Irbil raid produced evidence of connections with the Ansar al-Sunna, a Sunni jihadist group that happily killed Kurd and Shia alike. Connections similarly were charted between the Iranians and elements within the Mehdi Army, even though its leader Muqtada al-Sadr insisted he was an Iraqi nationalist and bulwark against Iranian influence. Furthermore, Muqtada's people regularly clashed with the Badr Brigade in the south. Reviewing this material, British intelligence analysts came to the conclusion that Iran would back anyone who undermined the Coalition project in Iraq and produced a weak, compliant neighbour. The captured material could not answer questions such as whether Iran's President Ahmedinejad or Supreme Leader Ayatollah Ali Khamenei had directed the Quds Force to set up these networks.

The picture uncovered by these raids was so complex that it required new language among the Coalition intelligence analysts. If people within the Mehdi Army were taking Iranian money and weapons to carry out attacks on Coalition forces or elements from the Badr Brigade were doing the same, when the political line of both movements excluded direct confrontation with Coalition troops, how should they be categorised? The analysts initially called them Secret Cells, and later Special Groups, but the idea was that they were Iranian-funded extremists who had a parasitic existence within broader Shia political movements. They were, to coin the phrase applied to Sunni extremists at the time, 'irreconcilables'. As such, the Special Groups were deemed suitable for the JSOC treatment – if, of course, they did not strike first.

It was a meeting typical of the security coordination machinery all over Iraq. An American police liaison team had gone to the Provincial Joint Coordination Centre in Kerbala, south of Baghdad. The soldiers came from an airborne artillery battery based at Forward Operating Base Kalsu, near Iskanderiyah. Their mission that day in Kerbala was to discuss security precautions for the forthcoming Ashura celebrations. As one of the main Shia pilgrimage sites, Kerbala could expect hundreds of thousands of visitors and with them the threat of al-Qaeda suicide bombing. The pattern was already too well established for such attacks, designed to sustain the outrage caused by the Samarra bombing and many other sectarian provocations, to be ignored. So the Americans were meeting Iraqi security chiefs to discuss what needed to be done. Places like the Joint Coordination Centre had sprung up all over Iraq and were a hallmark of the Coalition trying to concert a joint approach to security as they turned over authority for policing province by province. Sites like Kerbala were heavily fortified and the American soldiers, once they'd avoided the perils of the drive from the FOB, tended to relax.

It was around 5.45 p.m. when a convoy of black GMC Suburban SUVs came into the Centre, pulling up by the Americans' parked Humvees. Movements by such vehicles were so routine in the comings and goings of contractors or the shadier US government types that the Iraqi guards simply waved them in. The impression of normality would only have been enhanced by the fact that the dozen or so men in the vehicles were wearing the new-pattern American combat clothing and carrying M4 assault rifles.

Acting on excellent information, a couple of the GMCs moved around to the back of the building closer to where the security meeting was taking place. On a signal, men moved from the vehicles to attack the building front and back, initially throwing in stun grenades. They swiftly took two American officers from the meeting, dragging them out to the GMCs while a second group assaulted an upper floor. A grenade killed one and wounded three other Americans meeting in a police office. A third group of gunmen attacked one of the parked Humvees, dragging two US soldiers from it.

Little more than ten minutes later the attackers, with their four captives bound, drove out of the compound. The Iraqi police were soon in pursuit, heading east across the Euphrates. The gunmen eventually took the decision to abandon their prisoners and vehicles in order to make good their own escape. Before they did so all four Americans were shot in the head.

The Kerbala attack came as a body blow to the Americans. Five soldiers had been killed. Its audacity and sophistication ranked far above anything the average Iraqi insurgent network was capable of. The US Army initially put out a story that the four men had been ambushed on patrol. But the real version – that they had been abducted and murdered, with suspected Iranian involvement – was soon being broadcast. A few days after the incident, the *Washington Post* was given a detailed briefing on the new CII mission, presenting the revelation to its readers with the shock headline 'US Troops Authorized to Kill Iranian Operatives in Iraq'.

The *Post* article carried the unmistakable hallmark of an authoritative public warning to Iran. Less well-sourced articles appeared too, alleging the Kerbala operation was an attempt to kidnap counterhostages for the 'Irbil five', that a mock-up of the Joint Coordination Centre inside Iran had been used to train operatives for the raid and that two senior police officers in Kerbala were under investigation for tipping off the attackers about the meeting with the Americans.

In the aftermath of the Kerbala attack TF-17 were infused with an even stronger sense of purpose. But al-Qaeda and its jihadist allies demanded attention too. On 22 January multiple attacks killed 130 people in Baghdad. Early in February a huge truck bomb claimed 135 lives in the Sadriya district of the city. Intelligence analysts worried that the fighters driven out of Ramadi late the previous year had simply headed for Baghdad or the belts around the city, towns such as Yusufiyah or Baquba from which many of these attacks were launched.

The commander of Delta, Colonel *Grist*, still had the TF-16 mission of hunting down AQI and its associated groups. A new colonel, in charge of the 'white' or overt Special Force Group HQ posted to Iraq, ran TF-17. 'It was an uncomfortable relationship,' says one who watched them face off at Balad. 'You got this competition for resources, scarce things like aircraft or detainee facilities.' *Grist* could hardly be expected to hand over his people or indeed the JOC at Balad itself to the CII team whenever they needed it.

Lieutenant-General McChrystal wasn't comfortable with this arrangement either, and soon had the special forces colonel in charge of TF-17 replaced by someone from the inner team, a lieutenant-colonel from Delta Force. Although this rearrangement of command roles was achieved without too much ill will, the original arrangement lived on in one important aspect. The Tier 2 special ops units posted around the country, particularly the US Army Green Berets mentoring Iraqi elite units, became actively involved in the campaign against Iranian-backed Special Groups, whereas they had only occasionally supported TF-16's fight against al-Qaeda. In this respect the widening of JSOC's target set was at least accompanied by a significant increase in the number of troops available to conduct takedown operations.

What was Britain's role in this? To many in London, particularly on the political side, Bush's tough public rhetoric seemed like irrational hubris – why pick a fight with a major regional power or indeed Iraq's Shia majority when Sunni militants were still so dangerous? The counter-Iran strategy also seemed like a deliberate slight towards the great and good of the US Iraq Study Group who had recommended the previous December that the administration reach out to Iran in the search for solutions.

In MI6 headquarters at Vauxhall Cross, or at Hereford, opinion however had hardened against Iran. The evidence of Iranian involvement, at first regarded sceptically, had become compelling.

British soldiers were being killed by Shia special groups at a depressing and, it appeared, rising rate. Some of those who studied the UK intelligence picture at this national level reached the conclusion that Iran saw Britain as the soft underbelly of the Coalition. '[It's] pretty hard to understand it in any other terms,' one such official told me. 'It's pretty clear the Iranians would like to say they've forced our withdrawal.'

Those who shared this analysis could see no problem with attacking Iraqi members of the special groups, although there were clear UK orders that Iranian nationals should not be taken by Task Force Knight. The British government also decided to exclude its forces from certain intelligence-gathering measures being taken to prepare possible strikes against Iran. All of those who I have asked insist, for example, that the SAS did not carry out operations inside Iran. But while the Coalition analysts in Iraq understood better as a result of the Baghdad and Irbil raids how these Iranian-backed groups worked, there were doubts that the British task force in Baghdad could do much about them, even within their own defined area of operations. This became a major priority for Richard Williams, the CO of 22 SAS, who once more deployed Task Group HQ to Iraq early in 2007. The new deployment, codenamed Operation TRACTION 2, was part of a specific drive to target Shia militants, particularly in the south.

Britain had, by early 2007, devoted a huge amount of intelligence effort to building up a better understanding of the rat lines used between Iran and Iraq. This took the form of building up agent networks who understood the movement of people or goods to and from Iran and of surveillance operations along the border. It also involved some exotic new intelligence techniques. Prior to America's move to a 'kill or capture' policy on Iranian agents, dozens had been arrested and then released. Many of these men were 'biometrically logged' and this was done in such a way that their identity could be quickly confirmed when they were arrested.

By early 2007 British intelligence people felt increasingly confident that they understood infiltration routes from Iran, but the question of how to combat the Quds Force remained a vexed one. The Iranian officers were careful enough not to carry weapons or bombs themselves and used fake IDs. If the Iranian consultants were off limits for political reasons, what about the Iraqi management of the Secret Cells? New targets could certainly be developed for Task Force Knight, but many still harboured doubts about the possible consequences. And while this question was debated by those in charge the wind of change swept through the headquarters of the Multi-National Force. For General Casey had finally run out of road with his political masters. He had departed, and his successor arrived in Baghdad.

15

AMERICA'S SURGE

On 23 January General David Petraeus stepped into the room for his confirmation hearing in front of the Senate Armed Services Committee. He moved forward with his distinctive gait, to a chorus of photographers' shutters. With the announcement of his appointment to succeed George Casey and implement the new Bush Administration strategy, Petraeus had become an intensely newsworthy and controversial figure. Little wonder he quipped that morning that he had received many e-mails with the subject line 'Congratulations – I think'.

The challenges facing US forces in Iraq were bewildering. In Washington there was a widespread assumption that Iraq was already a lost cause. Petraeus himself conceded that events had produced the prospect of a 'failed Iraqi state'. But there was something else in the atmosphere that morning – something toxic closer to home, a taste of the bitter partisanship generated by the President's war. Critics of the invasion had taken a full-page advert in the *New York Times* with a picture of the nominee for command in Baghdad and a headline 'General Betray Us'.

To many of that growing number of Americans who opposed the Iraq war, General Petraeus seemed to be the man being sent out in a desperate attempt to get the President off the hook. In addition, the way in which the White House had formulated its new policy – politely greeting but ignoring the broad-based Iraq Study Group report and opting instead for the 'Choosing Victory' blueprint of a right-wing thinktank – had angered some on Capitol Hill.

Petraeus knew that some in that Senate committee were willing the whole endeavour to fail. He pleaded for time. He insisted that the new strategy was different because 'for a military commander, the term "secure" is a clearly defined doctrinal task, meaning to gain control of an area'. Petraeus said that although the new approach was a comprehensive one, involving many political or economic aspects, it was essential for security to be improved first, particularly in Baghdad. In his prepared remarks, he refrained from accusing Iran by name of involvement in the insurgency, instead referring only to 'regional meddling'.

Nobody had seriously thought that the general would not be confirmed in his post. Although there were some inevitable barbs from senators critical of the administration, there were equally many who paid testimony to the man's long service.

Petraeus was a paratrooper by training who had survived serious accidents on the firing range and drop zone. He had led the 101st Airborne Division into Iraq in 2003, taking control of the northern part of the country, including the city of Mosul. During his time there he had launched many programmes to win over the local populace and the city, despite its dangerous multi-ethnic mix, had not produced the flashpoint many had predicted.

Things changed once Petraeus left. As a three-star and head of the Transition Command he had been given the job of licking Iraqi security forces into shape. There were those within the army who argued that responsibility for the failures of the Iraqi army, such as during the 2006 Baghdad Security Plan, rested at least in part with Petraeus. He had left Iraq in September 2005 to run Fort Leavenworth, the army's command and staff college. There he headed the panel of officers that issue the counterinsurgency manual, which contained ideas, for example about securing the population, that had already been proven in Ramadi.

The general had promised the senators that he would give them regular reports on the progress of the new strategy and in doing so demonstrated a political astuteness many colleagues had already seen. His choice of words was so careful – for example he avoided picking a fight with Iran in his hearing – that he was able to shape his message to any particular audience with great deftness. Once on his way to Iraq, Petraeus stopped in London.

He had to brief Tony Blair on what he intended to do. He also needed to gauge the depth of Britain's commitment to remaining in Iraq. Petraeus knew only too well that the war had become a political millstone around Blair's neck, but needed to get a feel for the bilateral issues including whether the British division in the south would continue to withdraw come what may, and whether Task Force Knight would remain committed to the Baghdad fight. The new commander seemed sanguine about the British drawdown in the south and, alluding to the more secret aspects of what the country was doing, told one person who met him in London that 'the UK brings considerable assets to this in the intelligence world and other areas'. Petraeus had some personal business too. He wanted to make sure that the British government would extend the tenure of his British deputy, Lieutenant-General Graeme Lamb.

Lamb and Petraeus had become firm friends during their time as divisional commanders. One officer describes them giggling together during a command presentation late in 2003. Both, apparently, could detect the idiocy in some of the Coalition's early plans. Knowing early in 2007 that the tenure of the Senior British Military Representative in Iraq was normally six months and that Lamb was already more than halfway through, Petraeus needed to get it extended. He had been in frequent e-mail correspondence with Lamb during the autumn and knew something about the work the British general was doing with the Awakening movement. The new commander wanted continuity in this vital task and the British government agreed to be flexible.

During his short stop in London, the aspects in which Petraeus really valued Britain's contribution thus became clear: he wanted the SAS, he wanted MI6 and he wanted Graeme Lamb. He rated the Iraqi Prime Minister as weak and inexperienced. If Maliki wasn't up to it, the Coalition needed to drive the reconciliation process.

The first surge brigade into Baghdad, one belonging to the 82nd Airborne Division, arrived in February. In all, the Pentagon planned to add five extra brigade combat teams, two more US Marine battalions and a variety of other units totalling nearly thirty thousand. Doing this required them to strain every sinew – extending some units from twelve- to fifteen-month tours, shortening time between tours and stopping many soldiers leaving.

Despite the effort involved, the peak troop strength would only be achieved for a short period between April and September 2007. The surge was not sustainable – not with regular units at least. The 'Choosing Victory' paper had envisaged a large mobilisation of National Guard brigades for a second phase, if one was required, but few regarded this prospect with relish.

Petraeus had to deliver improvements in Baghdad, mollify critics in Congress and somehow – the most nebulous part of his mission – create a breathing space in which Iraqi politicians might operate more effectively.

With these huge additional forces involved and such important political stakes, it might be wondered what role Petraeus envisaged for JSOC and Task Force Knight in all this. He told many people during those early weeks, 'You cannot kill your way out of an insurgency.' That was precisely the approach some of the door-kickers felt they had been applying. But, above them, McChrystal and others knew both that they were not trying to kill their way out of the insurgency (their tactics involved many captures too) and that under their new commander the special ops takedowns would continue to have a vital role in reducing the suicide bombing threat in Baghdad while thwarting Iranian influence. In fact, with the coming of General Petraeus the message to the secret warriors was to redouble their efforts.

Once Petraeus was hard at work in Baghdad a great many advisers were able to shape his ideas. In the case of Graeme Lamb, the plain-speaking Brit was able to move his efforts to woo tribal sheikhs into a higher gear. He was also influential in formulating new strategies to combat the car bombs in Baghdad. Petraeus was determined to put high concrete T-walls around certain markets or neighbourhoods in order to control access. He called it creating 'gated communities'.

Petraeus's ideas on Iran and the Counter Iranian Influence mission were only half formed when he arrived in Baghdad. He believed the Irbil raid had worried the Revolutionary Guards in Tehran but thought that any further steps needed to be considered with great care. He was particularly worried about being drawn into stand-up fights in places like Sadr City before the Sunni insurgency had been tackled.

Lamb provided a concept of operations at this time, called the Squeeze Box. One special operations officer who was briefed by the general recalls:

[Lamb] produced this spectrum chart. On the right was lethal Iranian influence and on the left was al-Qaeda in Iraq. In the middle you have the 'squeeze box', ordinary people you needed to win over. By using Task Force 17 to neutralise the Iranians and Task Force 16 on al-Qaeda you could allow the middle ground to escape the influence of the extremes.

Petraeus endorsed these ideas and added his own political top-spin. He leant on Nouri al-Maliki, the Iraqi leader, to publicly condemn Iranian interference and to support the removal of senior government or security forces figures found to have coop-erated with the Shia militias. It was vital for the new effort to be seen as even-handed, or at least more so than the security drives of 2006. This was not just a matter of political stage management; it also reflected the reality that Shia militants were killing grow-ing numbers of Coalition soldiers at the same time as the Sunni strike rate was showing some signs of slackening. The drive against the Special Groups was about to move into a different gear. The trigger would prove to be an operation by Task Force Knight.

16

THE KHAZALI MISSION

On a mid–March night some members of G Squadron found themselves aboard a Hercules, deploying once again to Basra. In the near darkness of the cargo hold, men listened to their iPods or dozed. The blades rotating through their duty at Task Force Knight had become used to shuttling back and forth, but this tour of G Squadron, which was coming towards its end, had seen more of it than most. The higher tempo of strike operations started the previous autumn by Major–General Shirreff had not stopped with his departure. Although the SAS presence at Basra Palace had been upgraded through the formation of Task Force Spartan early in 2007, extra people were sometimes needed for big jobs, and this was one of those occasions.

One senior Coalition commander told me, 'Even in late 2006 there was a recognition of how involved the Iranians were in a number of issues. They had in mind a compliant and weak Iraq. They'd been getting an absolutely free ride for some time.' This latest serial in Basra was a further attempt to do something about it. It was a result of intelligence-gathering on a player called Qais Khazali. The 'find' part of the F3EA (find-fix-finish-exploit-analyse) doctrine had not been hard. Reports from human and other sources gave him a central role in organising militant break-aways from the Mehdi Army.

Qais Khazali was a Shia cleric who had studied under Muqtada al-Sadr's father before Sadr senior's assassination by the Saddam regime in 1999. Khazali had been close to Muqtada after the US invasion, acting for a time as his spokesman. But following the Second Sadrist Rising of late 2004 the two men had fallen out, with Khazali favouring continued operations against Coalition forces and Muqtada a ceasefire. The two had drifted in and out of alliance, Khazali all the time gaining importance and follow-ers. By mid-2006 Khazali had secured leadership over a group of rejectionists within the Sadrist movement who were taking large amounts of cash and weaponry from Iran.

Moving against Shia extremists was a particularly delicate issue with the Iraqi Prime Minister Nouri al-Maliki. His own small party, bereft of a militia, was in coalition with other Shia move-ments that had much to lose from any attempt to shut down their armed groups. General Petraeus and US Ambassador Ryan Crocker thus spent much time during the early weeks of 2007 convincing Maliki that their surge against the extremists required an even-handed approach – it could not simply be an anti-Sunni campaign. 'Dave and Ryan were working Maliki day and night,' says one senior US officer. But they found that Maliki had a naïve faith in the likes of Muqtada al-Sadr's assurances that his people were not attacking Coalition forces or contributing aggressively to the problem.

So Petraeus and Crocker started briefing Maliki with sensitive intelligence material, including telephone intercepts of some of his Shia allies crowing about how they were pulling the wool over the Prime Minister's eyes. Someone party to those briefings remarks, 'We showed him what those assholes were doing.' Maliki's attitude started to change but, lest he be saying one thing and planning another, the Americans leaked that they were listening in on the Prime Minister himself. It was all a process of what the senior officer describes as 'manipulation'. Maliki, says another player in this high-level intelligence gambit, 'goes from "the Shia can do no wrong" to a situation where he's listening to tapes and seeing product which made him think certain people were making a buffoon of him'.

In the case of Qais Khazali, Coalition intelligence had been aware of his role as an Iranian proxy for some months. But the officers briefing Maliki found '[Khazali's group was] allies of some kind with Maliki, they had something on him, which gave them some kind of political top cover.' It was only once the Iraqi Prime Minister had finally been convinced early in March to agree to an operation that the Khazali target pack could be passed to British special forces.

The operation against Khazali, due to take place on the night of 20 March, first required the SAS to 'fix' him. One member of the regiment says their trip to Basra that night was the logical result of 'a lot of exploitation of human intelligence in southern Iraq over a period of eighteen months'. The picture built of rat lines from Iran into Basra had allowed certain locations to be pinpointed. Another figure connected with the operation says, 'Once we decided to target him, it all happened amazingly quickly,' adding that their intelligence analysts had realised 'hit these dudes and we're laughing'. The trigger was specific information about the place where Khazali might be found.

The ground assault force was duly dispatched into the darkness in Basra. They hit the house where Khazali was staying without injury on either side.

Having found, fixed and finished the operation, it entered its critical phase. For it was in the exploitation and analysis that this raid was to emerge as the most significant Task Force Knight action of the entire Operation CRICHTON saga. In the house in Basra were several other people. Among them was Laith Khazali, Qais's brother, and a middle-aged Arab man who pretended to be deaf-mute. Along with the arrests came a haul of critical documents.

One of these papers was a twenty-two-page report on the Kerbala raid two months earlier. It described in great detail preparations for the operation and its execution. It identified Azhar al-Dulaimi as the commander responsible for this sophisticated raid, which resulted in the deaths of five American soldiers. A month after G Squadron seized these papers, Dulaimi was killed by US forces. The Kerbala memo also contained entries of a high political significance: indicators that Iran's Quds Force had approved the operation.

There were other memos too. Some listed attacks on British bases such as the Palace and Shatt al-Arab Hotel. Others indicated payments ranging from $750,000 to $3 million per month. Analysts who studied the documents considered that the payments were linked to performance in the execution of attacks on the Coalition. Perhaps the most extraordinary information yielded by that night's raid, though, concerned the manacled man who was taken northwards by Hercules soon afterwards, still pretending not to be able to hear or speak.

After three weeks of dumb-show, confronted by his interrogators with detailed information seized in the raid, the prisoner revealed that he could talk – and with a Lebanese accent. His name was Ali Mussa Daqduq, and since 1983 he had been a member of Hezbollah, the militant Shia group in his country.

Daqduq had risen to positions of considerable responsibility, at one time running Hezbollah leader Mohammed Nasrallah's bodyguard team, at others leading some of the movement's highly effective military units. Once Daqduq decided to talk the Coalition intelligence people learned a great deal.

Daqduq had been brought in by the Quds Force leadership in Tehran as a sort of insurgent management consultant. Since Hezbollah had become so expert in IEDs and other techniques during its long war with Israel, could they not raise the game of those fighting the British in Basra? He described how he had travelled from Lebanon to Tehran in May 2006 to receive his orders from the deputy commander of the Quds Force. He had then made four trips into Iraq where he reorganised the Shia Special Group cell structure, reported on their indirect fire as well as IED attacks and organised groups of Iraqis to travel into Iran for further training.

One of the Britons analysing the take from the 20 March raid in Basra argues, 'The case was proven from an intelligence point of view long before Daqduq.' The captured Hezbollah officer's debriefing, when set alongside other information gathered by the Coalition, demonstrated – and in a detailed way that could be publicly exploited – the role of Iran's Quds Force in funding and directing operations that had killed US and British soldiers. The only real issue outstanding was whether specific leadership figures, including Ayatollah Khamenei or President Ahmedinejad, had given clearance for operations like Kerbala.

General Petraeus changed his previously cautious public line about Iranian proxy operations in Iraq. Shortly after reviewing the intelligence seized in the SAS's Basra raid, he said at a press briefing, 'The Iranian involvement has really become much clearer to us and brought into much more focus during the interrogation of the members – the heads of the Khazali network and some of the key members of that network.' The SAS mission, just like Delta's January move in Irbil, had made a strategic impact. In this sense the Khazali operation ranked alongside LARCH-WOOD 4 as the most significant of the entire British special forces campaign in Iraq.

This new explicit language about Iran carried with it profound implications. Many in London or Washington wondered whether the US was about to go to war with Iran. Petraeus did not want this, but he did direct contingency planning for air strikes on Revolutionary Guard facilities inside the country. The raids would be launched if an attack attributable to Iran claimed the lives of many US soldiers – the exact number was not revealed. At the same time, the Americans resolved to use diplomatic channels to warn the Iranians about the possible consequences of what they were doing.

Since Petraeus was about to confront al-Qaeda in Baghdad and nearby Baquba in late 2007, the last thing he needed was an open fight with the wider Shia community or the Mehdi Army. So the CII covert operation, TF-17, was his weapon of choice. It would be used to step up raids against those acting as Iran's hitmen in Iraq. The information from the Khazali raid that resulted in the death of Azhar Dulaimi was just one aspect of this. Since the Coalition had leaders of the Special Groups in custody, their mapping of its networks received a huge boost, triggering raids throughout April and May. It was not a deniable or completely black campaign, but it was one in which the agility of special ops soldiers would be used to keep the profile low, thus avoiding the crisis that something like a full-scale offensive in Sadr City might cause.

In order to mount these operations Task Force 17 relied a good deal on the US Army's Green Berets mentoring teams with the emerging ISOF (Iraqi Special Operations Forces) units. The Americans had embedded what they called 'A Teams' or ODAs (from Operational Detachment Alpha) in outfits such as the Iraqi

National Intelligence Service's special forces and the Iraqi army's commando brigade. These US units, of around twenty men, became during the course of 2007 the key to Coalition operations in provinces such as Dhi Ghar or Maysan, where the British had pulled back. One senior American figure comments, 'It is hardly recognised how the entire situation in the south depended upon a very small number of US special forces soldiers.' Acting as mentors to Iraqi SOF, the use of these teams also ensured that operations in Shia militant strongholds had an Iraqi face to them – something of great symbolic importance in the US relationship with Iraq's government. Of course the American A Teams did not at that time have the run of Basra. Task Force Spartan was to be highly active throughout 2007 but, as the British discovered, the dynamic of confronting Iranian influence was quite different for them.

At 10.30 a.m. on 23 March a group of fifteen Royal Navy sailors and Royal Marines had gone in two inflatable boats to investigate a vessel in the lower part of the Shatt al-Arab waterway. It was just three days after the Khazali raid and naval officers had noted an upward trend in Iranian Revolutionary Guard violations of waters claimed by Iraq.

The British mission that day was to board a ship carrying cars to make sure it was not involved in smuggling. Their parent ship, the frigate HMS *Cornwall*, stood off in deeper waters while the search was made. *Cornwall*'s helicopter, which had originally covered the boarding, providing vital surveillance over the horizon, returned to the ship after a quarter of an hour in order to refuel. It was at this moment that two speedboats belonging to the Revolutionary Guards moved swiftly to the boarded craft, apparently catching the British naval party by surprise before they had completed their mission.

As soon as the Iranians told the members of the *Cornwall*'s crew that they were under arrest, a further six Revolutionary Guard speedboats were launched to cover the operation of removing the British. The sailors and marines were disarmed and, while an Iranian cameraman filmed them, sped under arrest back to a nearby naval base. Under the rules of engagement then applied by the Royal Navy, no attempt was made to stop them.

Iran's seizure of the boarding party soon developed into a major international incident. Much attention was focused on the lone female captive, the chain-smoking Faye Turney. Iranian TV showed footage of the British officers apparently confessing their 'mistake' in being in Iranian waters at the time of capture.

In Baghdad the capture prompted immediate contingency planning for a British rescue effort. Although the practicalities of mounting such an operation into Iran were far less promising than those of getting two SAS men out of the Jamiat, JSOC responded in similar spirit. A Predator drone was swiftly scrambled to assist the British.

Other preparatory steps were taken to facilitate a rescue mission. The Task Force Knight helicopter detachment at BIAP started to prepare for a move down south. An SAS liaison officer went down to Basra to discuss what might be done. The British divisional commander was by this point Major-General Jonathan Shaw, who had a poor working relationship with Lieutenant-Colonel Richard Williams, the SAS commander. Shaw was named joint commander for any rescue mission by PJHQ in Britain, so the two men would just have to get along.

However, the window for any rescue soon closed as intelligence and media reporting revealed that the captives had been taken north to Tehran. Britain used the diplomatic avenues open to it to pressure Iran, and on 4 April the detainees were duly released following a grand piece of political theatre, over which a beaming President Mahmud Ahmedinejad presided. In front of the world's press he decorated Iranian naval officers for their steadfastness and vigilance before releasing the sailors and marines with a gift of new suits. 'The Islamic government and the Iranian people,' he said, 'with all powers and legal right to put the soldiers on trial, forgave those fifteen. This pardon is a gift to the British people.'

So ended the drama of the Royal Navy's captured patrol. Media attention was focused on their behaviour and indeed whether they had really been inside Iraqi waters. Little was given to the issue of whether Britain was paying the price for the increasingly aggressive campaign against Iranian agents in Iraq. Certainly MNF headquarters in Baghdad had been sensitive to the possibility that strike operations like that against the Khazalis might expose Britain to retaliation in Basra or on the border. In an apparent attempt to deflect attention, some journalists had been briefed that American special forces had carried out the raid. And while direct action by Iran to embarrass Britain had always been feasible (other boat crews had been detained on the Shatt al-Arab waterway before), friends of the Khazalis also had the capability to strike back within Iraq.

This retaliation came in May 2007, when a convoy of heavily armed 'police' turned up at the Finance Ministry in Baghdad. They quickly found a British computer expert and the five bodyguards detailed to look after him, and spirited the men away. A nightmare had begun for the hostages, this time without the chance of a political showman like President Ahmedinejad turning it into a bloodless piece of propaganda.

The technique used to take the men was a trademark of the Special Groups – up to forty men in police commando uniforms with official-looking vehicles. It had been used against the Americans in Kerbala and to kidnap Iraqis belonging to the country's Olympic committee. It guaranteed passage through Baghdad's many checkpoints, and the large number of gunmen involved served to intimidate any bona fide policeman with suspicions, or indeed a western private security detail.

In their communiqués the kidnappers did not refer to themselves as Special Groups, a term developed by US intelligence, but as a resistance group called Asaib Ahl al-Haq or the 'League of the Righteous'. The League was in fact a name used by associates of Khazali, fellow breakaways from the Mehdi Army who were firmly in the pro-Iranian extremist camp. After initial public demands for the withdrawal of British troops from Iraq, the kidnappers revealed their true purpose. In return for the hostages they sought the release of the Khazali brothers and other named individuals detained under the Counter Iranian Influence raids.

Over time, the Finance Ministry kidnap affair showed the dangers of Britain adopting the CII mission, and specifically of G Squadron's raid in March. The Asaib Ahl al-Haq, like Iran itself, appeared to see the British as a softer touch than the Americans. Having detained the Khazalis and others, Task Force Knight had handed them over to US custody. The issue of whether the Special Groups or Quds Force prisoners should be freed therefore became a tricky bilateral question for America and Britain.

These political hazards were far from the only difficulties confronting G Squadron during the final weeks of its tour. The dangers of the job itself, particularly at the breakneck pace demanded by JSOC in confronting both Sunni and Shia extremist threats, carried plenty of risks of its own.

Task Force Knight had by early 2007 conducted so many takedowns that it had considered pretty much every aspect of the risk involved. It had lost just two men in Iraqi house assaults but had a great many more wounded, some seriously. Different methods were open to an assault force in hitting their Alpha, ranging from fast roping from a helicopter on to the roof to blowing their way in through walls with explosive charges. In most cases, particularly once a compound had been breached, there was no choice but to go from one room to another.

One veteran of many such assaults sums up the matter with dry fatalism: 'Going in, the bad guy is not going to be straight ahead of you. He is either to the left or to the right. At that point it's fifty-fifty really. You cannot look both ways at once, so you take your choice. If you enter and look left and he's on your right, you've got a problem.'

The regiment had done what it could to mitigate the risks, and body armour had been upgraded. Since 2005 the SAS had tried something quite new too. On certain assaults specially trained dogs had been sent into the Alpha. Those outside would then wait to see if the dogs flushed anybody out. But despite these new techniques the dangers of assaulting could not be eliminated. During the spring and summer of 2007 the regiment had several men seriously wounded, as it extended its operations into Sadr City, a particularly dangerous environment where, due to its built-up nature, it was harder to employ heavy weapons.

One issue thrown up in these months was the difference between UK and US rules of engagement, as well as in their general approach. The Americans, after some costly setbacks assaulting houses, were quite ready to drop a bomb, as in the Zarqawi case, or strafe a car from a helicopter gunship if their intelligence told them that the person inside had a history of taking life and could be about to do so again. One SAS officer characterises with brutal frankness the JSOC practice for dealing with its targets by this time: 'The only reason to capture someone in those circumstances was for intelligence. We were beyond the martyrdom argument, it had become an attritional campaign – we had to take them apart.'

British special forces went into Iraq with rules of engagement closer to those of their 'green army' colleagues. For a long time the DSF and CJO would not authorise the bombing of a house unless its occupants had shown signs of resistance, most obviously by shooting at Coalition troops but even, in some cases, simply by revealing weapons. Even then, if an assault had been ordered for intelligence-gathering purposes they could not necessarily shoot anyone inside who offered resistance. This produced much negative comment from Task Force Knight operators. Over time, Task Force Knight's rules of engagement had in fact been brought closer to those of the Americans. By 2007 they were, under certain circumstances, allowed to attack a house or car if they believed those inside to be terrorists about to perpetrate an act of violence. Even so, the anecdotal impression given by some British operators is that the Americans were more ready to authorise pre-emptive use of force in this way, and that the gap between approaches was never completely closed, despite changes to the Task Force Knight rules of engagement.

If the risks of storming an Alpha were greater for the British than the Americans, the odds of getting there unharmed were, some felt, better. Between January and April 2007 eight US military and two civilian helicopters had been shot down. This brought inevitable questions about whether the Iranians were supplying insurgents with new shoulder-launched anti-aircraft missiles or whether they were coming from some other source, since those left over from Saddam's army were by this time considered quite out of date.

In the first months of 2007 a series of complex ambushes had been laid for American helicopters. This produced some understandable nervousness in the RAF, but their pilots generally retained a confidence that their Pumas had superior defensive aids – countermeasures against the missiles – and their flying routines were constantly varied. 'If the Americans flew the same way, same day, same height, they were asking for it,' observes one Task Force Knight aviator. But the business of manoeuvring up to a dozen aircraft, at night, in unregulated airspace was inherently dangerous. On 15 April the Baghdad Puma detachment discovered just how risky it could be.

Task Force Knight's operation that early morning was a standard house assault against a suspected Sunni insurgent leader near Taji, twenty kilometres north of Baghdad. Taji was one of the classic Baghdad belt al-Qaeda strongholds and the scene of several previous raids. Because of the semi-rural nature of the target it had been decided to prosecute it with an air assault force. Both the blades and their support platoon from Task Force Maroon were to be landed in fields near the Alpha, a task requiring several Pumas.

The crews had a midnight briefing at MSS Fernandez and the mission got under way at 00.40 on 15 April. Eighteen minutes later the aircraft made their final approach to the landing zone. Or at least to the ground identified by the lead Puma's skipper as the landing zone. Dropping down from three hundred feet after crossing over some power lines, the first two helicopters, flying side by side, began their landing.

At this point the crews realised that they were off target, about to land in the wrong field. They had to make a snap decision. They could have flown forward, circled around and come in again. But the lead aircraft went into a hover and then began to fly backwards. It didn't go far, only about fifty metres, but it backed into the dust cloud billowing up just behind it. As the aircraft beside the lead ship executed the same manoeuvre the two helicopters lost the normal safety distance that ought to have separated them.

The first aircraft touched down and the SAS men started to leap out, but at that moment the rotors of the second Puma touched theirs. The tail boom of the first aircraft collapsed as a rotor sliced into the Puma's side and it tipped over. The second aircraft, just above the ground at the moment of the rotor strike, yawed violently.

Watching from above through his night-vision goggles, the pilot of the third helicopter in the operation was shocked to spot 'two people fall out of the right-hand door . . . it was very quick, just a flash'. In fact, three people had been flung out of the second helicopter: Sergeant Mark McLaren, one of the RAF Puma crew, Staff Sergeant Mark Powell, and another SAS soldier. The men had unclipped from their safety harnesses knowing they were about to touch down. The Puma crashed the last few feet to the ground and immediately tipped over, on top of the three men.

The shower of shattered rotor blades and other debris injured several other men on the ground. As the comms came alive with a mayday, soldiers from the first helicopter combined with survivors from the second to try to help their crushed colleagues. In the cases of McLaren and Powell, they struggled in vain. The other SAS soldier, seriously wounded, was flown to the Combat Support Hospital in central Baghdad where his life was saved.

Incidents like this during the final stage of G Squadron's tour showed how difficult the SAS's task had become. Its commanders had longed to operate at the same level as the Americans, out every night against a variety of targets. But Task Force Knight was operating with far less back-up against enemies hundreds of miles apart in Basra and Baghdad. The squadron had lost a man and had a dozen wounded – casualties amounting to around one third of those who embarked on the tour. And as their successors in A Squadron began to deploy, the pace of operations seemed to be increasing still further.

17

AL-QAEDA'S SURGE

The Iraqi parliament building is in fact an old conference centre from the Saddam era. In its central hall a band of murals looms high above those who enter. It shows doves of peace and stylised scenes from Iraqi history, a little like a Bayeux tapestry of Ba'athist cliché. On the first-floor mezzanine is a cafeteria where MPs gather for coffee and gossip.

By April 2007 the country was in a state of governmental and parliamentary gridlock. Nouri al-Maliki's national unity government appeared to form and dissolve, baffling the American diplomats who tried to bring the different sides together. For the lawmakers chewing over issues in the café, bills such as those to govern the extraction of the country's oil wealth or regulating militias became interminable struggles. At stake were sectarian, party and regional advantage.

Life as an Iraqi MP was, it can be imagined, hardly a bed of roses. Some had been murdered in their homes. Others faced constant threats. In the parliament building at least they could turn their minds to the job they had been elected to do. Entry to the Green Zone required special screening and, even once through that, there were two more security checks to get into the building itself.

Despite this, on 12 April a suicide bomber made his way up the stairs to the cafeteria. Finding a group of parliamentarians sitting at the tables he moved purposely onwards and detonated his device, killing himself and three MPs. Elsewhere in the city that day so many bad things were happening people dubbed it Black Thursday. Al-Qaeda destroyed a bridge at Sadriya that day too, killing eleven people and disrupting communications on a key Baghdad artery.

Strikes like the suicide bombing in parliament or the Sadriya bridge suggested to the Sunni militants that they could hit people pretty much wherever they wanted and that they could target national infrastructure too. Far away on Washington's Capitol Hill, Senator Joe Biden pronounced 'This war is lost.' The surge, he added, was not achieving anything. But the surge had barely begun, and in certain places al-Qaeda's power had been hardly touched.

The southern suburb of Doura had in its time been one of Baghdad's playgrounds. It was multi-ethnic, home to many professional families, thriving markets and restaurants. Doura's cafes had been choked with customers on spring evenings, smoking the *nargila* or hubble-bubble pipe while playing dominoes and watching the world go by. The area had even boasted some nightclubs.

By April 2007 it had been the scene of full-scale sectarian warfare for many months. Most of the Shia had been driven out and many Christians had taken their cue to leave when a suicide car bomb had been driven into one of their churches. The Mehdi Army retaliated by dumping murdered Sunnis outside one of the schools. One local man told me that he had stopped sending his children to school when the appearance of bodies, some with their eyes gouged out or showing signs of torture with electric drills, became an everyday occurrence.

Among the Sunnis, extremism was the order of the day. Reviewing security across the capital that summer, an Iraqi blogger described the situation: 'Doura is not under the authority of the Republic of Iraq. It is currently an Islamic emirate with its own departments and ministers.' Those who tried to contest al-Qaeda's power, like one local 1920 Brigades commander, were swiftly murdered.

Into this maelstrom were sent soldiers from 2-12 Infantry Battalion. They were ordered to establish a combat outpost (or 'Cop') in the heart of what had once been Doura's flourishing market. Fuelled by the new doctrine that security required American troops to live among the people and not 'commute to war' from the FOB, a few dozen soldiers camped out in abandoned shops, where I joined them as an embedded journalist in late April. Defended by little more than a few concrete blast walls and some razor wire, their situation felt intensely vulnerable. An Iraqi police station a few hundred yards away had been hit by a truck bomb, killing more than a dozen officers. General Petraeus's new ideas about securing the population required his men to take great risks. When a Cop outside Baquba was hit by a complex al-Qaeda attack on 24 April, nine American soldiers were killed.

Petraeus chose Doura as an early test ground for his new doctrines. By late April a few dozen shops had opened (although commanders claimed it was two hundred) and some at headquarters were hailing signs of progress. Any success at that moment seemed tenuous because al-Qaeda was conducting its own surge in the area.

The soldiers at Gator Cop, as Alpha Company's base in the market was called, were hit every day. Their Humvees got blasted with IEDs, RPGs were dropped into the base and snipers tried to pick off anyone who showed themselves in the streets. The market really only operated for two hours a day and once people had scurried home with the essentials they needed to subsist, the streets were largely deserted. Under strict Islamic law there was no question of the restaurants opening or men meeting to smoke and play dominoes.

Those on errands darted from one doorway to another and civilians with gunshot wounds were frequently brought into the Cop for treatment by its medics. Both al-Qaeda and some of the police, whom the locals considered a uniformed branch of the Mehdi Army, seemed to shoot people at random. The soldiers in Gator Cop reacted with gallows humour, having T-shirts printed with the slogan 'Doura Market – Shop 'til You're Dropped'.

In a place like this, both the ground-holding force, 2-12 Infantry, and special operations forces were free to mount operations in the *muhallas* or city blocks. But there was inevitably a hierarchy in the way these were applied. The infantry operating out of Gator Cop were under pressure to mount a raid every night, just as the OC of Task Force Knight was. But going out was so risky nobody wanted to do it for dry holes or to pick up an innocent man. Undoubtedly, though, they sometimes did, even if their record was generally a good one.

Accompanying Gator Company one April night we were joined by an NCO from the brigade's Tactical Humint Team – the equivalent of British Army Field Humint Teams run by the Defence Humint Unit. He brought with him an agent from one of the *muhallas* who was dressed up as an Iraqi interpreter, complete with balaclava to disguise his identity. Once inside the target house this agent discreetly identified two suspects. One proved to be a suspected bomb maker who had been organising IED attacks, the other was an innocent man who was released a couple of hours later with an apology.

At the same time that operations like this were being prosecuted every night, outfits like Delta and Task Force Knight, with their responsibility for the Baghdad area, were also free to work up target packs on networks in neighbourhoods like Doura. While this might have seemed like a recipe for conflict, it actually allowed ground-holding troops to exploit the special operators' natural competitiveness to their own advantage. In this situation, says one Task Force Knight veteran, 'liaison officers and OOB [out of bounds] boxes became the order of the day'. When a takedown operation was planned the liaison man would arrive with the local unit, install himself in their ops room and keep routine patrols out of their area of interest.

Members of the FHT attached to Task Force Knight therefore made it their business to cultivate the intelligence officers of the various American battalions around Baghdad. 'Delta thought it was beneath them but we were absolutely ruthless,' says one British humint operator. 'We would talk to anyone who could give us the information to get started.' Thus the arrival of Pumas became a regular event at FOB Falcon, a couple of miles to the south of Doura. There the British met the intelligence officers of US units operating in the Rashid District of southern Baghdad, which included such al-Qaeda strongholds as Doura. Task Force Knight also started to focus its attention on Arab Jabour, an area of farms and market gardens several miles further south, and another al-Qaeda bastion. If the American officers were agreeable, an agent meet would go ahead with the British there too. In this way the British developed takedown operations that had a direct impact on the fortunes of the ground-holding unit here, and therefore of the tentative progress of Petraeus's new approach.

The picture of al-Qaeda that emerged through humint operations in places such as Doura or Arab Jabour was of a very different organisation from the one that had baffled the spymasters in 2003 and 2004. It had gone from a small conspiracy dominated by foreign fighters into a widespread franchise, growing rapidly as the mercury of sectarian conflict had risen. In many places AQI used its reputation, money and profile to swallow up groups that had previously been loyal to less militant nationalist parties. One British officer comparing the intelligence he read in spring 2007 with that of an earlier tour notes the reporting featured 'the same tribal names, and the same towns on the outskirts of Baghdad were targeted – but they had changed allegiance from the Ba'athists to al-Qaeda'. During late 2005 and early 2006 this shift of tribal allegiances had in many places made life hell for Coalition troops and non-Sunni families because it added to the ranks of the militant organisation faster than JSOC could take people down. But this growth also opened greater possibilities for the penetration and neutralisation of al-Qaeda cells. This applied not only to humint organisations but to the burgeoning Awakening operation. For just as tribal sheikhs had switched the allegiance of their followers from the Ba'athists to the jihadists, so they might be persuaded to rent them en masse to the Awakening.

Even so, al-Qaeda's strength in places like Doura or indeed Baquba in the Baghdad belt posed some disturbing questions. If, as many people accepted by the spring of 2007, the extremists had been dealt with a few months earlier in Ramadi, was it not the case that they had simply shifted to Baghdad and Baquba? Some analysts wondered whether Petraeus would just be playing whack-a-mole, hitting al-Qaeda in one place only to see them pop up elsewhere.

For those waging the secret war of intelligence-gathering and strike operations, this new phase of the conflict required them to increase their tempo still further. If al-Qaeda could be defeated in Baghdad, just as they had been defeated in Ramadi, then the Coalition could claim a strategic victory. In mid-February 2007 Petraeus had launched a third version of the Baghdad Security Plan, called this time Operation Fardh al-Qanoun, or Law and Order. The al-Qaeda upsurge of April was clearly designed to break this new initiative, but could the organisation sustain its own surge?

During those early months of 2007 the organisation had shown its continued ability to perpetrate murder on a massive scale: a huge truck bomb in Tal Afar on the Syrian border had killed 152 people in late March; two days later eighty-two had died in multiple bombings of Shia neighbourhoods in Baghdad; a further wave of bombings claimed two hundred lives in the capital on 18 April; four days later eighty perished in a VBIED attack in Kerbala. Perhaps only a fool or an incurable optimist could have detected signs of hope in this. Yet among the intelligence analysts there were some who eschewed the apocalyptic.

In the first place, although some al-Qaeda cells still showed themselves capable of multiple suicide bombings or complex attacks the scale of these did not seem to match some of the earlier ones – for example the fourteen car bombs of 29 April 2005 or the huge attack on Abu Ghraib prison in the same month. Secondly, some began to wonder whether the new peak in activity of April 2007 carried an element of 'use it or lose it' among the car bombing cells. Their infiltration routes had become more difficult due to the large number of *Sakhwa* or Awakening groups mushrooming across Anbar. These groups were also being established in the Baghdad belts. On 2 May one of these Awakening groups, operating near Taji, had eliminated a minister in the jihadist Islamic State of Iraq. Jihadists driven out of Ramadi or other parts of Anbar appeared in places like Doura and they did not make themselves popular. Anxious to step up attacks on US forces and for the implementation of strict sharia, they soon alienated many of the city dwellers.

There were also those at Camp Slayer, where MNF Iraq's intelligence chief sat, and in the spooks' talking shops around the green zone who began wondering whether April's high levels of violence disguised an important underlying trend, which was that while the totals might still be going up, it was Shia militants who accounted for a growing proportion of this. Were attacks by Sunni jihadists actually falling while those by Shia were going up, boosting the aggregate total? Some American commanders in Baghdad were by that spring saying openly that Shia militants were responsible for the majority of attacks on Coalition forces.

Regardless of who was killing whom – and the issue was complex when US lives were taken by EFP bombs or other weapons supplied by Iran to extremists on both sides of the sectarian divide – the trend was still depressing. During the early part of 2007, anxious lest domestic support collapse, JSOC had briefed certain senior visitors on its covert campaign and Lieutenant-General McChrystal's view that al-Qaeda could not carry on taking this level of damage. Visitors were given JSOC's estimate that by early 2007 it had killed two thousand members of the Sunni jihadist groups as well as detaining many more. TF-16 was often mounting six raids per night. TF-17 could produce something similar. The effectiveness of these raids was increasing too.

McChrystal's high-tempo onslaught had begun in earnest barely two years earlier. JSOC's intelligence database had grown with each network it rolled up. 'The campaign matured,' argues one SAS officer, commenting that agent networks among the AQI cells were at last delivering good information. In fixing these targets, the growth of Iraqi mobile phone use to millions of subscribers and a steady increase in the number of drones available for surveillance meant time was on JSOC's side. The real issue, then, was whether the US political will to keep going with the surge would falter before JSOC's takedowns, the Awakening and the activities of ground-holding troops like 2-12 Infantry could exhaust al-Qaeda's supply of people and bombs.

From the parochial viewpoint of Task Force Knight, it entered May with new kit and new people. A Squadron was taking over from G, after its exhausting tour. The troops had been given new transport, an armoured vehicle far better protected than its old Humvees. Improved night-vision aids had come into use during the preceding months.

The SAS also donned new combat uniforms. They had for years been free to adopt a wide variety of camouflage, depending upon where they were operating. The new clothing, made by a firm called Crye Precision, was quite distinctive – darker than standard British desert camo and browner than the American combat uniform. Quickly dubbed Crye Kit by the blades, it was also used by Delta Force. The switch to these darker uniforms stemmed largely from a realisation that the sand-coloured desert uniforms used by both the US and British military made them too visible at night, when most of their operations were conducted.

As G Squadron quit the MSS for home, a new tour was starting. A tour that was to coincide with a new chapter in Iraq as a whole.

18

THE TIDE TURNS

The arrival of A Squadron at MSS Fernandez produced a certain nervous tension among the supporting players of Task Force Knight. 'The rivalry between squadrons was massive,' explains one intelligence specialist. 'They were obsessed with the tally they had achieved and outdoing the previous squadron.'

In truth, the kind of start that A Squadron wished to make depended to a considerable extent on the target packs that had been nurtured but not executed by G Squadron and other predecessors. One SAS operator notes, 'We inherited a very well-developed intelligence picture. It had become a well-functioning factory by that point and one squadron fed off the work of another.'

When one outgoing squadron departed, exhausted after six months of adrenaline-fuelled contacts, the new men would arrive full of enthusiasm. One intelligence operator who saw them come and go records: 'The squadron would turn up in country and say, "We're going out tonight, what have you got?" They would actually want a job on their first night. They would put the most intense pressure on for the intelligence needed to maintain their strike rate.'

This aggression was felt in the Task Force Knight helicopter detachment too. They had been chastened by April's fatal accident. However, as one pilot notes, 'the SF guys are hard people to say no to. They are charismatic. People don't want to say no because they want to be part of that legacy.'

Some, like D Squadron's OC the previous summer, tried to stand back a little and reflect on their target sets before throwing themselves into the fray, but the OC of A Squadron was cut from different cloth. Major *Kennedy* was the first squadron commander to come back into Iraq after serving there as a troop leader a few years earlier. He had been with Richard Williams's G Squadron as the insurgency got under way during the summer of 2003. Having been guided by the hard-fighting Williams at that formative stage, both men had gone up a step in rank.

'[*Kennedy*] had been brought on by Richard Williams . . . when he went back in command of A Squadron he proved to be even more operationally aggressive than Colonel Williams,' comments one of those who served under *Kennedy* in 2007. Another frontline observer remarks that A Squadron arrived with a highly competent, experienced selection of Team Leaders, making it 'a dream team across the board'. These five or six captains and staff sergeants worked away on target packs and missions – sometimes more than one a night – were cued up for the blades. With Task Force Knight operating as a highly tuned machine under a hard master, the contrast with the British effort in southern Iraq could not have been greater.

*

Back in February Tony Blair had confirmed in the House of Commons that Britain's plans to turn over security in southern Iraq would proceed apace. He justified this partly in terms of the success of Operation SINBAD. The military officers who sought to move on to Afghanistan and close the Iraq chapter as swiftly as possible deployed other arguments. The presence of British troops in the centre of Basra was itself attracting a great deal of militia activity. So many rockets or mortars were fired at the Palace or the Shatt al-Arab Hotel, with so many missing and falling into neighbouring civilian areas that, to quote one officer at the time, 'consent is evaporating'.

If this smacked of capitulation, SINBAD had at least demonstrated that the British army could not do much more, since the UK chain of command would not commit additional troops and the Iraqi security forces were keen to get the British out of the way too. All of this informed the appreciation of Major-General Jonathan Shaw, the commander of Multi-National Division South East for much of 2007. A senior American tells the following anecdote:

> I went down there because the situation in Basra was dire. I asked him [Shaw] 'What can we do to help?' He told me that he didn't need any help, that he had decided to withdraw his division to the airport where it would wait the decision to pull out. I looked at him and said, 'Well, thank you for your clarity. You have at least told me exactly what you are going to do.'

The British army was entering its final and most controversial phase in southern Iraq. Those who watched from Baghdad were saddened or even disgusted. One SAS man quips, 'Defeatist doesn't quite cover it.' A senior officer who worked in the capital reflects, 'The British in Baghdad actually made the intellectual adjustment that MND South East never made.' In his interpretation, those who acquired the Baghdad mentality had absorbed the American spirit of aggression, problem-solving and critical self-examination. The Basra crowd, by contrast, never escaped the collective cynicism of a professional group that had gone to Iraq thinking it knew better, and then blamed others for its failure.

Jonathan Shaw, in his defence, was operating under the directive of the Chief of Joint Operations back in the UK and indeed what happened next was simply the fruition of a plan laid out by the Prime Minister himself in February. The Old State Building (a small base right in the city centre) and the Shatt al-Arab Hotel were handed over to the Iraqi army and Provincial Iraq Control, or Pic, had been signed off in Maysan in April.

British troops left at the Palace became the focus of every militia mortar-man or IED-layer in search of a payday. Under constant bombardment, losses grew alarmingly as even supply runs produced intense street battles. The battlegroup based there was not supine: it mounted several strike operations, and one mission in April in which it had driven into the Hayyaniyah, effectively challenging the Mehdi Army to a fight. The British claimed to have killed two dozen militia without loss on their own side, but everybody in the city understood the way events were going and on 2 September Basra Palace was evacuated. The column of Warriors moving from the city centre to the airport flew British and Welsh flags as the Rifles and Fusiliers rumbled out.

For many Basrawis this withdrawal marked a final disappointment by the British. Places that had once been relaxed and secular, such as the university or the corniche, had fallen under the baleful influence of militia puritans during the preceding years. It was not as if this imposition of Islamic sobriety brought peace in its wake. Instead, Badr Brigade gunmen fought the Mehdi Army and the police often clashed with the army. Not long after the British evacuated the Palace the city Chief of Police lamented that 'they left me militia, they left me gangsters and they left me all the troubles in the world'.

The controversy of the British withdrawal was succeeded by one concerning dealings with the militias. The SIS in Basra played a central role in this. As part of broader negotiations with the Mehdi Army, the British government agreed in August 2007 to release two dozen senior detainees after the Palace had been evacuated. These included Sajjad Badr, whose July 2006 arrest in a strike operation spearheaded by G Squadron had prompted a large-scale battle. The deal was allegedly negotiated with another man taken in an SAS-led strike from his prison cell at Basra airport. As part of a broader accommodation with the militias, the British agreed not to conduct further strike operations in the city in return for a ceasefire with militant groups there.

Some British officers had feared that, having left the Palace under a barrage of indirect fire, the militia would soon be rocketing the airport. However, once agreement was reached firing at the British base stopped almost completely. After years of intelligence analysis that described the insurgents in the city as splinter groups or offshoots, they almost all heeded an order to cease fire with remarkable discipline. Under these new arrangements the SIS had been withdrawn too, as had the SAS Task Force Spartan. With strike operations suspended there was little further role for special forces in Basra.

The story of that summer in Baghdad and the belt of communities around it was, by contrast, one of offensive action, spurred on by troops infused with new ideas of how they might beat the insurgency and backed up by considerable reinforcements. At

MNF-I headquarters, Camp Victory or in the Green Zone there was quite a bit of disparagement of the British. The top British general in Iraq, taking part in the morning BUA and bereft of anything positive to report from the south, would refer day after day to the results produced overnight by Task Force Knight. 'The SBMR-I would do anything he could each day to try and impress Petraeus,' recalls a jaundiced SAS observer of the morning briefings. 'We became his best card.'

These operations consisted of takedowns against Sunni and Shia militant targets. During May and June many Shia arrest operations were conducted by special ops units, including the SAS, but increasingly through TF-17's Green Berets and the Iraqi commandos they mentored. The sense that the Prime Minister and the US were united against him caused Muqtada al-Sadr initially to flee to Iran, fearful for his own liberty and later, in August, to declare a Mehdi Army ceasefire with the Coalition. The fears raised by naysayers who had argued the folly of confronting Shia extremists were thereby shown to be groundless.

During those same summer months of 2007 Petraeus's surge reached its climax. In Baghdad neighbourhoods including Adhamiya or Doura the erection of T-walls around particular *muhallas* allowed access to be controlled. This was followed by house-to-house sweeps. These had been done many times before, but this time with a difference, according to soldiers like those of the 2-12 Infantry in Doura. Insurgents who might previously have assumed themselves safe because they could escape over the back wall of a compound once the approach of Humvees was heard now calculated that they could not get across the new barricades. Afraid of getting cornered in the enclosed *muhallas*, many started to keep their distance. With this declining jihadist presence local citizens flocked to the Awakening forces and the success that had been achieved in rural Anbar was replicated in Baghdad. Many insurgents were hired in these days, turning for the princely sum of three dollars a day to fight on behalf of the Iraqi government rather than against it.

The toughest battle of that summer actually occurred outside Baghdad. It was in Baquba that many of the al-Qaeda men made their last stand. There had been bitter sectarian conflict in the city and the surrounding communities of Diyala Province for many months. It may be that the sense that they were all about to be murdered by the Shia made the Sunni population in that place harder to turn than they had been in Anbar or Baghdad. Jihadists had also declared Baquba to be the capital of the Islamic State of Iraq, having previously given that same distinction to Ramadi.

During early operations around the city's outskirts in March and April US troops had got a taste of what was to come. In one two-kilometre stretch of road they discovered thirty IEDs. On 6 May a huge deep-buried bomb hurled a Striker armoured vehicle into the air, killing the six American troops and one journalist inside. Fighting their way into the narrow alleys of Baquba's historic old city the American troops went house to house, finding hundreds of booby traps and running firefights. 'It was like World War Two,' says one senior American officer. 'It really was that intense.'

With so many more US troops fighting, casualties mounted quickly. In April 104 US soldiers were killed, in May 124 and in June 101. By July and August, though, these shockingly high figures had started to drop.

In places such as Doura the change brought about by the summer's fighting was dramatic. Dubbed 'the worst place in Iraq' by some earlier in the year, the streets had become quiet enough for the local battalion, 2–12 Infantry, to patrol by foot. One of the soldiers I had met during April's embed sent me an e-mail saying that they had complete freedom of action on the streets.

As Doura became calmer operations were stepped up just to the south, in Arab Jabour. Here too conventional forces, setting up Joint Security Stations, worked in tandem with the special operators. One US special forces officer serving with the ground-holding troops gives this example of what happened:

> The special ops people targeted Taher Razuq, one of the main leaders in Arab Jabour. They put two five-hundred-pound bombs through the roof of his house and killed him. There were two real consequences. Firstly, people felt more secure and that meant intelligence went up. Secondly it forced al-Qaeda underground.

In Washington the long-expected high noon between General Petraeus and the critics of the surge proved to be something of a damp squib in September. He and Ryan Crocker faced days of probing by Senate and House committees, leaving the latter to quip that it would be the first time he'd be glad to get back to Baghdad. But some of the fight had already gone from those who had previously condemned it all as ill-conceived. The indicators, in terms of falling violence in Baghdad and losses of US soldiers, were beginning to bolster General Petraeus's narrative. Even the killing by al-Qaeda of Sheikh Sittar, the key Awakening leader in Anbar, just after the congressional hearings could not dampen the mood of cautious optimism. Sittar was soon replaced by one of his brothers on the Awakening Council and many more sheikhs who had previously backed the insurgency now seemed ready to turn their backs on it.

Task Force Knight and JSOC's role while all of this continued was, to quote one American commander, to act as 'a hammer which could be used to smash insurgent groups against the anvil of conventional forces'. Given the high pitch that the various agencies providing targeting information had reached, a steady stream allowed the SAS to make nightly excursions from the MSS.

One of the particular features of A Squadron's operations under Major Kennedy was their tight focus. He did not have to worry, for example, about Basra since duties there were initially handled by Task Force Spartan, and after Britain's withdrawal from the city centre there was no further demand for strike operations. Instead, he was given the absolute priority of targeting the remaining al-Qaeda VBIED – car or truck bomb – networks. The great majority of the leads prosecuted by Task Force Knight's intelligence people proved to be in a triangle with Doura at its apex, Arab Jabour to the south-west and Salman Pak to the south-east. A Squadron's battleground was therefore one of city *muhallas* in the north, market gardens and date groves further down, and open farmland along the banks of the Tigris in the south.

When I asked one participant in these operations to nominate the most spectacular or successful raid of Major *Kennedy's* tour during the summer and autumn of 2007 he told me that it would not be possible because 'it was probably the most mechanistic tour . . . what we were doing as an accumulator. It wasn't about single operations but about their cumulative effect on the whole operation.' As part of this, British humint teams worked up intelligence with the US ground-holding units, sometimes using small SAS squads farmed out to them in order to react rapidly, moving in to arrest bomb makers or others who emerged from intelligence analysis.

In many cases these takedowns were violent. Reservations that the UK might once have harboured about US rules of engagement had by this time been assuaged. Under certain circumstances Task Force Knight could use pre-emptive force against known insurgents. They were operating in the style of Delta, killing dozens during those summer months.

Inevitably, with operations at this intensity, there were casualties on both sides. On 5 September A Squadron went to hit a target in Baghdad. They were searching for a leading member of a Sunni group and the operation was carried out in the usual style by an assault team of SAS backed up by Paras from Task Force Maroon. Two teams assaulted the Alpha, one of them led by Sergeant Eddie Collins. The sergeant, thirty-three, had started his tour in Basra but ended up in Baghdad as operations there were wound up.

Having broken into the house, the two assault teams began room clearing. As in many Iraqi houses, there was a staircase to the roof and the task of scaling it was considered particularly dangerous. Going through a door laid you open to attack from one side or another, on a roof the danger could come from any angle. An insurgent was lying in wait as Sergeant Collins emerged, shooting him with a 9mm pistol. The round struck Collins's neck and proved fatal. Other members of the team swiftly killed the gunman.

A Squadron's pace of operations throughout the summer meant its people were often pitched into situations for which they were unprepared. This produced a major drama near the end of their tour, on the night of 20 November.

The mission selected for Task Force Knight that day was a typical takedown. The teams woke around 2.30 p.m. and prepared themselves during the afternoon. There would be four Pumas, two Lynxes and a couple of other aircraft taking part.

During the early evening everything the blades and their supporting aircrews had been told changed. They would now be going after a different target, a Sunni insurgent whose position had been fixed to a rural area near Salman Pak, forty-five kilometres south-east of Baghdad.

Setting off into the early evening darkness the choppers flew low over the city's roofs. Two Lynx machines were in the lead, followed by two pairs of Pumas. In the first pair of troop transports were members of the SAS. The second wave carried Paras who could act as a Quick Reaction Force or cordon as required.

As with many of these missions around the city, the flight to the target area passed quickly and uneventfully – but then everything started to go wrong. One of the Lynxes flew too far ahead of the target grid reference and the formation commander, an RAF squadron leader in one of the Pumas, could not reach the Lynx by radio. Rallying the two SAS Pumas and the other Lynx he devised a new plan but the fix on their target now shifted. Information came from the orbiting command aircraft that the man was moving.

Down below, insurgents had been alerted by the arrival of the helicopters and their orbiting as new plans were put together and dictated over the radio. Through their night-vision equipment, the personnel in the circling aircraft could see men whom they believed to be insurgents moving in trees beside some fields. They illuminated these fleeting figures with one of the powerful searchlights carried for just such purposes. The door gunner of one of the Pumas opened fire. The air was crackling reports now – one pilot reported return fire from the ground.

Six helicopters and a number of other aircraft were wheeling over a moving target in a hazardous aerial ballet. So many of Task Force Knight's operations were routine house assaults, but this was panning out very differently. As one of the special forces aviators reflects, 'it's when it goes hot and dynamic, that's when it gets tricky'.

Major *Kennedy*, aboard one of the helicopters, decided to get his men on the ground. One chopper touched down; the other, dropping vertically from seventy-five feet, came close to the ground and was engulfed in dust. The Puma pilot decided to shift his landing position at the last moment, but with an urgent warning that a Lynx might be passing right over him he took the Puma up and then swiftly down again. The Puma hit the ground hard and almost immediately rolled on to its right side.

Just as with the April accident, men were thrown out of the chopper's side door by the force of impact. Three were pinioned underneath it as it smashed into the ground. Two SAS soldiers and one RAF man were trapped.

Those who had got away quickly organised themselves for a rescue attempt. But as Major *Kennedy* rallied his men around the wrecked Puma flames started licking the aircraft's gearbox. The RAF man was freed with SAS medics tending him and one of their own who had been hurt inside the aircraft. The two blades trapped under the fuselage, Sergeant John Battersby and Trooper Lee Fitzsimmons, could not be shifted.

In what seemed like moments the Puma was engulfed by fire. Rescuers facing into the heat soon heard rounds from the aircraft's door-mounted machine gun cooking off, as well as the whoosh of burning flares. The subsequent inquiry noted that 'the aircraft was completely ablaze and therefore unreachable within four minutes of coming to rest, with no further attempts being possible after this relatively short time'.

Even as the tragic outcome of this accident became clear Major *Kennedy* was talking to the surveillance aircraft overhead. The target had arrived at a second house in his car. One of the Puma crewmen piped up over the radio, disagreeing with the surveillance aircraft about which house he had entered. *Kennedy* made the decision to prosecute his original target. Organising his men away from the burning helicopter, the OC gave quick battle orders. There was a rapid house assault but the target had escaped.

With its mission over the team embarked on the remaining Pumas, returning to MSS Fernandez. Having recovered the bodies of Sergeant Battersby and Trooper Fitzsimmons, and having made attempts to sanitise the burnt-out Puma, an air strike was called in to finish the job.

This second helicopter incident caused some to question the way in which Task Force Knight did business. The inquiry flagged up the technical reasons for the pilot's crash landing. It also alluded to many aggravating difficulties including the way army Lynx and RAF crews inter-operated, the fact that the SAS did not like to strap in and the pressures put on the helicopter operation by the operational tempo. Asked about the two Puma incidents of 2007, one Task Force Knight aviator blamed 'toxic management'. Asked to elaborate, he explained that some of their commanders were 'like baboons in a tree – seen from above they presented smiling faces but to those lower down they were arses'.

A Squadron's tour ended on this difficult note. They had lost three men and several had been wounded. Nonetheless, its time was considered by JSOC and the SAS to have been outstandingly successful. Major *Kennedy* was decorated. One commander notes, 'they took apart the al-Qaeda VBIED network'.

From May to November A Squadron had mounted raids almost nightly, during which it arrested 335 people and killed 88. The latter figure in particular marks a stark contrast from the squadron's deployment of late 2005, when it took just one life. Few statistics demonstrate better the extent to which the SAS's mission in Iraq had changed. By locking his task force tightly into JSOC's operations, Lieutenant-Colonel Williams had succeeded in his ambition of raising the regiment's speed, accuracy and effect. The sharp increase in lethality between these two A Squadron tours shows that due to the improvement of intelligence (achieved in large part by working so closely with the

Americans), Task Force Knight was targeting the violent extremists rather than the old Ba'athists who had been led quietly from their homes in 2004 or 2005. For Williams personally, though, storm clouds were gathering. His period in command of the regiment was coming to an end and it was not destined to be a quiet departure.

19

THE V WORD

In the murky gloom of a C-130 high over Anbar an SAS assault force stood up and shuffled its way towards the aircraft's tail ramp. Each blade had a parachute strapped to his back, a weapon to his side and his assault equipment to the front. With a mechanical squeal the ramp lowered and the men walked forward to its lip, peering into the Iraqi night below.

The soldiers were from B Squadron of 22 SAS and early in 2008 they were about to notch up a first for the regiment in its six-year campaign in Iraq: an operational high-altitude parachute assault. Their target was a man who was making money for al-Qaeda – literally producing counterfeit dollar bills – on a remote farm.

Stepping into the night sky the SAS soldiers experienced a brief freefall before opening their parachutes. The technique known as High Altitude High Opening or HAHO allowed them to glide many kilometres while keeping the noise of their Hercules far away from their intended target. The soldiers hit the ground, threw off their parachuting rig and moved on foot to assault the house. Once again the SAS got its man.

B Squadron's stint in Baghdad generated some controversy within the regiment. 'Each unit tries to demonstrate how it's different from the one before,' remarks one SAS officer a little wearily. 'Well done for jumping, but was it strictly necessary? Isn't that why helicopters were invented?'

Just a few months before A Squadron had achieved extraordinary impact, 'smashing the Baghdad VBIED network'. The boss of B Squadron perhaps understood that with AQI reeling it would not be possible to achieve the same focus, geographically or in terms of the target set. The success of B Squadron's previous tour (November 2005 to May 2006), in which the LARCHWOOD 4 operation gave a start point for the Zarqawi operation and Norman Kember had been freed, added to the pressure.

Early in March Task Force Knight's intelligence team developed an operation against a bomb maker. He was believed to have fled Baghdad for a former powerbase of Saddam Hussein to the north of the capital in the so-called Sunni Triangle. SAS operations in this city were quite unusual, for Task Force Red, one of JSOC's American units, was based nearby. But the British followed their leads to a substantial property in an affluent part of town: the bomb maker had none other than the police chief, a judge and the commander of the local police response unit as neighbours.

Having fixed their target, B Squadron hit his house at 2 a.m. on 26 March. They first called upon the target and another man to come out. After receiving no response the SAS stormed the house. But not for the first time during their years in Iraq was there someone lying in wait and the entry team stepped into a hail of bullets. Four men were wounded, one of them fatally. As the team dashed out of the house grenades were thrown and gunmen from a neighbouring building joined in the fusillade.

The SAS returned fire, with support from circling helicopters. Within moments a general firefight had developed with tracer zipping around the suburb's streets. A missile was fired from a circling aircraft into one of the houses being used to fire upon the special forces. Following an explosion that brought down part of the building, the two targets of the operation ran from it into a neighbouring house where they either took hostages or persuaded several women and children to come with them. As they crossed open ground this group was engaged from the air.

Coalition spokesmen said that two suspected terrorists and seven civilians (three of them children) had been killed in the operation. Locals told the BBC that the civilian death toll was actually sixteen. The Ministry of Defence kept the dead SAS soldier's name secret, along with where it had happened. During the days that followed local anger produced several gun battles with the American ground-holding unit. Its commander told BBC correspondent Paul Wood that the lesson of the raid was that 'aggressiveness meets aggressiveness'.

In some respects this battle was regrettable but not unusual. The number of 'Echos and Kilos', or women and children, killed during SAS operations in Iraq is very hard to estimate because many raids had to be so fast there could be no waiting around for a definitive assessment of Iraqi casualties. It is safe to assume that by 2008 the total killed during the regiment's years of operations may have been as high as fifty. Many in the special ops community would dispute that figure, arguing that it was significantly lower, but in truth the chaotic circumstances of many of these contacts makes hard and fast calculations difficult. The regiment also lost one of its own people there, the fifth to die in a house assault. The confusion about where the insurgents were at some times during the operation was another regrettable feature of assaults mounted at such short notice, with limited intelligence.

There was something else notable about the operation, and this was the regiment's use of a specially trained dog to enter the Alpha at the start of the assault. Squadrons posted to Baghdad had in fact been using this technique since 2005, but when the inquest on the dead B Squadron man was held in the UK several months later it emerged as a significant issue. He had by this point been named as Sergeant Nick Brown. The dead soldier was what might in former times have been called a 'child of the regiment', having grown up in Hereford while his father was serving in the SAS. When his father, John, and his widow asked searching questions at the inquest they carried considerable weight.

The court heard that the 34-year-old sergeant in B Squadron had gone into the building after the dog sent ahead of the entry team had been killed. He had been shot in the back and mortally wounded by someone lurking in the building. His relatives wanted answers at the inquest about why the men had gone in when they already believed their search dog to be dead. In the end, with the coroner citing security concerns about not prejudicing operational techniques, the issue did not receive the full and open discussion that it might. But while the violence with which the special ops people had prosecuted their assault shocked many local Iraqis, the issue it highlighted for many in the regiment was quite different. They wondered whether, despite the gradual changes in British rules of engagement, the Americans would ever have assaulted under similar circumstances, or whether, instead, they would have hit the Alpha from the air once they had evidence that the people inside were willing to fight.

By March 2008 the climate for mounting aggressive special

forces operations of this kind was changing. The Sunni insurgency was waning rapidly, and being hired to serve the government as Sons of Iraq. Stirring up communal anger with a raid of this kind damaged that process. One SAS operator remarked to me that after an operation, 'We disappear into our helicopters and the local unit is left to feel the pain.' This approach had been acceptable during the desperate months of 2006 and early 2007 when it felt as if all of society had become unhinged by murderous violence. But by the summer of 2008 the American battalion or brigade commanders responsible for holding sectors of Iraq had been thoroughly inculcated in General Petraeus's new doctrine, which stated that their primary mission was safeguarding the population. Patrol bases or Joint Security Stations were rapidly expanding the ground-level intelligence picture and helping to stamp out sectarian violence: if JSOC's raids miscarried they could damage this progress.

So, just as British special forces had roamed far and wide in search of a target they might be able to prosecute during their early months in Iraq back in 2003, five years later they were trying to find places where they might do some good. During B Squadron's tour their operations extended to Anbar and Tikrit. But whereas operations years before had been limited by the dearth of good intelligence, during the final period of the SAS's stay in Baghdad the analysts sat within a sophisticated information-gathering web, but had to look harder and harder to find a target worthy of them.

The Americans had developed their mobile phone database into a fearsome analytical tool and fielded dozens of Unmanned Aerial Vehicles. Cover from Predators was supplemented by cameras mounted on tethered balloons or fixed on the roofs of buildings. Using gamma-ray imagery of cars, American analysts were able to study their 'unblinking' record of the city's main thoroughfares.

About a hundred thousand defectors from Sunni militant groups enrolled in the *Sakhwa* or Awakening militias known as Sons of Iraq, giving what the intelligence analysts called granularity to their picture of militant activities in most of Iraq. Some pockets of AQI, including of foreign fighters, remained, for example in the northern city of Mosul where bitter intercommunal violence opened up a toehold in the community just as it had in Baquba in 2007. Overall, though, the picture of violence was one of steep decline, particularly in Baghdad. MNF Iraq's Sigacts data showed bombings in the city down by 250 per cent in the summer of 2008. The graph of ethno-sectarian deaths showed a steady fall from its peak of more than two thousand in December 2006 (across Iraq, with Baghdad accounting for around 1600) to a few murders during April 2008 and a flat line thereafter.

Among the blades the evaporation of worthwhile targets soon had an impact. 'They got very low-level operations to go and get mortar teams and people who should have been the responsibility of the Iraqi Army,' explains one former operator. 'People got disillusioned.' Smart young soldiers coming through special forces selection and hearing tell about the intensity of combat in southern Afghanistan started to gravitate towards the SBS which was operating there: 'People want to go where the action is.'

While B Squadron tried ever harder to make an impact with its operations Richard Williams, who had until December 2007 been the Commanding Officer of the SAS, faced an uncertain future. He had left the army with his marriage broken, while dealing with post-traumatic stress. To compound his personal situation, Williams was briefly investigated by the Director of Special Forces for his use of official expenses. There had been no wrongdoing, and he was soon exonerated.

When Williams handed in his resignation the previous

summer, the fact had soon appeared in the press. Obsessive and aggressive, the former CO had made plenty of enemies. Williams had emulated his hero Stan McChrystal in spending much of his time during 2005 to 2007 personally directing operations in Iraq, pushing his people hard. *The Times* commented that his leadership style 'has drawn criticism from the army hierarchy, which believes that commanding officers, whether they are in the SAS or in conventional regiments, need to be less involved in frontline combat and more concerned with the "big picture".'

Talking to participants in these operations it was obvious that Williams's period in command still evokes strong emotions. One leading (non-special forces) figure in Baghdad said he regarded the SAS leader as 'a victim of Hereford politics, and it is a place where there are bitter rivalries'. Such is the strength of these animosities that one officer who had served in the SAS in Baghdad alleged to me that Williams had actually been forced out early, or effectively sacked.

In fact this is untrue, as is the suggestion that he had blotted his army record by leading from the front. One general who could have influenced Williams's promotion prospects had he remained in the army says, 'Had he stayed I have no doubt that he was destined for three- or four-star rank.' A more junior figure, a veteran of Task Force Knight, told me candidly that he had bitterly resented Williams's pressure at the time, but had come to realise that his boss had provided the impetus necessary to make their operations really bite.

Any supporter of Richard Williams could point out that the regiment's period of maximum effectiveness in taking down terrorist networks – from the summer of 2005 to late 2007 – coincided almost exactly with his tenure as CO. Before he arrived, due to differences with the Americans over detainees and command arrangements, the SAS had been achieving only a limited impact. They had rounded up old men, Ba'athists whose detention made little difference to the carnage on the streets. Once Williams had gone the aggression he had insisted upon, telling each squadron commander they must complete at least one mission a night, seemed to fall away too.

There is without doubt an element of coincidence. In particular, the improvement of security in Baghdad, and more widely during 2008, rapidly cut the ground from underneath the special operations people. That had nothing to do with who was running the SAS, Task Force Knight or indeed JSOC, for Lieutenant-General McChrystal was gone by then too. It was however in taking the SAS to its high-gear, high-impact operations against al-Qaeda, often in the teeth of opposition from his boss, Major-General *Peter Rogers* – that Williams made his greatest personal impact.

In some ways Williams came to symbolise a deeper clash of cultures within the British system. For, talking to many of those who were involved, the debates about Williams or the SAS's role in Baghdad were clearly suffused with a theme of pro- and anti-Americanism. These arguments about the rights and wrongs of George Bush's war or the often disastrous early conduct of operations in Iraq provided a subtext to so many of the discussions in the SAS, MI6, the Foreign Office or Army. Many of those who favoured the British caveats on Task Force Black's operations during 2004 to 2005 shared a scepticism about American goals and methods that bordered on hostility. Issues such as detainee conditions or rules of engagement were exploited to keep British operations semi-detached. 'The British, when we went there, were very sniffy about the American way of doing things,' reflects one commander who started off in the sceptic camp but ended up realising that JSOC 'was doing it in a rather templated industrial manner and in the end we came around to their way of doing things'.

Williams believed that the SAS could never be truly effective without harnessing the massive intelligence resources at JSOC's disposal. But he was also an unashamed Americanophile. One SAS officer told me 'the thing about Richard is that he would probably have preferred to have commanded Delta', but the idea of the SAS commander sitting at the Joint Operations Center at Balad running the whole US–UK black operation in Iraq could never be. The United States simply had too many of its top covert operatives and too much of its sensitive intelligence technology at play in Iraq to allow a foreigner, even a Brit, a turn at command. The other pivotal pro-American in these debates was Graeme Lamb. As Director of Special Forces he had launched the SAS into its Baghdad mission cooperating closely with Delta Force. Later, when wearing the two hats of deputy commander of MNF-I and Senior British Military Representative in Iraq, he not only played a key role in the Awakening but also kept a paternal eye on UK special forces operations.

The record of squadron operations perhaps provides the best vindication of those who argued that UK special forces could only achieve the same results as the Americans if they were led with comparable aggression and supplied with comparable intelligence. During the middle part of 2003, during A Squadron's tour that operated closely with the Americans, it raided eighty-five properties. Four years later, after various UK national caveats had been removed, the same squadron mounted almost twice as many raids. In fact, the rate was not dramatically different because the first tour had lasted four months and the 2007 one six, amounting to an average of five operations each week on the first tour and almost seven on the second. In between these two highly successful deployments, however, the British had for much of 2004 to 2005 removed themselves from JSOC's operations against Islamic militants and concentrated instead on

Former Regime Elements. During this period the tally fell dramatically, reaching its nadir during the C Squadron (SBS) tour of 2004, when fewer than two dozen raids, or an average of 1.3 each week, were mounted.

On the same March day that B Squadron's raid in the Sunni Triangle unfolded, the highways to southern Iraq began to hum with military traffic. On 25 March Nouri al-Maliki had taken the decision to bring forward an operation against Shia militias in Basra. The 7th Iraqi Division was dispatched southwards with hundreds of armoured vehicles and teams of embedded US advisers. The 14th Division, trained by the British to operate in the city, was also stood by for action.

When convoys of Iraqi Army vehicles began snaking into the city thousands of black-clad Mehdi Army fighters took to the streets. General Petraeus and Ambassador Crocker had spent the past year convincing Maliki that he had to break the power of the Shia militias, principally the Mehdi Army. They had succeeded to such a degree that by March 2008, according to one senior US figure, 'we almost had to stop him taking a gun and going to Basra to join in the fighting'.

It was just as well that Maliki restrained his impulse because during the early days of Operation Charge of the Knights his army suffered some embarrassing reverses. One of the British-trained brigades of the 14th Division 'collapsed', with hundreds deserting. British Merlin helicopter crews sent to the Palace to pick up Iraqi casualties reported having to beat back dozens of terrified Iraqi soldiers who were trying to escape on their aircraft.

The operation pitted twenty-seven thousand Iraqi security forces against an estimated five to six thousand militia. Around two hundred US and British embedded advisers with these units were able to bring in artillery, helicopter and other support. During street-to-street fighting the government lost more than two hundred soldiers. The militia's casualties have been estimated at up to six hundred killed. At one stage, against military advice, Maliki allowed a ten-day ceasefire for negotiations.

On 19 April, four weeks after the operation had been launched, Iraqi troops walked into the Hayyaniyah. In that one-time militia bastion that the British troops had dubbed the Shia Flats, people came out onto the street to applaud their soldiers. Resistance was over and for the first time in years the spell of intimidation that the gunmen had woven across the city was broken. Young women returned to the university without veils and the corniche once again thronged with couples arm in arm.

Although General Petraeus and other senior officers in Baghdad had been dubious about the timing of the operation they celebrated its results. In the corridors of the Republican Palace or Camp Victory the American brass drew its lessons. Many Iraqi generals and a small band of British officers, including many from the special forces, saw things in much the same way.

Operation CHARGE OF THE KNIGHTS had demonstrated that the Shia militia in Basra could be beaten. It was not a permanent solution, for that could only come through politics, but it did scatter and suppress the city's armed gangs. The negativity and hesitancy – or 'defeatism' as one SAS officer characterised it – of many of the British officers who had served in Multi-National Division South East during the previous years had however been exposed. People like Major-General Richard Shirreff, who had argued that Britain could not leave the power of the militia intact and had tried to confront it, found little support from head office at the Ministry of Defence or from the wider British public.

The more politically savvy British officers argued that flushing out the militias, with all the bloodshed and destruction that involved, was something only the Iraqis could do, and that the confidence of Maliki's forces had received a boost as a result of the operation's success. But US actions in Ramadi late in 2006, in Baghdad early in 2007, or in Baquba in June of that year had confronted opposition even more intense than that seen in Basra and defeated it. The view that Britain had been defeated in Basra became widespread among the American top brass. Yet their perceptions of what had been achieved by the small British special operations task force in Baghdad could not have been more different.

On 30 May 2009 Operation CRICHTON, the UK special forces deployment in Iraq, ended. A small party from G Squadron left Baghdad airport and headed back to the UK. In some ways the work of Task Force Knight was unfinished. Iranian influence remained strong and the search for British hostages taken at the Finance Ministry in 2007 continued. There was still some low-level political killing in the country. But Baghdad felt like a city transformed. Levels of violence had fallen away, there were few tasks left for Coalition special operators. Moreover, the Iraqi government, while agreeing to the future US presence in the country, no longer wanted the British to operate.

During six years in Iraq a British special forces task force that rarely exceeded 150 had killed or captured 3500 people. Of these, the great majority were captured. Precise tallies of the dead are difficult because in places like Ramadi in 2003 or Yusufiyah in 2006 blades have told me they had to leave before bodies were counted. However, the number killed by British special forces, based on estimates of those involved, was probably 350 to 400. The equivalent figures for JSOC's US operations across Iraq during the same period can be estimated at a total of eleven to twelve thousand, of whom around three thousand may have been killed. A higher proportion of British captured to killed is apparent, but this pattern was set in the years where their main mission was taking down Former Regime Elements, relatively few of whom put up any resistance.

These stark estimates hint at the deeper story of the Coalition's secret war in Iraq. Certainly many of those involved would accept that it was bloody, but argue that in the maelstrom of violence that wracked the country it was necessary to meet fire with fire. They assert, furthermore, that the campaign masterminded by General Stanley McChrystal succeeded in breaking al-Qaeda in Iraq. JSOC captured or killed the organisation's members faster than it could recruit new ones. What some refer to as the martyrdom argument – that killing an insurgent simply causes others to step forward in his or her place – needs to be re-evaluated in the light of JSOC's campaign. No doubt there were many who wished to avenge killing by the Coalition's special operators, but it was General McChrystal's operational design that eventually made it impossible for them to do so.

In many counterterrorist campaigns the limitations of intelligence, special forces numbers or political will mean that strike operations can never account for more than a small percentage of the enemy organisation. Dead men's shoes are quickly filled. What happened in Iraq was different. By insisting that each of his five or six task forces carry out multiple takedowns every night, McChrystal set a pace of operations that probably removed from the streets (by arrest or elimination) most of the membership of AQI. One senior British officer who watched it happen asserts that 'the US tempo proved irresistible and decisive'.

Of course credit in the American success of bringing Iraq back from the abyss was claimed by many people outside JSOC. One US officer with a special forces background who served with the regular army unit south of Baghdad at the time of

A Squadron's many raids in the area during 2007 argues that the key building block in the Coalition's success was the establishment of dozens of Joint Security Stations. These places combined US and Iraqi security forces and enhanced people's safety while offering an easy local address to those who wished to give information. On the other hand, a ground-holding commander in the Rashid district of southern Baghdad told me that the entire Coalition effort was secondary to the shift in Sunni opinion to rejecting the insurgency during 2007.

In September 2008, during the course of a long BBC interview with General Petraeus in Baghdad, I explored his perceptions of how the tide had been turned. Petraeus had banned his staff from using the 'V word' and told me that he didn't think he ever would. The situation was too tenuous and the general too careful to claim victory. As to the ingredients, he laid emphasis on the Anaconda Strategy, his comprehensive approach that stressed everything from political reconciliation to economic progress and conventional and special operations forces. Giving the example of the elimination of Abu Musab al-Zarqawi in June 2006, Petraeus asked, 'Did that make any difference in the violence? Well, it undermined, certainly, leadership for a while in al-Qaeda but someone else popped up and there was again a continual standing up.' While special ops 'may conduct the most important operations of all, and they typically do', the effect of changes in the way intelligence was gathered and shared proved critical. 'In fact,' he argued, '*the* breakthrough is not any one technological capability or intelligence advance: it is the fusion of all of those.' The way in which General McChrystal had built his own network at Balad had, implied General Petraeus, cascaded through Tier 2 special forces to conventional units and even Iraqi ones.

In evaluating the relative role of what Petraeus referred to as 'special mission units' – the classified forces or JSOC – the general was obliged to take a line in which due acknowledgement had to be given to his new operational approach of making the people the centre of operations and to increases in the number of conventional forces: the surge. None of the key players, not even General McChrystal himself, appears to believe that a stand-alone special operations campaign of increasing intensity and size could have been the panacca for Iraq's security problems. It is also obvious that constraints, from the political to operational ones posed by more limited intelligence, prevent the application of the JSOC Iraq model in many other parts of the world. However, it is clear that the covert offensive against al-Qaeda in Iraq and Iranian influence played an important role in bringing the country back from the brink of anarchy.

It is also clear that key aspects of the campaign against the Sunni insurgency were gaining traction before Petraeus and his Anaconda Strategy were in place. The Awakening movement (with British participation) was already delivering important results in the second half of 2006. The JSOC campaign in the Triangle of Death had also started to degrade al-Qaeda's ability to mount complex large-scale attacks. That the overall tide of violence was still rising at that time was due in large measure to the Shia insurgency being sponsored by Iran. The great achievement during the Petraeus period was to take on the irreconcilables of both sides at the same time and for this the Anaconda or comprehensive approach was vital.

As for Britain's involvement in Iraq, the picture is more straightforward. The green army arrived in the country with the conviction that it knew best how to conduct a counterinsurgency. Words like smug and complacent are sometimes used by officers who witnessed the UK approach in the south. Instead, Basra and Maysan provided a bitter learning experience. The overt military mission ended with recriminations and suggestions after Operation CHARGE OF THE KNIGHTS in spring

2008 that the Iraqis had been forced to do a job Britain was unable to perform. As for the other parts of the UK's involvement, it is important not to overlook the command element in Baghdad – the Senior British Military Representative in Iraq; British members of the MNF staff; the embassy; and the MI6 operation. Certainly there were times when SIS provided an element of coherence that was lacking from the American intelligence operation. The role of the SBMR-I – particularly Lieutenant-General Graeme Lamb in late 2006 and early 2007 – was also significant in developing the Awakening strategy.

What is clear is that Britain's special operations task force in Baghdad provided the one clear success of the nation's controversial involvement in Iraq. Task Force Black, then Knight, played a role completely disproportionate to its numbers in improving the security situation. For this reason the top American commander used clear language about UK special forces, words of a kind that he had hesitated to deploy with regard to his country's own. General Petraeus, in an interview with *The Times* in August 2008, said the SAS 'have helped immensely in the Baghdad area, in particular to take down the al-Qaeda car bomb networks and other al-Qaeda operations in Iraq's capital city, so they have done a phenomenal job in that regard'. He added 'they have exceptional initiative, exceptional skill, exceptional courage and, I think, exceptional savvy. I can't say enough about how impressive they are in thinking on their feet.' This praise gives some sense of how the small, secret British contingent in Baghdad counteracted the impressions some Americans formed in the south, preventing the UK's involvement in Iraq from being seen as a debacle. Lieutenant-General Rob Fry, who had served as the Coalition number two in Baghdad in 2006, later described the role of British special forces in 'defeating' al-Qaeda as being of 'an absolutely historic scale'.

*

While the SAS role in taking down al-Qaeda was 'phenomenal', their campaign against the Shia Special Groups produced more problematic results. The arrest of the Khazali brothers and their Lebanese adviser by the SAS in March 2007 was an event of strategic importance. But it produced retaliation, both in the arrest of British naval personnel and the Finance Ministry kidnapping, that was hard for the British government to deal with. The wider JSOC and Counter Iranian Influence campaign against Shia militants demonstrated that Iran could be deterred from further escalation of its covert activities and the militias checked. But since Iran would continue to be Iraq's neighbour and the Shia would form a majority of Iraq's population, these efforts could only achieve containment rather than the knockout punch given to al-Qaeda.

During 2009 there were a series of developments that underlined the temporary effect that JSOC and its British allies were able to have on the Shia extremists. In May, the 'Irbil Five', the Iranian officials seized by Delta early in 2007, were released. A couple of days before the end of the year, Peter Moore, the surviving British hostage taken at the Finance Ministry, was freed. In return Qais Khazali, taken by the SAS in Basra in March 2007, was transferred from US to Iraqi custody with the understanding that he too would soon be released. Other veterans of the Special Groups had also been quietly let out. From the point of view of those who had masterminded the Counter Iranian Influence campaign of 2006–7, there were obvious risks with these deals that the fires of sectarian or anti-western violence would be kindled anew. But in truth, the Prime Minister was seeking to garner support with the Shia community prior to elections, the releases were a reminder of what those who sought Mr Maliki's approval early in 2007 to move against these 'irreconcilables' had long understood, which was that the communal and political ties between elements of the Shia community were hard to break.

It was then in the role of Task Force Black, then Knight, in taking down so many members of al-Qaeda in and around Baghdad that Britain can find its 'V word'. Guided by intelligence teams, and with considerable US assistance, British special forces waged a campaign against one of the most ruthless and violent enemies of modern times. Al–Qaeda in Iraq was a movement for whom killing a hundred shoppers in a busy market with a truck bomb or videotaping the decapitation of a western hostage was considered a good day's work. By playing a key role in neutralising this network, the British task force helped to create an opportunity for peace.

On 2 October, an unseasonably warm autumn morning, a procession made its way into Hereford Cathedral. As the organist played a Bach fugue the city's dignitaries made their way inside. The programme for that morning's service read 'A service of Thanksgiving to mark the completion of the Iraqi campaign by 22nd Special Air Service Regiment including an act of commemoration for those who were killed in action'. There were many members of the regiment lending their voices to the opening rendition of the national anthem. The lessons were read by the Director of Special Forces and the Commanding Officer of 22 SAS.

During the hymns and prayers there was plenty of time for contemplation of what had happened in Iraq and its human cost. The SAS prides itself on the dedication of those who embark on selection for and service in its ranks. Its soldiers sometimes refer to themselves as pilgrims because of the journey of faith this involves. Appropriately enough, the hymn of Bunyan's 'Monk's Gate' boomed out of the cathedral, ending 'He'll not fear what men say, He'll labour night and day to be a pilgrim'. The regimental sergeant-major picked up this theme with a stanza from 'The Golden Journey to Samarkand':

We are the Pilgrims, master; we shall go
Always a little further; it may be
Beyond the last blue mountain barred with snow,
Across that angry or that glimmering sea.

The cathedral service was followed by a special dinner in the sergeants' mess at Credenhill. This gathering was addressed by General Stan McChrystal. Almost all of the key figures in the six-year drama of the regiment's service in Iraq were there to hear him – directors of special forces, commanding officers, senior NCOs and old sweats. In all, something like 360 people were crammed into the mess for what McChrystal called a 'unique gathering'. The commander of Delta Force was there too, and several other Americans. The general had taken time from directing Nato operations in Afghanistan and arguing the case with his President for more troops. It was a measure of the importance of his bond with the SAS that he kept his appointment to address the dinner. All of those who heard his oration were left in no doubt as to the respect in which he held the British contribution to the secret campaign and its importance in preventing Iraq's descent into chaos.

One of those at the dinner gave me this epitaph for their struggle: 'Al-Qaeda came to raise the standard of the caliphate in Iraq. We stood toe to toe with them. They were contested and found wanting. Their image, their franchise, got a bloody good shoeing.'

Just a few months after Operation CRICHTON ended, during the summer of 2009, Baghdad witnessed several bloody car-bomb attacks. The violence continued sporadically in the months that followed. Even if the scale of these incidents was far below that of the carnage of 2006, many people worried. Was the serpent of sectarianism raising its head again? Was the violence latent in Iraqi society bound to break out as soon as the Coalition's special operators left? Did the renewed attacks demonstrate the futility of the UK–US onslaught against the bombers? Those involved in the secret struggle of 2005 to 2008 argue that it was precisely because their mission had ended that the bombers got a second chance. The special operations campaign in Iraq could never produce a final answer to the problems of Islamic militancy or sectarianism. It could, however, provide a breathing space, an opportunity for political resolutions or indeed for the Coalition's withdrawal. That, with great secrecy, intelligence and ruthlessness, was what it did.

Index

INDEX

INDEX

INDEX

Operation TRACTION 2: 214
Operation VIDETTE 193–4
overwhelming force, doctrines of 56

Page, Mike (Sergeant-Major in G
  Squadron) 15–16
Pakistan, alleged jihadists from 57, 62,
  68, 135
Palestine, jihadists from 36
Palestine Hotel (Baghdad) 23
parachute assaults 259–60
Parachute Regiment 1, 14, 18, 65, 90,
  167, 255
  Task Force Maroon 141, 143, 254
parliament building, Iraqi 236
Patey, William (British Ambassador to
  Iraq) 109–10
Patterson, Sergeant Norman 200
Pentagon 19, 20, 32, 35, 37, 52, 54,
  80, 153, 161, 165, 174, 207, 219
Petraeus, General David 186–7, 197,
  216–18, 220, 238–9, 241–2, 250,
  263, 269
  Anaconda Strategy 272, 273
  his evaluation of campaign 272–3,
    274
  Iran issue and 217, 218, 220–1, 226,
    227
  Graeme Lamb and 186, 218–19
  al-Maliki and 219, 221, 223–4, 268
  political criticism of in Washington
    216–17, 220, 252
  SAS and 219, 220, 274
Plank, Corporal Ian 28–9, 30–1, 200
police force, Iraqi
  in Anbar Province 179, 183, 184
  attacks against police stations 79,
    238
  in Basra 42, 95, 97–8, 99–102,
    103–7, 194–5, 202–3, 249
  British mentoring of 95, 97, 107
  corruption and 95, 96, 97–8, 166,
    202–3, 239
  Captain Jafar 95, 96, 98, 202–3
  Jamiat incident (19 September 2005)
    and xiii, 95, 96, 99–102,
    103–6, 107–8, 202–3
  Mehdi Army and 166, 203, 239

militia penetration of 97, 99, 108,
  166, 203, 239
  in Ramadi 179
  Serious Crimes Unit 95, 96, 202–3
  training of 42
  US army liaison teams 210–11
Pontrilas training area 90, 92
Powell, Staff Sergeant Mark 235
Predator drones 40, 64, 71, 80, 85,
  119, 179, 207, 244, 263
  hunt for Zarqawi and 64, 79, 84,
    160
  Jamiat incident and 100, 101, 102,
    105, 116, 229
prisoners
  detention and interrogation facilities
    54–5, 67–8, 72, 86, 131,
    148–50, 159
  handing over of to US forces 54,
    57–8, 62, 72, 231
  interrogation of 36–7, 54–5, 67–8,
    148–50, 159
  lack of SAS detainee facilities 40
  language barriers 37
  mistreatment/abuse of 54, 55, 60,
    61–2
  'national caveat' over Balad 67–8,
    72, 73, 75, 86, 91–2, 116, 265,
    266
  rendition of 57–8, 62–3, 200
  Tactical Questioning of 128–9, 130,
    131
Provincial Iraqi Control ('Pic') strategy
  107, 248
Puma helicopters 1, 2, 72, 88–9, 137,
  140, 233, 234–5, 254–7

al-Qaeda 2, 4, 26, 37–8, 47, 66–7, 68
  9/11 attacks xiv, 8
'al-Qaeda in Iraq' (AQI)
  in Anbar Province (western Iraq)
    178–80, 181, 182–5
  announces 'Islamic State of Iraq'
    (October 2006) 183–4
  attacks (early 2007) 242
  attacks in Baghdad (early 2007) 212
  Baghdad and 165, 212, 237, 238–9,
    240, 241–2

INDEX